Praise for From Aid to Trade

In their book, *From Aid to Trade*, Daniel Jean-Louis and Jacqueline Klamer draw from years of working with entrepreneurs and businesspeople to offer a refreshing look at the problem of poverty—one that shifts the focus from aid and assistance to the productive capacity of people.

They show how the current model of development is misaligned with the needs of the people, and how aid agencies, charities, and NGOs have delayed the development of Haiti. Jean-Louis and Klamer call for a move "from aid to trade" but recognize that this can only happen when local enterprise flourishes. In a discipline dominated by social engineering and the latest fad, they call for a renewed appreciation of the role of the business and market exchange in getting people out of poverty. They argue that NGOs and aid agencies can play a positive role if they work within the local economy, not with "public-private partnerships" or crony capitalism, but by engaging local business to supply goods when possible.

From Aid to Trade is not just about Haiti. It is about creating the conditions for the poor to create prosperity in their own families and communities, and should be read by anyone who is concerned about poverty and economic development.

> Michael Matheson Miller, Director/Producer, Poverty, Inc.

Daniel Jean-Louis and Jacqueline Klamer are right: If you keep doing the same thing over and over, you cannot expect different results. Yet, that is exactly what has been happening in Haiti for decades. This book is a wakeup call. It provides a blueprint for a new Haiti through both in-depth analysis and real life stories and is a must-read for all actors in the Haitian government, the Haitian private sector, and the international community.

> Ted Boers, Author of *Demons of Poverty*

Jean-Louis and Klamer offer thoughtful insights as to why Haiti remains a poor nation amidst the ongoing aid, and how changes can be obtained when NGOs collaborate with Haitian businesses. This book is a must read for those seeking to bring about market-based solutions to economic problems in Haiti and around the world.

> JoAnn Flett, Board Chair of Capital for Good; Director of MBA Economic Development, Eastern University

This book presents a detailed review of the impact of ⸱ Yet, more importantly, it provides a comprehensive re strategies to transform Haiti from the "Republic of N(in the 21st century global market place.

> Firmin Backer, President, Haiti Renewal Alliance (HRA)

The 2010 earthquake in Haiti was catastrophic, yet the aid that followed was destructive—undercutting numerous local industries and contributing to a failed state. The post-earthquake context is a sad illustration of the saying that "the road to hell is paved with good intentions."

Lessons can and must be learned and applied around the globe. In the context of Haiti, Jean-Louis and Klamer capture the tragic historical events and the rickety development efforts thereafter. Yet, they also prescribe a constructive path forward, where aid organizations and businesses can work together to transform developing nations and their economies.

This well-written and most helpful book should be a mandatory reading for NGO leaders, donors, and business people who are serious about serving people and building nations.

MATS TUNEHAG, Chair of Business as Mission Global Think Tank

Daniel Jean-Louis is a visionary whose work inspires many of his generation and generations to come. He is someone with a different approach when it comes to doing business in Haiti, and his insights on business solutions within a developing economy speak volumes. This book provides crucial information when it comes to doing business in Haiti, and how to transform your passion into something that contributes to shared success and impacts.

DAVIDSON TOUSSAINT, CEO of Haiti Tourism Inc.

This book embraces the whole paradigm shift Haiti needs to move forward. It provides key insights about negative impacts of aid and gives perspectives on the need to organize the Haitian economy around a model based on business development and growth. Not only do Daniel and Jacqueline go into an in-depth analysis of the issues, but they also support their arguments with facts. I would recommend this book to anyone who is trying to find the best way to help Haiti.

ROCK ANDRÉ, Economist & Entrepreneur, Founder of Center for Entrepreneurship and Leadership in Haiti (CEDEL HAITI)

From Aid to Trade is a must read if you care about Haitians or any other economically struggling people! This book offers great insight into the economic woes and opportunities of Haiti's people—from Haiti, written by a Haitian, for the *shalom* of Haiti's people. Daniel Jean-Louis brings expertise, experience and heart to bear on the devastation unthoughtful aid has brought to his country, and the hope that lies in promoting and unleashing the trading capacity of her people. Read and learn!

DR. DRU DODSON, Author of *Kingdom Outposts: A Fresh Theology of Relief and Development*

FROM AID TO
TRADE

How Aid Organizations, Businesses, and
Governments Can Work Together:
Lessons Learned From Haiti

Daniel Jean-Louis & Jacqueline Klamer

From Aid to Trade:
How Aid Organizations, Businesses, and Governments Can Work Together:
Lessons Learned From Haiti
Copyright © 2016 by Daniel Jean-Louis and Jacqueline Klamer

Developed with assistance from Somersault.

Library of Congress Control Number: 2015959768

ISBN 978-0-9980044-0-2 (softcover)
ISBN 978-0-9980044-1-9 (ePUB)
ISBN 978-0-9980044-2-6 (ePDF)

Cover design: Anne Huizenga
Interior design: Beth Shagene
Photographer (unless noted otherwise): Jacqueline Klamer
Edited by: Lori VandenBosch, Christopher Cartright, and Andrew McGinnis

Printed in the United States of America

16 17 18 19 20 21 22 • 11 10 9 8 7 6 5 4 3 2 1

Baton ede pye pou pye ede baton.

(The walking stick helps the foot as the foot helps the walking stick.)

Contents

Foreword

Haiti is a beautiful country with pristine beaches, a vibrant culture, and a resilient population. Given all of its assets, it might be surprising that it is the poorest country in the Western Hemisphere.

Over the last ten years, I've watched as Haiti received over $5 billion (USD) in aid, and yet the country has not seen much change. This raises the obvious questions: Where has all the money gone? What has it accomplished? Why are people still so poor?

Haiti in fact is caught in a vicious cycle where the main actors in its development—the government, the private business sector, and nongovernmental organizations (NGOs)—have repeated a failed strategy over and over again for decades. The precepts of this approach are that the government is too corrupt to be trusted and that the private sector appears nonexistent and antiquated. In response, the international community has implemented its own formula where NGOs serve as tools to address needs of the local population—including health, education, infrastructure, access to water, livelihoods, and every other sector you can imagine under the sun. Billions of dollars have been poured into the well, and to everyone's dismay, Haiti remains poor.

Many of the financial resources of NGOs are used to bring in donated or subsidized imported goods, which are then distributed to the community or network of people they serve. This only results in huge market distortions in Haiti. When donated or subsidized goods are distributed below market value, NGOs simply kill the incentives for the private business sector to invest to meet these needs.

These products have seized many sectors in Haiti's market. Viable companies that have been in business for decades have gone bankrupt as a result of such practices. People I know personally have had to shut down production in Haiti and lay off their staff.

From my own experience as owner of Farmatrix, a pharmaceutical production company based in Port-au-Prince, I've found it alarming that within the pharmaceutical sector in Haiti, NGOs supply an estimated 50 percent of the total market. One can easily understand why Haiti can count merely three local pharmaceutical manufacturers, while the Dominican Republic lists 101 equivalent companies for roughly the same size population.

Case in point: To combat the cholera outbreak of 2010, our company had developed a hand sanitizer with alcohol and benzalkonium chloride, which is better suited than other products to protect communities against the outbreak. After buying our branded packaging labels, containers, and setting up this new formula within the production line, we had to stop production completely for one reason: there was an influx of donated hand sanitizers—only alcohol based—that were given for free by the NGOs to communities of customers we were already serving.

Furthermore, keep in mind that for the fiscal year 2014–15, Farmatrix gladly paid over $200,000 in taxes, including payroll and income taxes, to the government. Any successful product launch we have increases our profits, giving us the means to reinvest, hire more employees, raise salaries, and add to the taxes we pay.

If the private business sector brings significant value to the table, why are NGOs still operating under the same model—and, for the most part, ignoring any collaboration with businesses in Haiti?

When talking to the NGO community, three major issues often surface in their reasoning against local procurement: price, quality, and scalability of production.

All these are legitimate concerns that should be addressed. It is true that Haitian businesses tend to be small and operate in a somewhat informal manner. But we must also understand that major players in business will always be reluctant to enter a market where more than 50 percent of the demand is out of their reach. Reaching economies of scale, which could address the issues of price and quantity, is currently difficult for businesses in Haiti, and even impossible under these conditions. The end result is underfunded companies with low-yield, noncompetitive prices, and lower quality products that do not meet buyer needs and expectations.

How do we move forward from here, and without finger-pointing? How do we go from a vicious to a virtuous cycle? The authors of this book propose to answer these difficult questions. Daniel Jean-Louis and Jacqueline Klamer have highlighted a clear plan to move from this rampant problem to a solution. Their plan, with case studies for support, demonstrates how proper investments in market opportunities will create sustainable companies, increase jobs, generate taxes, and take Haiti out of its downward spiral. Their plan is straightforward and includes these key strategies to support the long-term growth of Haiti's business sector:

- Buying locally
- Creating platforms for connecting the main actors
- Advocating policy changes
- Investing in viable business opportunities

Implementation of this strategy will be a perilous and long-term endeavor. There undoubtedly will be many occasions when relief actions to situations such as natural disasters will derail the implementation. By staying true to the course, however, there will also come a time when NGO relief and development efforts, if done well, will strengthen local companies instead of competing against them. Some will argue that local goods, even when they reach quality standards and meet quantity requirements, might still be more expensive. In response, we must jointly—as NGOs, businesses, and governments—engage these following questions: How has a country, which NGOs love and to which they give, become poorer because of their actions—even actions with the best intentions to help? What is the cost to the people that NGOs have fed for years who have no jobs after they exit NGO programs? How is it possible that injecting money in particular ways actually breeds more poverty? What impacts do some businesses' decisions to not pay taxes—on the premise that the government will only steal the money—in addition to corruption within the NGO community itself, have on Haiti's future? What needs to change both horizontally and vertically to strengthen Haiti's market-based system?

Government corruption can and should be tackled. Dancing around the problem doesn't solve it. NGOs need to realign their strategy to Haiti's market-based system. And entrepreneurs and investors need to take risks to achieve long-term sustainable growth and create jobs within the country.

When it comes to Haiti, we all need to change our mental structure. We need to look at Haiti the way we do any other country and see the potential Haiti has to achieve its own unique future.

There are countless good, honest citizens in Haiti. The entrepreneurial spirit is alive and strong. Volunteers and development professionals from around the world truly have our nation's best interest at heart. We have the potential to be a country where corruption, if tackled head-on, is lowered and vibrant companies are manufacturing with certified processes and high-quality goods at competitive prices in the domestic and global markets.

Yet, for this change to happen, the government, the private business sector, NGOs, and the international community need to be *all in*. It will be a long, strenuous battle, yet one we can all win together. This book is a stepping-stone pointing us in the right direction.

RALPH EDMOND
Cofounder and President of Farmatrix S.A.
Port-au-Prince, Haiti
June 2015

Preface

Humans are created and mandated to help each other. Reflecting on the earthquake in Haiti on January 12, 2010, I recognize that now more than ever before.

Though a myriad of aid critics have hit the headlines in recent years, I have learned from my own experience that the desire to support others and build a flourishing culture of mutual care is not the problem. Rather, it is the way humans often go about aid that is problematic. We need to adapt the current models that have been implemented in developing economies and communities of high unemployment for decades.

When I returned to Haiti after completing my university studies in the United States, I was thrilled at the potential of collaborative efforts to fight poverty in my country—an optimistic perspective soon shattered by the unsustainable practices I witnessed on the ground.

These flaws were only exacerbated by the earthquake. I watched as vast amounts of resources, mostly allocated through nonprofits and NGOs (nongovernmental organizations), soon dissolved and disappeared without improving people's lives or resolving Haiti's underlying challenges.

Most aid organizations did not partner with Haiti's business sector.

Instead, these organizations provided foreign aid that undercut Haitian businesses' ability to compete in the local market and serve their respective communities. Just twelve months after the earthquake, the Associated Press stated that out of every $100 spent by US organizations in Haiti, only $1.60 was won by Haitian contractors—a mere $1.60!

At first, my frustration only grew.

Albert Einstein supposedly once said that insanity is doing the same thing over and over again and expecting different results. In Haiti, the same attempts, the same poverty-reduction strategies, only continued.

As I interacted with various professionals helping with post-quake disaster response, I overheard an international aid worker joking that she wished there would be another earthquake so that she could take another helicopter ride. Foreign doctors and nurses streamed into the country, truly seeking to help, yet rarely joined forces with the network of Haitian medical professionals, including my own friends and colleagues with decades of experience who were pushed to the sidelines even in their own medical facilities.

Such attitudes and mindsets were the norm in a post-earthquake recovery environment flooded with millions of dollars in cash and the inevitable false sense of hope.

The worst part? Most aid and development workers weren't willing to adjust their strategy in Haiti, a country known by many as the "Republic of NGOs."

The biggest competitor Haitian businesses faced was the frantic distribution of donated cash and subsidized imported goods—especially the distribution of products for free or below market value. For weeks, then months, then even years following the earthquake, that strategy only caused NGOs to compete with the daily organic business transactions that are the backbone of Haiti's market-based economy.

Despite the prevalence of existing models of aid in Haiti—alarmingly the country with the second highest number of NGOs per capita in the world—and vast amounts of aid poured into the country in recent decades, Haiti has always been, and still remains, a market-based economy in which businesses intend to meet consumer demand with quality products.

Having grown up in Haiti and living there now, I feel deeply connected to the climate, the culture, and the livelihoods of my own family and those around me. Yet, after experiencing other cultures and contexts from my own perspective, I want to help change the way people view my country; I want to reduce the gap in perception between what people see and how Haiti really is.

Haiti's real problem is not the absence of an economic framework. Rather, it is the continued disregard of the one structure in the country capable of bringing about real, lasting, and sustainable growth: Haiti's existing market-based system.

Surely, Haiti has a purchasing power problem. Many people today do not have the means to buy what they need to live, grow, and thrive. Yet the key way to solve this problem is through viable sustainable employment. And the best way to create real employment is through sustainable, viable, and profitable business opportunities.

In this book, I, along with my colleague Jacqueline Klamer, propose a new model. Foreign aid needs to align itself with the market-based economy in which it operates to create jobs and truly have sustainable impact.

Through interviewing dozens of business owners, we found stories of Haitian businesspeople and NGOs partnering through trade to strengthen the Haitian economy and ensure the dignity and self-sustainability of Haitian society for the benefit of all.

It is easy to catalog Haiti's long list of problems: poor infrastructure, weak governance, corruption, lack of education, a culture resistant to western approaches. These observations abound.

But there are also underlying human needs: a mother needs to feed her children; a family needs to care for themselves and their neighbors; people need jobs.

These are real problems. And these are real opportunities for Haiti today.

In the course of writing this book, we realized that our findings reflect not only our two viewpoints, but also that of many others. In addition to interviewing the dozens of business owners and workers you'll find in the case studies, we surveyed over twelve hundred Haitians and internationals in the field. We also included our own personal experiences in Haiti, as well as insights from a broad network of businesspeople, investors, community leaders, government representatives, and development professionals who share this vision for Haiti's future.

The message is simple: Anyone who truly desires to help Haiti must realign their strategy to help create legal, profitable business opportunities in the country. For example, a nonprofit organization might advocate against corruption, or a lending institution might provide affordable access to credit for small businesses. An NGO might equip business owners through training, or a business association might connect Haitian companies with investors. An orphanage manager might intentionally serve healthy meals sourced by local farmers instead of cheap, donated imports, or a representative in parliament might work to enact economic policies that favor business growth. Each of these strategies align with Haiti's market-based system and can help create an environment in which Haitian businesses drive the development of the economy and its impacts on broader society.

This book is not an attempt to offer an unproven theory to be read and placed on a shelf. Instead, we invite all actors to embrace market solutions to Haiti's myriad challenges. We need to stop distorting Haiti's market-based system, and instead build on its emerging opportunities to enable the sustainable growth Haiti so desperately needs.

To clarify, we aren't simply presenting import substitution or social enterprise as miraculous solutions for the current situation. We are also not promoting consumerism as the sole means to development—though we recognize that people should have the opportunity to choose the products that are best suited to meet their families' needs at the right price, whether the products are imported or not.

What we do hope you find is that, in the midst of today's challenges, Haitians continue to transact each day—from purchasing a meal from a street-corner vendor, to producing smart phones and tablets to sell locally and for export.

The power of transactions in Haiti's market economy must not be underestimated.

We should not ignore—no, cannot ignore—the strengths, the innovation, the entrepreneurship, and the endurance that Haiti and her people have to offer.

Daniel Jean-Louis
Port-au-Prince
July 2015

Acknowledgments

We owe a debt of gratitude to Jack and Carol Van Der Ploeg for their extraordinary encouragement and support to make this book a reality.

We also would like to thank our advisors and colleagues—Mats Tunehag, Roxanne Addink de Graaf, Roland Hoksbergen, Doug Seebeck, Dave Genzink, Raulin Cadet, JoAnn Flett, Fred Eppright, Reagan Stricklin, Michael Matheson Miller, Ted Boers, and Ralph Edmond—as they lent us wise counsel to share this message that is so deeply needed in Haiti and beyond.

Our sincere thanks also goes to those who assisted in the research, development, and editing process, including Lori Vanden Bosch, Christopher Cartright, Drew McGinnis, Jeff Bloem, and Jamie Cartright.

I (Daniel) have been blessed to work with my talented and dear friend Jacqueline Klamer, who took the risk and pushed me with her unique insights and endurance as we wrote this book together (literally word-by-word via Skype) throughout the process. My love goes to my wife, Ketia, and our children, Meyer and Brianne, who supported me and sacrificed our time together in the writing of this book—though thankfully my office is two doors down from our home and family reunions were frequent.

We are grateful for the guidance provided to us by the Lord through-out these efforts and in every step ahead.

Last, we give our thanks to the many business owners and development practitioners in Haiti who provided their stories and case studies and, more importantly, continue to make this message ring clearer each day.

CHAPTER 1

The Tragedy
of Auguste Savonnerie:
How International Donations Killed
a Successful Haitian Business

As he guides us around his family's factory on a quiet Sunday afternoon, Laurent Auguste tells us the story of Auguste Savonnerie, once Haiti's third-largest soap manufacturer.

Laurent's grandfather started the business more than four decades ago, basing it near Cité Soleil, which eventually became one of Haiti's most dangerous slum neighborhoods. By age eleven, Laurent was already working in the family business. He would head straight from school to the factory every afternoon, where his grandfather created new products, where his father treated buyers with respect, and where his older brother would test new recipes, striving to create the highest-quality soap product in Haiti. Laurent earned a bachelor's degree in industrial design in the United States, then returned to Port-au-Prince to add value to the family business.

With their college degrees and a strong family work ethic, the Auguste children could have moved to almost anywhere in the world to make a better living—perhaps Brussels, Montreal, Los Angeles, or New York. Certainly, Haiti's political instability and economic fragility make it a difficult place to operate profitably. But the family has intentionally remained in Port-au-Prince. Their roots are here, and Laurent says his family loves the country and its culture too much to leave. But he also displays a sense of civic responsibility. Laurent says that their business has helped to transform the lives of its thirty employees and the thousands of customers from the lowest social class the enterprise serves. As business owners in Haiti, the Augustes seem well aware of the importance of job retention and ethical practices in Haiti's growing yet fragile economy. His family's enterprise embodies how innovative, customer-first businesses can survive and thrive in Haiti's competitive free market.

Yet, despite the myriad challenges the Augustes have endured in Haiti, the one threat the family business would not survive was an unexpected influx of foreign aid following the cholera epidemic of 2010. The influx of donated soap into the market distorted the economy and drove their enterprise out of business.

Ethics and Innovation

So how did the Augustes run a profitable enterprise in Haiti, the least-developed country in the Western Hemisphere? And how did they last for over thirty years? First, they exceeded customer expectations. Second, they met the needs of their employees. Third, they competed and adapted to a local market. And fourth, they met social needs through their business.

Exceeding Customer Expectations

Soap is a basic necessity of modern life, in Haiti as much as anywhere else. But some Haitians have specific needs attached to their soap consumption. According to Laurent, villagers in the rural and mountain regions need a biodegradable product to ensure the livelihood of fisheries and communities downstream, and they requested it of manufacturers.

To meet the specific needs of those customers, Laurent's grandfather launched Auguste Savonnerie in 1978. "We listened to our customer," explains Laurent. The company supplied affordable yet high-quality soaps to customers whose needs were not being met by imports. "They especially loved it because it lathered well," he says.

According to Laurent, his grandfather and brother have spent years specializing their recipe to create a product that goes beyond customer expectations. Laurent explains that the knowledge, risk, and financial investment needed to produce high-quality, biodegradable soap in Haiti has been immense. And, as three generations of entrepreneurs committed to grow their business in Haiti, the Augustes continually invested in research and development and mechanization.

Although soap is a common purchase across social classes, Laurent's market research has taught him that consumer demand is driven by income stability as much as by need. This demand fluctuated regularly according to his customers' income and even by season. "During summer, people wash clothes more frequently due to the hot weather," he reports.

By 1995, the Augustes' company held over 10 percent of the national market and became the third-largest soap producer in Haiti, constantly innovating to thrive in Haiti's free market. Their primary competitors? Two large national corporations that, according to Laurent, produce semi-boiled soap, a lower-quality industrial product that does not last as long as the Augustes'.

By targeting the rural poor and by supplying affordable, high-quality, biodegradable soaps, the company's sales rose steadily. At its height in 2011, Auguste Savonnerie sold nearly $250,000 (USD) of product a month.

Meeting the Needs of Employees

Through the years, the Augustes went beyond the needs of their customer base to address the needs of the workforce. "Our employees had a sense of ownership in our company," says Laurent, who describes his workers as valued members of his organization, not an anonymous labor force—which is how many Haitian employees are often treated by local businesses and international corporations alike. The company valued its staff, offering opportunities for personal and professional growth. The family employed disabled people who could not find work elsewhere, including an aging, blind man who worked for the company for more than twelve years in packaging. Regarding the Augustes' implementation of some of the best manufacturing principles in the world to improve quality and production, Laurent says the family made each decision after much research and consideration of the livelihoods of their employees, who lived in the immediate surrounding communities.

Maintaining market presence while protecting employees' jobs meant using effective management strategies to remain competitive. "You'd never train one employee to know the entire secret method," Laurent says with a grin. The Augustes kept soap recipes a family secret, which Laurent says was essential to maintaining competitiveness in the national and international markets.

They also offered their staff flexible days and hours. "Our competitors were working their staff six days a week," says Laurent. Auguste Savonnerie gave employees the opportunity to decide together to fulfill contracts within three days of long hours if they needed extended weekends. The business also provided professional development opportunities for the staff. "We employed thirty instead of one hundred, but it was a career for them," says Laurent, "not just a seven-hour-per-day job where they weren't recognized and had no opportunity to grow."

That concern for staff led to a mutual respect. When the company upgraded its factory site in 2009, the thirty employees helped build the security walls that stood around the factory just blocks from Cité Soleil. When the January 2010 earthquake destroyed that very same wall, many employees slept outside around the factory to protect the property until its safety was once again ensured. "They knew this is their company," he says. "This is their livelihood, their opportunity for innovation, their pride."

Competing in and Adapting to the Local Market

Competing in Haiti's soap market was made more difficult by the Augustes' two largest national competitors, who together held close to 90 percent of the market. These companies often dropped their sales prices to flood the market. Since the Augustes could not maintain profitability at those levels, they had to maintain consistent prices—despite their competitors' fluctuation. But their customer base proved faithful. "We weren't playing games," says Laurent, "and they respected that."

Beyond consistency, the Augustes' enterprise remained competitive through strategic investment in research and development and in production. In 2005, Auguste Savonnerie invested in some of the best equipment in the world and achieved a more efficient and cost-effective production that produced a higher-quality soap. "Every five years, we moved into R&D, studying to see what was next," says Laurent. The company quickly doubled production, but Haiti's market absorbed it easily. "Having been here so long," says Laurent, "we can tell you that Haiti's always going to be developing." According to Laurent, opportunities to meet new market demands will only grow.

Instead of investing heavily in marketing, the Augustes passed on savings to their low-income customers. "It's a lot more personal here," says Laurent. "We've hardly ever spent anything on advertising because the soap spoke for itself." The product's quality created a demand that eventually developed its own value chain. "We actually created wholesalers," Laurent reports.

Free competition was a foundational aspect of ethical business for the Augustes. Even when given the opportunity to monopolize the market, the Augustes actually assisted their competitors when they faced transportation challenges. Laurent explains, "We believe in free competition. Competition is good for me. It pushes me to be better. Other people in Haiti believe the opposite. They think by crushing competition, they can monopolize. But they don't realize that they plateau the market by being the only person in the market with no innovation. We've always practiced fair business, and it's paid off." As Laurent notes, the company's fair business practices have led to an increase in customer loyalty over the years.

Meeting Social Needs through Business

In Laurent's experience, he has seen how well local businesses can adapt to meet community needs—often better than foreign businesses and even NGOs. In 2007, Laurent and three other business owners operating near Cité Soleil—one of the several "red zones" identified by the United Nations and Haitian national police[1]—decided to ask the community how local businesses could help.

Laurent reports that the community asked the business owners to build a school. To his surprise, the residents were not requesting the establishment for their own children. "They wanted a school for all the kids on the streets who don't have parents and can't pay for schools, because tomorrow these kids are going to be enemies of the kids with parents, and out on the streets."

Laurent calls it the opportunity of a lifetime. He and his partners began seeking nonprofit NGOs with whom they could partner, and they approached well-known international organizations that could potentially fund the project. He was again surprised to find that one such organization held a $9 million budget that had to be spent in the red zones within two years.

Laurent and his partners quickly organized a meeting for business owners, community leaders, and representatives of NGOs. The first meeting would be the last. Laurent reports that one foreigner representing the NGO with the seven-figure budget stood up to discuss how they should build a proposal collectively to request the funds. "The only thing we need to report is that this area is full of hoodlums and gangsters, and this is how donors will be more than happy to give money," she said. In response, one nineteen-year-old resident spoke up: "Excuse me, ma'am. If you need to call me a gangster, a murderer, a thief, please take that money and shove it." According to Laurent, he and his partners did not hear from that NGO again.

Still, the business owners were not deterred. They raised the funds themselves, providing more than enough from their own profit and that of other businesses nearby. "Four of us put up and paid for the school," Laurent says, reporting that the school cost nearly $50,000 to establish.

Now, just five years later, the school serves 385 students each year and boasts a 97 percent graduation rate, in accordance with the tests required to pass kindergarten through sixth grade. The building has six classrooms, and adult education is provided in the afternoon.

"Everything is community-based," says Laurent. "We don't depend on anything [outside the community]." Other area businesses provide food for student meals. The school even sends food home with children who would otherwise go hungry.

Laurent visits the institution regularly to spend a day with the children. Their poverty has not ceased to affect him, though significant progress has been made. "If I spend a couple of days down there, I start crying," he says.

The Catastrophe of NGO Donations

With a manufacturing site in Cité Soleil, the company had seen its share of ups and downs over the years, enduring not only the political unrest of the 1990s through the early 2000s, but also managing to survive amid the continuous gang violence that permeated the surrounding area. Like many Haitian entrepreneurs, the Augustes have received multiple death threats. In 2005, during the United Nations' mandate to disarm and secure the red zones, civilian riots and an unending string of gun battles between the local gangs and UN forces rocked Cité Soleil. Hundreds of bullet holes are scored in the factory's cinder block security walls.

But while Auguste Savonnerie survived those years of chaos and bloodshed, the ever-increasing number of free goods distributed by international NGOs disrupted Haiti's market in an even more catastrophic way. In October 2010, cholera broke out. In March 2011, Auguste Savonnerie closed its doors. In less than a year, donated soaps had done what riots, gang violence, and death threats had been unable to do: put the Augustes out of business.

According to Laurent, before 2011 between three and four million bars of soap were imported and distributed for free in Haiti each year. Health and sanitation organizations, and other NGOs running those kinds of programs in the country, often distribute soap to combat the spread of disease. Laurent expresses respect and appreciation for the initiatives, which help Haitians "in regions we knew our businesses couldn't reach."

But international organizations, wary of the Haitian private sector's oft-publicized corruption and lack of quality, rarely purchase goods locally and prefer imports often purchased or donated in their own economies. Still, for years Auguste Savonnerie had been able to predict and adapt to the sporadic competition from donated goods.

After the cholera outbreak that began in October 2010—caused, ironically enough, by the poor sanitation practices of UN military forces[2]—the United Nations imported forty million critical items, including bars of soap to combat the spread of the disease,[3] as well as other NGO imports distributed below market value. From one year to the next, Auguste Savonnerie went from competing with three to four million bars of free soap to an overwhelming increase of soaps and other substitute products.

The free soap bars were rapidly distributed under the emergency-response phase of Haiti's earthquake recovery. This context allowed for little oversight, and the United Nations had a vested interest in distributing the soap as quickly as possible to prevent the cholera from spreading on their watch. Later, a large portion of the soap was reported stolen. It reappeared on the market soon after, being resold for one-tenth of market value. Demand for soap plummeted and prices followed. Suddenly, the Augustes could not break even at any price.

While the free distribution of goods like soap in developing countries ostensibly aims to help the poorest people on the planet, larger economic interests are also served by this practice. Large manufacturers in developed economies often overproduce in order to guarantee supply, yet oversupply quickly satisfies demand, leaving an overstock that lowers profits. When the United Nations declares a health emergency in a country like Haiti, some of the world's largest corporations have an opportunity to quickly shed overproduction and recuperate capital without driving prices down at home.

Laurent recalls his wholesalers approaching him with news of cheaper goods now available through various sellers who had acquired the donated soap. He told them they could very well purchase at the bid the illegal sellers were offering, knowing they would have to make the most economical decision for themselves. As a result, within months, the Augustes manufacturing site shut down.

Laurent Auguste, an authentic businessperson to the last, says it was his fault. According to him, Auguste Savonnerie should have predicted and adapted to competition from the free NGO imports. But while hindsight is 20/20, in 2010 the market for soap in Haiti was distorted far beyond what any strategist would have been able to forecast.

Ultimately, the influx of free, imported products wiped out a profitable business that supplied quality biodegradable soaps at an affordable price to the Haitian poor. When the donations ran out, prices rose again, and the market was saturated with lower-quality, less environmentally responsible goods. When the Augustes went out of business, jobs were lost and a source of tax revenue for the state also dried up. Every time a profitable, registered Haitian business goes under, municipal and national infrastructures take a hit. The livelihoods of the business's employees are significant, but the ripple effect on the local consumers, transporters, wholesalers, and retailers who also rely on that business is catastrophic, not to mention the effect on local infrastructure, which relies on tax revenue for support.

Moving Forward

So where do we go from here? What can we learn from the story of a Haitian business struggling to compete, not just against other local businesses—or even against Haiti's natural catastrophes and political instability—but against a constant influx of donated goods that poison the market and distort the economy?

In chapter 2, we will examine the major players in Haiti's economy: business, government, and nongovernmental aid organizations (NGOs); we will review some basic economic theory, including the role of businesses in generating resources, and the role of governments and NGOs in distributing those resources. Then, in chapter 3 we will review the history of Haiti's market economy, and in chapter 4 we will demonstrate how the power of transactions in Haiti has been undermined by prevalent NGO strategies, subsidies, and donations. But the subsequent six chapters are why we are really here. In these chapters we develop answers to questions arising from stories like that of Auguste Savonnerie. We believe aid organizations and businesses can collaborate. Instead of ineffective and detrimental international intervention and aid, we advocate a system of opportunity-based economic development through trade. Haiti, while poor, is a market-based economy, and must be treated as such for any sustainable progress to take hold. Trade—not aid—holds the key to the economic future of Haiti as a truly developing nation, not as a Republic of NGOs.

CHAPTER 2

Business, Government, and NGOs:

The Major Players in Haiti's Economic System

Why should we care about the fate of a company like Auguste Savonnerie? Because, to put it simply, a country's economy grows if and only if its businesses grow. In a market-based system, a country's economic growth is equivalent to the growth of all businesses, on average, that exist in the country. Governments, NGOs, and businesses have revenue and expenses. However, business revenue comes from sales, while government revenue comes from taxes and NGO revenue comes from donations.

In short, businesses are resource generators, creating wealth rather than collecting or redistributing it.

RESOURCE GENERATORS: Business

How do businesses create wealth and thus become resource generators? A business acquires material and human resources, then transforms them into a good or service that has value for customers. When a business makes enough sales to cover its costs, it breaks even. When sales, or revenue, exceeds the cost to provide the good or service, the business can grow. So, if the business can deliver a satisfactory product for a price that exceeds the costs and the customer is willing to pay, the customer makes a purchase that results in a profit for the business. This balanced transaction creates wealth that did not exist before: customer satisfaction and profit. In turn, this growth allows the business to further invest in its operations, employ more people, and pay more taxes.

Here's an example: A business spends a dollar to produce a product, then sells the product to a retailer for $1.50. The business makes a fifty-cent profit and thereby a 50 percent return on investment. The retailer sells the product to another customer for three dollars, but in the meantime has distribution expenses of fifty cents, on top of the $1.50 it paid for inventory. The retailer therefore makes a dollar in profit and also a 50 percent return on investment. Finally, the customer purchases the product, which adds value to his or her life. In this win-win-win situation, the business, the retailer, and the customer are satisfied by a balanced transaction.

What Are Balanced Transactions?

Transaction is the world's primary method for sustaining life. As do most countries around the world, Haiti relies on transactions to sustain and grow its economy, whether through international trade or domestic market exchange.

In a transaction, one person or entity exchanges goods or services with another person or entity. The earliest forms of exchange were often performed through bartering: the direct exchange of one good for another. But people soon discovered that bartering did not always allow for the most efficient satisfaction of demand. In response, humans developed other mediums of value, such as gold and other precious metals, then printed money, and now credit cards and other forms of electronic payment. Still, throughout history most societies and civilizations have used some form of transaction to meet their needs.

A balanced transaction is the healthy result of supply and demand through which the customer's need (demand) is satisfied and the business's good or service (supply) yields a profit. The opposite would be an unbalanced transaction in which either or both customer satisfaction and business profit are not achieved.

Price is an essential component in balancing supply and demand, thereby determining the success of a transaction. A balanced transaction can be as big as buying a house for $250,000 or as little as purchasing a shoelace for fifty cents. In each of these examples, the three components—supply, demand, and price—must be in harmony to achieve a balanced transaction. In other words, price often determines both whether the customer will leave with the desired item and whether the business will make a profit. The basic reality is this: anything that needs to be acquired in a market-based economy falls within a dynamic of supply and demand.

The global economy functions and grows because together we make billions of balanced transactions every day. What we may not realize is that our transactions have a multiplying effect on the stability and growth of our market-based economy, both locally and globally.

Transaction as a Key Factor in Economic Growth

Transactions are the engine of economic growth, but for sustainable economic growth to happen the transactions on average need to be satisfactory and profitable, which in economic terms is called market equilibrium. Just as the global population grows one child at a time, the global economy grows one transaction at a time. The more balanced transactions that are made, the greater economic growth will be. The opposite is also true: A lack of balanced transactions, or an increase in unbalanced transactions, will weaken a market-based system.

We must understand business and transaction as distinct elements in a market dynamic. A transaction may be the engine of growth, but it is simply a trigger that jump-starts momentum within a larger business strategy. Transactions function much like the human heart. The heart is not intelligent. It does not strategize or even think. Its primary purpose is to distribute blood throughout the body. When parts of the body need oxygen, the heart reacts based on that need. Transactions can be understood in the same way. The most basic function of transaction is to facilitate exchange, as is the case when any product is purchased. Transactions facilitate that exchange within the ecosystem of price, supply, and demand.

While transactions are like the heart, businesses are like the brain. They have the intelligence to direct the heart, or transactions. They have strategic plans to respond to emergency situations, to increase or decrease the rhythm of transactions, and various other strategies. A business might realize that the flow of supply isn't meeting customer demand, and it can increase production or adapt distribution. Regardless of whether profit or customer satisfaction are achieved, transactions will occur as soon as there is supply, demand, and both parties are willing to transact and exchange at an agreed-upon price.

For transactions to lead to economic growth they need to take place within profitable business models. Business is the best channel by which balanced transactions occur because it allows for the outcomes that are essential for economic growth. One key outcome is profit, which can be reinvested in the business or in the market at large, adding value and triggering future transactions.

Balanced transactions lead to economic growth, which leads to industry growth, market development, and job creation. Entire value chains can be sustained in this way. As businesses create wealth and customer satisfaction, they also create employment, raising the population's purchasing power. Balanced transactions grow an economy by generating resources, tax revenue, and purchasing power.

According to a recent report in *The Economist*, nearly a billion people have risen out of poverty in the last twenty years because assets and liabilities have been leveraged into opportunities in countries around the world. Global poverty was cut in half between 1990 and 2010 as economic growth rates in certain developing countries grew from a previous average annual rate of 4.3 percent in 2000 to 6 percent in 2010. Some estimates attribute two-thirds of poverty reduction in a particular country to this kind of economic growth.[1]

RESOURCE DISTRIBUTORS: Government and NGOs

While businesses generate resources through balanced transactions, government generally does not generate resources, nor does it create wealth directly. Rather, in market economies, governments draw most of their revenue from taxes. Therefore we can understand governments as resource distributors. Tax revenue is collected from a variety of sources, including private businesses and employees. That revenue is used to provide public services, such as the legal system, public education, and the police, and to invest in infrastructures that increase business opportunities and the quality of life. When a government collects enough taxes to cover its expenditures, it breaks even.

The simple collection of taxes from businesses and individuals can support a nation's entire operational cost. But for an economy to grow, government—as it fulfills its own role to serve and strengthen society—needs to invest the taxes collected back into the economy by partnering with businesses so that the private sector can make more transactions, thereby creating a healthy environment in which the country's wealth and resources continue to grow.

Like the government, most NGOs are resource distributors. They gather revenue through donations, then distribute resources for free or at subsidized prices under their nonprofit charters.

Ultimately, governments collect taxes and then distribute that wealth and resources, NGOs collect donations and distribute resources purchased, but it is businesses that generate the wealth and resources that governments and NGOs distribute. A simple chart on page 34 summarizes the difference.

When businesses make balanced transactions—transactions that generate resources for the business (revenue) and meet the needs of the customer (satisfactory products or services)—they can grow, thus supporting the needs not only of the private sector, but also of the public sector (government) and even NGOs. Business alone has the ability to generate resources that no other entity can. But when the government or NGOs unknowingly upset the balance of business transactions, as happened in the case of Auguste Savonnerie, catastrophe results. And instead of growth, the country experiences a downward spiral.

Challenges have been prevalent in Haiti throughout its history, including political instability, natural disaster, poor infrastructure, and a lack of long-term vision and investment. Yet from our findings, Haiti's downward spiral has also been exacerbated because the government and NGOs have disrupted the natural process of balanced transactions. On the one hand, the government fails to promote the healthy business climate needed to increase balanced transactions. On the other hand, misaligned NGOs distribute

	REVENUE	EXPENSES	IMPACT
BUSINESSES (Resource Generators)	By selling goods and services, businesses generate revenue by providing something of added value worth the price a customer is willing to pay to satisfy a need.	Businesses have fixed costs and variable costs, including raw materials, production, marketing, distribution, human resources, taxes, and loan interest rates.	Businesses generate resources by creating profit. A business not only distributes goods and services, but pays income to its employees and taxes to the government. It also provides direct return on investment to customers and shareholders.
GOVERNMENT (Resource Distributor)	Most taxes for national and local governments come from businesses: sales, income, payroll, and property taxes, customs and other duties—all generated through for-profit businesses or their indirect impact.	Government uses tax revenue to cover expenses such as investment in infrastructure, public safety, the legal system, public education, and other social services such as welfare and healthcare.	Government distributes wealth and resources generated by for-profit businesses. It provides taxpayers and society as a whole an indirect return on investment.
NGOS (Resource Distributors)	NGOs have multiple revenue sources, including government grants, private donations, and foundational donations—the majority of which are sourced from wealth and resources created by for-profit businesses.	NGOs spend money on operations and material goods in their work toward social and humanitarian relief services, distribution of free or subsidized goods and services, or long-term developmental programs.	As nonprofit organizations, the majority of NGOs pay little or no government taxes. Instead, they distribute resources generated by businesses. Donors do not receive any direct return on their investment, and many donors do not require full audits or reviews of NGO spending.

resources in an unsustainable way. Although we will make some comments on rule of law and government policy, tackling government policy is not the focus of this book. Instead, we want to focus on the role NGOs play in the Haitian economy, and for more information to support this claim, will next review Haiti's market-based system throughout its history.

The History of Haiti's Market-Based Economy from the Precolonial Years to the Present

No matter the political framework, the economy based on trade is an underlying current of human life, and Haiti has always had a market-based economy. Through colonization, slavery, revolution, dictatorship, and democracy, Haitian life has been shaped by small and large transactions, the lifeblood of market economies.

This chapter is the foundation to help readers understand how Haiti's market-based economic situation has been an intricate part of its historical timeline leading up to where Haiti finds itself today. Since some readers may question this concept, in this chapter we will survey the major phases of Haiti's economic history to show how Haitians have survived over the last three centuries by transacting locally and internationally to meet needs profitably. Yet readers who are already knowledgeable about Haiti's market-based system over time may skip to the next chapter.

The Precolonial Era

While little is known of the Taíno and Arawak peoples who inhabited the island before Spanish colonization, we know that, over five hundred years ago, transaction through bartering supported communal life. Because of the absence of private property rights, a market economy as we know it did not exist. However, evidence suggests that the Taíno people were avid hunters and fishers, and traded among themselves, with other tribes, and even with other islands throughout the Caribbean.

In 1492, Christopher Columbus landed near what is now the city of Cap-Haïtien, and named the island Hispaniola. Just over a decade later, the first Africans were brought over to the island for labor. Within five years, the Spanish had established slavery. With the arrival of European explorers, the process of colonization reformed the island's economy.[1]

Colonization and Slavery

In 1592, Queen Anacaona, the leader of the last Taíno kingdom, was executed by the Spanish governor, but from the day Europeans set foot on Hispaniola, the economic framework of the island was turned upside down. All resources on the island were declared the property of the Queen of Spain, setting the stage for a market economy with the introduction of property rights. The notion of private property was further established as colonists built homes and plantations—and enslaved the remaining indigenous population, taking ownership of their labor.

The market-based system matured as Spain and France competed for the island. Colonists throughout the island sold goods to the Spanish and French governments, providing cotton, sugar, spices, cacao, and gold to the European markets. In 1625, the French settled on the northwestern region of the island, naming it Saint-Domingue. Port-de-Paix was founded to export the island's resources. Under the 1697 Treaty of Ryswick, Spain ceded the western third of the island to the French. By the start of the eighteenth century, Hispaniola was fully integrated into the global economic system of trade.

As Saint-Domingue grew, the French invested more heavily in the colony's agro-production, requiring a larger workforce. The indigenous peoples died from European diseases and forced labor, so Africans, turned slaves, were imported to take their place—a phenomenon already in practice throughout the Caribbean and North America. Because of the half a million slaves in Saint-Domingue by the late eighteenth century, the French were able to export increasing quantities of sugar and coffee, which were in high demand in Europe. Saint-Domingue quickly became the most prosperous colony of the French Empire, a leading economic force in Europe and the New World.[2]

The French colony was a success because they chose to produce staple foods that were in high demand in Europe. In contrast, the Spanish focused on mining gold and mineral wealth, and were late in moving into agricultural production. With its successful production methods and diverse revenue streams, Saint-Domingue became the most profitable slave-based plantation colony in the world, and was known by all as the "Pearl of the Antilles." According to economist Mats Lundahl,

> after 1680, sugar, a staple, became the main export product; indigo and cocoa were added toward the end of the seventeenth century. Cotton was exported for a while but suffered heavy competition from sugar, and did not come back until the 1750s. The overall value of exports expanded rapidly. In 1743, Saint-Domingue produced more sugar than all the British Antilles together. Saint-Domingue developed into France's most valuable colony: in 1789, it accounted for more than 40 percent of the foreign trade of France, and some 5 million out of 27 million French were estimated to depend directly on this trade, which rested on the labor of some 450,000 slaves. In the same year coffee exports, which had begun in the late 1730s, had expanded to the point where their value equaled two-thirds of the exports of raw sugar.[3]

In 1749, Port-au-Prince was established and named the capital of Saint-Domingue. Just two years later, the first slave rebellions began, led by Francois Mackandal. But despite these tensions, the market-based system of the western part of the island continued to grow.

Many colonists refused to feed their slaves and instead provided them with small plots of land. Slaves farmed their own lands after working on the plantations, growing enough food to survive, and eventually selling their surplus to each other or in the larger local market. From the elite landholders, to the merchant class, to the slaves, transaction sustained daily life and grew the economy of the island.

By 1789, Saint-Domingue produced 60 percent of the world's coffee and 40 percent of the world's sugar, which was exported in large part to the

French and British Empires. Saint-Domingue was the wealthiest colony in the Caribbean and one of the most prosperous in the world.[4]

The Effects of the Industrial and French Revolutions

The Industrial Revolution was born at the crossroad of the growing European population's increased demand for food, and the deterioration of forced-labor systems as the notion of liberty spread throughout the classes as a result of the American and French Revolutions. In the eighteenth century, Europe began to experience the population growth and economic advantage that made it the leading competitor in the global economy. Europe had accumulated much of its wealth through forced labor and slavery. But in the nineteenth century, new and more effective means of production began to emerge, giving birth to the Industrial Revolution.[5]

Social, political, economic, and industrial innovation made it cheaper and more efficient to use machinery than forced labor. The Industrial Revolution abroad informed the colonial revolution of the middle class in Saint-Domingue, who quickly pulled the slaves over to their cause by promising abolition.

As the world's population grew, so did demand for goods—from staple foods to spices and sugar. That demand had to be satisfied within the market-based system. That market did not dictate the use of slavery; rather, the market-based economy is actually the neutral platform upon which such decisions were made. The decision to implement the forced-labor system that cost the lives of hundreds of thousands of slaves in Saint-Domingue and around the world was based on the need to meet rising demand profitably. Once the Industrial Revolution created opportunities to meet that demand even more profitably through mechanization and mass production, the economic advantages of slavery subsided.

In response to the French Revolution of 1789, which produced the Declaration of the Rights of Man and of the Citizen, the free blacks and mulattoes of Haiti approached the government of Saint-Domingue to claim the voting rights that France had declared for all proprietors.[6] When they were denied, the voting rights movement grew, and soon the educated mulattoes revolted against the Empire, which led to the declaration of freedom for all slaves in 1793. This new conception of liberty, born in Europe, spread rapidly throughout the colonies and sparked the Haitian Revolution.

Independence and Abolition

As Africans in Haiti continued to organize and revolt, the Haitian Revolution accelerated and became the most successful slave revolt in history. On the night of August 14, 1791, Dutty Boukman, a voodoo priest, led a religious ceremony in Bois Caïman. Over the next week, slaves revolted, burning plantations throughout the colony. Over the two months following, more than one hundred thousand slaves joined forces, killing more than four thousand whites and burning hundreds of sugar, indigo, and coffee plantations. Within one year, the freedmen and former slaves controlled one-third of the island.[7]

The French Legislative Assembly decided to protect its economic interests by granting civil and political rights to all men of color in Saint-Domingue. However, other European nations and the new United States of America were concerned that France would lose control over the most profitable slave colony in the hemisphere. As the colonial wars raged on, the former slaves of Saint-Domingue allied with the English and the Spanish to stand against the French in the New World. In order to prevent a military disaster, the French governor of Saint-Domingue, Léger-Félicité Sonthonax, freed the slaves still under the Empire's control. In 1794, the French Empire abolished slavery in France and all of its colonies, but a forced-labor system continued nonetheless.[8]

By 1801, Toussaint L'Ouverture, leader of the Haitian revolutionary forces, issued a constitution declaring Saint-Domingue an autonomous and sovereign black state and pronouncing himself Governor for Life.[9] In response, Napoleon Bonaparte sent wave after wave of troops to attempt to regain the colony. In spite of the capture and exile of L'Ouverture, revolutionary forces, under the command of Jean-Jacques Dessalines, continued the fight against Bonaparte's armies.[10] Haitian forces recoursed to extreme measures upon Bonaparte's attempt to restore French control—burning plantations and destroying infrastructure under the order of Toussaint to keep Bonaparte's troops from reclaiming property and plantations—in the broader plan the Haitian leadership desired to protect the market-based economy Haiti held and to restore it.

On January 1, 1804, the French were defeated, and the colony became the first independent black nation in the world. As Saint-Domingue went through this profound revolution, the political system transformed from colonization to self-governance. The war had so completely destroyed the plantation system that, on the surface, it would appear that the market-based economic system in Saint-Domingue no longer existed.[11] Every aspect of life seemed fundamentally changed. But the economic framework in which needs were met through transactions lived on.

The Post-Revolution Economy

The continuation of the market-based system in the new Republic of Haiti was a conscious decision made by its Haitian leaders as the best way to rise out of post-war recovery and build prosperity.[12]

Prior to the previously mentioned invasion of French military leader Bonaparte and the subsequent burning of plantations, in 1801, when Toussaint L'Ouverture took control of the colony, he had adopted a policy in which large plots of land were distributed to army generals for the cultivation of crops such as coffee, sugar, and tobacco. Officers were provided smaller plots of land that produced vegetables and other crops. The land distribution was predicated on a market-based system of private ownership and trade. After the arrest and exile of L'Ouverture, Dessalines continued the same policy of land redistribution to develop agriculture and to meet needs profitably through market transactions. Small farms sprouted throughout the country. Haiti operated as a market-based economy that encouraged free enterprise and small businesses. Although the production was tightly monitored by the newest fragile government under military leadership, the small farm production made it directly to the local markets and continued to be exported.[13]

As the Industrial Revolution expanded in western Europe and the United States, Haiti maintained its presence in the global market by importing and exporting products such as cotton, tobacco, and coffee. Haiti became the second-largest trading partner for the United States, as a newly independent country in close proximity, and continued exporting coffee and other products within in the midst of its dictatorial framework early on.

For the first two decades following independence, the former colony was divided. The northern region was held by King Henry Christophe, who reinstated forced labor under a centralized government that continued exporting to foreign nations and entities. The western region was led by President Alexandre Pétion, who implemented a more decentralized economy, distributing small plots of land from the government to former slaves.[14] In either case, the large and small landholders alike produced and sold to each other and abroad, whether in wholesale or small, informal transactions.

In 1826, Jean-Pierre Boyer became president of the western portion of Haiti following the death of Pétion. He also occupied the eastern two-thirds of Hispaniola, or the present-day Dominican Republic, for twenty-five years, until he was ousted by Dominican nationals in 1844. During his first months as president, Boyer made plans to increase revenue by increasing the number of transactions within the same market-based economic system. He also initiated a policy to reevaluate the leasing of land through the government. Although his presidency was very different from that of his predecessor, he maintained the two layers of transactions at the national and international level.

Boyer's policies, however, had a detrimental economic and social impact. As economist Robert Lacerte summarizes:

> Boyer also attempted to increase export revenues by increasing agricultural production. In 1826, he promulgated a Rural Code based on forced labor. The Haitian land situation was a mixed one of large estates owned mostly by mulattoes, except for the North where there were black plantation owners, alongside whom existed small proprietors. The latter cultivated between ten to fifty acres given over to coffee trees and subsistence crops. The mulatto elite could not demand forced labor from the black majority with the same rigor with which Toussaint and Christophe had done without risking a caste war. They had to acquiesce to a growing number of peasant proprietors. The peasants, however, were not oriented primarily to

an export economy. Their coffee trees were allowed to run wild, were never replaced, and were worked only five weeks out of the year with the inevitable result that coffee production declined. At the same time, the blacks refused to work the large estates because of their association with slave labor. This meant that the mulattoes were unable to increase production on their plantations with the result that they gradually abandoned them. The movement of the mulattoes into the towns also had the disastrous effect of further tightening caste lines. Haiti grew increasingly divided between rural areas populated largely by blacks and towns which were predominantly mulatto.[15]

Despite these challenges, whether through agricultural development or urbanization, individual enterprises continued to sustain life by producing and selling goods and services locally and exporting commodities abroad. According to Lacerte, "by 1832, Haitian exports were valued at £1,250,000 annually of which the British share was one-half. Haiti came third, at that time, after Mexico and Peru as England's trading partner among the Latin American republics."[16]

Throughout the nineteenth century, the national constitution was constantly rewritten by Haitian heads of state as political turmoil reigned. In 1849, the Haitian Republic itself was overthrown by Emperor Faustin I. As a result, the economy stalled as the newly appointed government redistributed agricultural holdings again. The Haitian economy was also crippled by the reparations it had to pay to France, which equaled $21 billion in modern terms.

In the meantime, the United States did not acknowledge Haiti as an independent nation until 1862 due to US tensions between the North and South that would eventually end in the American Civil War and the abolition of slavery.[17] In 1865, the United States and Haiti signed a new treaty of commerce allowing trade between the two market economies, which equipped Haiti to step forward into the twentieth century. The last two decades of the nineteenth century were also marked by the development of the Haitian intellectual middle class, as well as urbanization as the market-based economy grew.

It is important to note that amid all of this political upheaval the fragile market-based system was still the backbone of the nation. During the first century following independence, no matter the political system, no matter the leader, all of Haiti relied on local and international trade to sustain life.

The 1915 American Occupation and Its Aftermath

At the start of the twentieth century, Haiti saw the arrival of Lebanese, German, Italian, French, and other foreign nationals who established themselves in the country and participated in the market by importing foreign goods and exporting Haitian goods.

From 1911 to 1915, six different presidents took power in Haiti, and each was exiled or killed. As communism and fascism spread throughout the world, the United States feared German influence on Haiti's fragile political system; Germans had quickly gained control of 80 percent of Haiti's foreign commerce, with a strong presence in the major ports of Port-au-Prince and Cap-Haïtien.[18]

As Haiti's political history unfolded, foreign nationals played a major role in the market economy through commercial ventures. An estimated fifteen thousand Syrian-Lebanese Christians, fleeing religious oppression and poverty in the Ottoman Empire, migrated to Haiti at the turn of the century. Lebanese and other foreign nationals invested in the food and textile industries, and adapted to the local market system of Haiti by importing foreign products to distribute in the country and exporting valuable goods such as coffee, cocoa, and other products. Foreign investors weren't too far behind. According to Brenda Plummer,

> the United States wasted little time in discovering the utility of the Syrian merchants. American trade with Haiti consisted primarily of the same dried staples and cloth that it had exported to the West Indies in colonial times. In the early 1900s, American firms provided 60% of all Haitian imports, most of which were sold to the peasant majority.[19]

The same spirit of commerce that pervaded Haitian society throughout the colonial and post-revolutionary eras remained strong. Even before the United States invaded Haiti in 1915, Americans were already vying with Syrians for influence in the Haitian market, because both nations exported textiles and clothing to Haiti's rural peasants.

In 1910 the US State Department backed a group of American investors in a bid to acquire control of the Haitian National Bank, the sole commercial bank in Haiti, which served as the national treasury, in order to diminish the influence of the Germans, who were an emerging global threat to western powers.

In August 1912, the Haitian American Sugar Company (HASCO), an American business venture of three investors registered in Wilmington, Delaware, began operations in Haiti with an initial capital investment of $5 million. A railroad system was installed throughout the country to transport sugarcane to the company's plant near the bay of Port-au-Prince. Beyond its political and diplomatic implications, the HASCO venture is just one of many examples of how foreign corporations were formed in Haiti to meet global demand for Haiti's agricultural production.[20]

Amid emerging political tensions at the start of World War I, Haiti began to reverse its isolationist policies and entered an alliance with the United States. However, when American bankers complained to President Woodrow Wilson about the amount of debt Haiti held in American banks, the United States invaded in 1915. The first American invasion came at the time when the United States feared that the Germans and the Syrians were gaining significant economic power in Haiti. The US strategy was to consolidate its economic interests in the Americas as the industrial nations of the world entered the First World War.[21]

In July 1915, three hundred US Marines invaded Port-au-Prince under the direction of President Woodrow Wilson, and the Haitian-American Convention was ratified for a ten-year period by the US Senate, which wielded veto power over all government decisions in Haiti. The United States dismantled Haiti's constitutional bylaws, which had originally prohibited foreign ownership of land. Through a newly ratified constitution, foreigners could now own land in Haiti, a right not previously granted in order to protect the economy from foreign intervention. During the occupation, US interests used up to 40 percent of Haiti's national tax revenue to repay decades-old debts to American and French banks.[22]

Ultimately, the repayment of these debts to foreign banks crippled Haiti's economic growth during the nearly two-decade-long occupation. During that period, the US government invested in Haiti's infrastructure, building roads and bridges, restoring irrigation canals, and constructing public buildings, schools, and hospitals—all to serve American business interests in the country. In Haiti's crippled economy, nonprofit development models, funded by the international community, began to emerge, such as the US military's efforts to increase access to drinking water.

In spite of Haitian resistance to the occupation, US forces remained until 1934, when critics in the United States saw the need to refocus the government's efforts toward the domestic economy during the Great Depression. Following the US occupation, Haiti underwent a period of political instability marked by predatory regimes and frequent coups. Though coffee remained Haiti's largest export, it would never again rise to the great production levels of the nineteenth century. The country also faced challenging relations with the Dominican Republic. In light of the Great Depression and the growing unemployment rate among Dominicans, in 1937, disputes over trade and land ownership near the border resulted in the well-known Parsley Massacre during which time nearly twenty thousand second-generation Haitians living and working as manual laborers were killed by Dominican troops.[23]

Finally, in 1946 Dumarsais Estimé was elected president, and Haiti entered a period of relative stability. President Estimé secured legislation on social security and equipped middle-class citizens and many blacks to play essential roles in municipal and national government, roles traditionally held by mulattoes and the elite. Of equal impact was Estimé's nationalization of the Standard Fruit Banana Concession, a step that drastically reduced the once privately held corporation's revenues. Estimé's decision to nationalize industry did not align with Haiti's historically market-based economy in which private business owners and investors—not governments—operated for-profit companies. During "the first half of the 1940s, bananas began to be exported, but the removal of the private export monopoly thereafter killed the new product."[24]

Though the US occupation and its aftermath had severe political and economic effects, nothing undermined Haiti's market economy as badly as the introduction of nonprofit development models and Estimé's nationalization of industry.

World War II, Communism, and the Duvalier Era

François "Papa Doc" Duvalier was appointed Director of Public Health under the presidency of Dumarsais Estimé before being appointed Minister of Public Health and Labor in 1949. After opposing the coup d'état that ousted Estimé in 1950, Duvalier sought asylum abroad. Six years later, he returned to Haiti as elections were being organized. In October 1957, he was elected president.[25]

After World War II, the nations of the world had little choice but to ally themselves to either the United States or the Soviet Union. Duvalier stood diplomatically with the United States in opposition to the rising influence of communism as many socialist revolutions took root throughout Latin America and the Caribbean. While neighboring Cuba's economic structure had transformed to adapt to a communist model in which citizens worked for the state, which redistributed resources, Haiti's market economy held strong. With little support from the Haitian government, private businesses continued to meet the population's needs.

In 1961, during the early stages of his dictatorship, Duvalier rewrote the Haitian constitution, appointed himself president for life, and established a paramilitary force, the Tonton Makout, whose sole purpose was to protect Duvalier's power. Through targeted killings and rapes, the Duvalier regime effectively repressed any opposition. His dictatorship caused further divisions between educated mulattoes, many of whom held positions in the military and public sector, and low-income blacks.[26] During this time "thousands of mostly middle- and upper-class Haitians" fled the dictatorial regime as refugees and were able to resettle abroad, representing a large percentage of professionals from the public and private sectors.[27]

As the brain drain continued, copper emerged as an export opportunity, and the Haitian government contracted international corporations to extract the commodity. Over a period of twelve years, the exports of copper alone injected over $21 million in revenue into the economy as 13.3 million tons of bauxite were mined and exported to the United States, accounting for nearly one-fifth of raw supply to the Reynolds Mining Company between 1959 and 1982.[28]

This arrangement favored foreign governments and businesses while the corrupt Haitian regime made its profit, bypassing the local private sector in myriad ways. While a market-based system of private ownership prevailed over the nationalization prevalent in the region, the Haitian government did not develop the nation's resources in a way that capitalized on economic opportunities for the private sector. Instead, the government sold those mining rights to foreign interests. Even at the government level, transactions that adversely affected the private sector were in practice. According to Lundahl,

> subsequently, however, these exports shrunk, one by one. Bauxite reserves were depleted. Sisal was finished by the mid-1970s, out-competed by synthetic fibers. The sugar trade lasted for another decade before low yields and political mismanagement strangled it. Cocoa exports declined as a result of unfavorable prices in relation to domestic food crops. Essential oils, which had shown an upward trend from the late 1950s to 1974, when they accounted for almost 10 percent of the total export value, were priced out of the market by a government export monopoly. Coffee production, finally, declined as the population grew and food crops gradually took over the land.[29]

Instead, Haiti delved into new opportunities on the global market, namely labor. In the 1970s, Haiti became a key manufacturing destination for the United States and other countries. Many Haitian and foreign companies producing in Haiti used cheap labor to assemble baseballs and garments in urban centers such as Port-au-Prince and Cap-Haïtien. In the 1980s, Haiti was the largest producer of baseballs distributed globally. However, unemployment hovered at 50 and 60 percent of the labor force throughout the 1980s.[30]

Reductions in exports led to import dependency, while the decision to import foreign goods instead of producing them locally led to the extreme exploitation of labor. Once again, Haiti had an opportunity for economic growth, job creation, and poverty reduction through market-based transactions; this time Haitians could have provided a workforce that met the demands of the global market while developing Haitian infrastructure and sustaining life.

Instead, the professional sector fled the Duvalier regime, exports declined, and the poor were forced back into the horrible labor conditions Haitians had sought to abolish two centuries before in the fight against slavery.

Aristide and the 1994 American Occupation

Following the ouster of Duvalier and a string of unsuccessful governments that ousted one another in quick succession, Haiti held one of its first successful presidential elections since the end of World War II. Jean-Bertrand Aristide, a former priest promising economic reform, was elected in 1991. During the first year of his presidency, Aristide pushed for social justice and targeted the Haitian elite, drawing attention to the endemic economic repression of the poor. In that same year, a coup d'état led by General Raoul Cédras, head of the Armed Forces, sent Aristide into exile.

Aristide's first term was so disrupted that none of his economic reforms took effect. The United States quickly placed an embargo against the new regime, but instead of hurting the regime, it cost Haiti an estimated one hundred thousand jobs and quickly halted Haiti's burgeoning economic growth.[31]

In 1994, the Clinton administration sent US forces to Haiti to restore Aristide to power; this support came with the condition that Haiti must reduce the import tariff on rice from the United States from 35 to 3 percent.[32] At the time, President Clinton argued that the tariff reduction would help Haiti develop its industrial opportunities by importing food from the United States instead of growing it in the Haitian agricultural sector, which was not mechanized and relied on human labor alone. These policies were supported and implemented by the International Monetary Fund and the World Bank, indicating the international community's consensus.

Compared to a mere 7,000 tons in 1985, US rice imports skyrocketed from 87,000 tons in 1994 to nearly 220,000 tons in 2000. Meanwhile, local production of rice in Haiti decreased from 110,000 tons in 1985 to 80,000 in 1995, just a year following the tariff reduction. And ninety-three thousand farming families, representing 20 percent of the population, lost their share of the market due to the cheap imports of US rice, and thousands of supplemental agricultural workers, local traders, and millers lost their jobs.[33] Within Haiti's rice market, the overall domestic supply declined from 47 percent in 1988 to merely 15 percent two decades later.[34]

In the 1990s, while almost every sector of agricultural production declined, the light-assembly industries[35] and low-paying manufacturing sector expanded. Emerging production industries included beverages (such as soft drinks, beer, and water as a commodity for purchase), detergent, flowers, soap, sugar, textiles and garments, and construction supplies. In addition, service industries developed, such as hotels, restaurants, and construction services. President Aristide's handpicked successor René Préval sought cooperation with technicians and specialists from Cuba to reopen a state-owned sugar mill, the same kind of state-owned corporation as those formed under the Magloire administration of the 1950s. As in other private-sector ventures, goods would enter the market and create transactions, but the profits went directly to the Haitian government. According to a report from Reuters, the sugar mill "produced 2,607 tons of sugar in 2005, its best year since restarting, but made no sugar in 2009, instead manufacturing syrup for alcohol distillers."[36] The government plant could not provide even 1 percent of the sugar consumed in the country at a cheaper rate than imports. "This meager output compares to the 250,000 tons of sugar that Haiti imports each year, from the United States, the neighboring Dominican Republic and other sugar producers."[37] Ultimately, the majority of sugar farmers stopped cultivating the crop and ventured into other, more profitable staple foods.

Recent Economic Developments

Despite all the political challenges and instability that have continued in Haiti since the 1990s, and despite the devastating blow of the 2010 earthquake, investment does continue to grow. Key sectors growing today include agribusiness, construction, energy, manufacturing, tourism, and telecommunication. Transactions too are growing, as Haiti continues to hold firmly to its market-based economy. Since 2011, under the direction of President Michel Martelly, the government and bureau of commerce have been emphasizing various industries as opportunities for growth. According to the new governmental brand slogan, "Haiti is open for business."[38]

Telecommunication is one of the leading industries today that supplies communication services throughout Haiti, including widespread cell phone services offered by competing companies such as Digicel, Voilà, and Haitel. From 2000 to 2009, the number of mobile cellular subscriptions in Haiti grew from 0.6 subscriptions per 100 people to 36.4 per 100.[39] Today, even the oldest generation in rural parts of Haiti is connected by cell phone!

With more than nine hundred kilometers of natural landscapes and relaxing beaches, Haiti's tourism industry has been relatively stable overall since 2007. In order to revive the long-lasting interest in Haiti as a tourist destination (with two well-known World Heritage sites), the governmental Center for Facilitation of Investments has goals to open more than thirty-five hundred new hotel rooms for short-term impact, and to attract more than $500 million of investments for private-sector hotel and convention construction projects and achieve $400 million in spending in the Haitian economy for medium-term impact.[40] And momentum is growing. In 2012, nearly three hundred thousand tourists visited the country, significantly more than in 2006, when 108,000 international visitors traveled to Haiti.[41]

The textile industry has also been a target market for foreign investors, with significant results in recent years. The Hope II Act of 2006, followed by the Haiti Economic Lift Program (HELP) Act of 2010, allowed tax-free access to distribute garments to the US market. Since then, the garment sector in Haiti has grown to thirty factories employing around thirty thousand workers throughout the country. The industry's exports have also grown to $730 million at a stable growth rate of just over 4 percent since 2011, and more than 40 percent since 2010 when exports were at only $512 million.[42] An industrial park in the northeastern city of Caracol, with close proximity to the international port of Cap-Haïtien, has seen significant growth through a public-private partnership of businesses, government, foundations, and NGOs. Based on an investment of $280 million, the industrial park was launched to host numerous domestic and international companies that would produce cutting-edge apparel for international markets. Among these companies was the leading South Korean apparel manufacturer, Sae-A, which became the park's anchor tenant. By May 2013, this company had hired 1,285 Haitians, and has significant plans to continue growing in coming years.[43] However, the need for tenants still remains. Despite the original goal to hire sixty thousand Haitians in the industrial park by 2015—and thereby to help decentralize Haiti's economy—only five thousand permanent jobs were created by the target date.[44] Yet through investment, innovation, and opportunities for trade and exports, there is still hope for this public-private partnership to move forward and create jobs on the north coast of Haiti.

HAITI'S MARKET ECONOMY: Past and Present

The underlying current of the Haitian market-based economy is transaction. People transact to sustain themselves. This has been the case, from even before independence from European powers to present day, as Haitians use transactions as their means to sustain their own livelihoods. Although Latin American neighbors such as Cuba have adopted other types of economic systems, the market-based system within Haiti has pervaded through the ages as the key means to satisfy consumer needs, to create jobs, and to continuously cycle revenue back into its economy as much as it can.

There have been, however, many different reasons why Haiti's market-based system has not been developed to its full potential. Amid the political instability and corruption, a lack of vision, high risks of reinvesting in business, and more recently the influx of aid, the pursuit of opportunities for long-term growth have been at stake. Furthermore, this "destructive aid"—and the prevalence of NGOs in Haiti as showcased in the next chapter—is currently undermining Haiti's market-based system that once competed on the global market and today stands as the key to sustainable economic change. Needless to say, transactions only continue. The present challenge is to address the underlying trends of aid, and evaluate ways to bring Haiti's market-based system back to the forefront of the discussion—to be prioritized, debated, and integrated into the long-term strategy for the betterment of Haiti's future.

CHAPTER 4

An Abundance of NGOs:

How International Aid Contributed to a Failed State

In the university business course Daniel Jean-Louis teaches, his first assignment to new students requires them to track how many transactions they perform in one day—from the moment they wake up until the moment they fall asleep. Perhaps a student showers with water purchased at a monthly rate and dresses in clothing bought at a retail clothing store. The student then leaves the house and quickly catches a tap-tap—a local form of public transportation—for a small fee. When the student hops off the vehicle, the scent of a breakfast pastry draws her into a café, and she purchases a morning snack. Upon arriving on campus, she takes classes paid for through her annual tuition. After class, she might head home on foot, but maybe she stops to purchase a phone card to top up her cell phone minutes. Perhaps the student enters a store to purchase school supplies or personal items. Leaving the store, she stops at a street vendor where she purchases vegetables, beans, rice, or other food to cook for dinner. Jean-Louis designed this assignment to make his students aware of how many individual transactions take place in just one day.

Haitian students practice the same regular pattern of transaction that is a given in any market-based economy. Whether the students pay annual or monthly bills, whether they purchase goods in formal businesses or on the informal market, all of these transactions rely on the exchange of currency for goods or services—and those transactions contribute to the nation's economic growth.

This process of transaction is apparent in any market economy. Now imagine a university student in the United States; we'll call her Kristen.

Kristen arises from a bed that she purchased from a store, wearing pajamas that she bought at another. She heads downstairs to the kitchen of a house that someone else owns, but that she rents month-to-month. After making a fresh pot of coffee—using organic coffee beans purchased through an online supplier—Kristen washes up using water purchased from the city and soap, shampoo, and conditioner purchased from a retail chain. Before even leaving the house, she relies on myriad transactions to complete the most basic tasks. Just as any other student, including those in Haiti, Kristen transacts in her own country's market-based economy to satisfy all of her needs.

But let's say Kristen wants to make a difference. She plans to go to Haiti, so she finds an American NGO to volunteer with. The organization asks that she bring school supplies for children at the orphanage she will visit. She purchases a plane ticket and fills an extra duffel bag with the goods, all purchased at home. Now, watch what happens when she travels to Port-au-Prince.

Once in Haiti, Kristen gets picked up by an aid worker in a pricey truck. Both the truck and the diesel, as well as the aid worker's salary, are paid for by donations. She travels to the orphanage, where she distributes the school supplies to the children. She eats a meal with the children. That meal is not only paid for by donations, but also consists of food purchased abroad. Furthermore, whatever services she provides for free compete with the local labor force, which is already woefully underemployed.

As noble as her intentions may be, Kristen's choices, and those of the NGO she volunteers with, are misaligned with Haiti's market-based system. Kristen's efforts fulfill the children's immediate needs; yet, she has not made any transactions in Haiti, and instead met those needs through transactions made within her home country's economy.

With the growing influx of nonprofit humanitarian and development aid organizations in Haiti, the model of transacting to meet the population's needs is under attack. As long as NGOs distribute goods and services for free or at a subsidized price, failing to support the daily transactions in the Haitian economy, they will have detrimental impacts on the market—reducing the chances for poverty reduction and sustainable job creation. Even worse, the implications of this misalignment have a snowball effect throughout the market, which multiplies those adverse effects. The abundance of NGOs virtually guarantees the downward spiral that we have documented in the previous two chapters.

HAITI: **The Republic of NGOs**

Haiti is often called, in ironic fashion, "The Republic of NGOs"—and for good reason. According to some sources, Haiti today has an alarming twelve thousand NGOs present,[1] meaning that Haiti has the second highest number of nongovernmental organizations per capita in the world.[2] Meanwhile, Mark Schuller, in *The Journal of Haitian Studies*, estimates that the number of NGOs in Haiti is anywhere from ten to twenty thousand.[3] In a country of just ten million people, this means there is roughly one NGO for every five hundred to one thousand people!

Many international development and humanitarian aid organizations are distributing goods and services for free or at subsidized prices, putting competitive pressure on the private sector. Most of these resources are produced and purchased abroad, creating fewer balanced transactions within the country and thereby decreasing the economic value added locally. Across the board, with best intentions, NGOs have replaced the balanced transactions that should sustain Haiti's market economy with unbalanced transactions and donations.

When existing businesses bring about balanced transactions to meet needs profitably, they can grow, thereby generating more revenue, increasing production, paying more taxes, and creating more jobs as resource generators. This is what can be described as an open-cycle, or a continuous creation of new resources. This cycle is an investment of assets that are then used to add value, which thereby can generate more profit, which can then be reinvested, which further generates more profit, and if all factors are aligned, the cycle only continues.

FIGURE 1: **Open Cycle toward Continuous Resource Creation**

INVESTMENT PRODUCTION TRANSACTION PROFIT REINVESTMENT

But the Haitian private sector cannot grow in a climate in which resource distributors have greater purchasing power than resource generators. In this case, resources run out when they are distributed faster than they are generated. The unbalanced transactions that NGOs create, distributing resources without creating new wealth, run contrary to the balanced transactions required for sustainable resource generation and economic growth.

The closed-cycle distribution of resources leads to the opposite effects of an open-cycle. In other words, in a closed-cycle, resources distributed are consumed, yet do not generate financial profit and reinvestment for growth. Therefore, no new wealth is created, as the opening story of Kristen illustrated so vividly.

FIGURE 2: **Closed Cycle Distribution of Resources**

RESOURCES DISTRIBUTED

RESOURCES RECEIVED

RESOURCES REQUESTED

The Detrimental Effect of NGOs in Haiti

NGOs have been in the country since the 1950s, when CARE and the Red Cross established branches to deal with the effects of Hurricane Hazel. A full history of the growth of foreign aid and NGOs in Haiti is beyond the scope of this book, but the 2010 earthquake affords us a snapshot of their devastating effects on the country. (For an overview of NGOs in Haiti and around the world, see the Appendix.)

After the earthquake, "Haiti received an unprecedented amount of support and aid in response. Private donations reached $3.1 billion. Individual Americans gave $774 million in the first five weeks." According to the Office of the Special Envoy to Haiti, $9.28 billion in humanitarian and recovery funding was pledged from 2010 to 2012, and 60.7 percent of those funds were disbursed by March 2012.[4]

Following the earthquake and throughout 2010, aid from official donors rose to over 400 percent of the Haitian government's domestic revenue.[5] For the fiscal year of 2011–12, the Haitian government budget barely exceeded $2.9 billion,[6] while the amount distributed in foreign aid was almost *twice* the government's budget.

In 2011, Haiti's gross domestic product (GDP), or the economic value of all goods and services produced, was $7.346 billion.[7] Meanwhile, $5.63 billion of resources were distributed in humanitarian and recovery funding between 2010 and 2012.[8] But while NGOs brought billions of imported products into the country, direct foreign investment in Haiti's private sector increased by a mere $181 million in 2011.[9]

According to the Center for Economic and Policy Research, between January 2010 and April 2011, the United States Agency for International Development (USAID) awarded 1,490 recovery contracts to numerous NGOs and businesses, totaling $194 million. Of those contracts, only 23 went to Haitian companies, at a value of less $5 million, or 2.5 percent of the total.[10] In a review of contracts twelve months after the earthquake, the Associated Press reported that only 1.6 percent of US government funded reconstruction contract dollars were won by Haitian firms. That's right: less than two cents out of every dollar.[11] When more than 98 percent of foreign aid is spent outside the country that is meant to receive the assistance, that doesn't leave much opportunity for resource generators—local enterprises in the market—to create wealth, employ people, and replenish the society's resources profitably.

Reporting on data released by USAID regarding its local contractors in Haiti as of April 2012, the Center for Global Development reports that the contracts added "up to $9.45 million, which is far less than one percent of more than a billion dollars spent by USAID. Over 75 percent of USAID funds went to private contractors inside the Beltway (located in Washington, DC, Maryland, or Virginia)."[12]

It is no surprise that resource-generating businesses in Haiti received so little in contracts, since the majority of funding was utilized internally by NGOs and donor nations, or used to transact with corporations based in the donor country. Furthermore, of the $2.43 billion committed or disbursed in humanitarian and development funding after the earthquake, 34 percent, or $824.7 million, was used to fund donors' own civil and military expenses—i.e., salaries, benefits, equipment, operations, and logistics—while 28 percent went directly to United Nations agencies and international NGOs for projects listed in the United Nations consolidated appeal process. Another 26 percent supported international NGOs and foreign private contractors, 6 percent was provided to unspecified recipients, and 5 percent funded the International Federation of the Red Cross and national Red Cross societies. In the end, 1 percent—just $25 million—was provided as assistance for the government of Haiti.[13]

In some cases, NGOs may have purchased products or services in Haiti to fulfill the particular needs of a project. However, as noted above in the report from the Associated Press, US contracts—which made up nearly half of foreign aid following the earthquake—were rarely accorded locally. It is likely that other foreign organizations transacted with Haitian suppliers very little as well.

Not only have NGOs transacted little with businesses in Haiti prior to and following the earthquake, but many also performed poorly in post-disaster efforts through inadequate methods and failures in their own internal operations. According to a study from the Center for Economic and Policy Research, the majority of USAID funding for Haiti assistance was channeled through private contractors and grantees, mostly based in the United States.[14] Subsequent USAID audits and evaluation programs presented alarming results, especially a significant "lack of effective oversight and a failure to meet, or even apply, basic benchmarks."[15]

Furthermore, foreign aid to Haiti was not the only funding source misaligned with Haiti's economy. As illustrated by Kristen's story, private charitable or community-based organizations are also a major source of donations. When combined, even small NGOs can have a massive effect in undermining Haiti's market-based system when vast amounts of goods purchased abroad are given away in Haiti for free or sold below market value.

Examples abound. In one case, a church in a small town in Wisconsin decided to help children in Haiti by requesting all people in the town to donate peanut butter, which they saw as an essential high-protein food to provide to malnourished children. Numerous NGOs, churches, schools, and even small businesses throughout the United States and other countries have been donating thousands of jars of peanut butter sporadically to Haiti over the years. In the midst of peanut butter drives, the majority of the time, donors have not even considered sourcing locally the Haitian peanut butter called *mamba*—one of the most popular foods known in Haiti. Peanut farmers and peanut butter producers alike have suffered from these charity efforts. Thousands of small, well-intentioned churches, schools, and non-profit organizations like these also have a detrimental effect on a country's market economy.

Unfortunately, regardless of size, many NGOs still practice the same strategy that has yielded little measureable improvement for the Haitian people for over sixty years. Those practices continue in various sectors. Haitian entrepreneurs have to settle for whatever share of the market has not been served by NGO donations.

AN ONGOING DISASTER: Misalignment with Haiti's Market-Based Economy

Today, with up to twenty thousand NGOs operating in Haiti, as well as thousands of donors with outsized purchasing power in a fragile economy, this continual misalignment can have a disastrous effect. Not only is this practice donation-based as opposed to transaction-based, but the commonly held strategy is to distribute resources to the Haitian population for free or below the market value—oftentimes without considering the ways in which Haitian enterprises could meet that demand.

This misaligned aid has such a strong presence in Haiti that it has become an overbearing parallel structure to Haiti's traditional market-based system. NGOs are in nature donor-based entities and are incapable of generating resources themselves, yet they continue to grow to meet demand, albeit in a misaligned way. However, through their generous donations, they distort the market and undermine opportunities for resource generators (businesses) to meet those same needs profitably.

While hundreds of millions—and now billions—of dollars are distributed through donated products and services in Haiti, the levels of poverty and unemployment have risen to nearly the highest rates ever. Haiti ranks 145th out of 168 countries in the United Nations Human Development Index, is characterized as a least developed country, and is well known as the poorest country in the Western Hemisphere. As of 2011, GDP per capita in Haiti was $1,034, compared to $8,651 in the neighboring Dominican Republic.[16]

About 70 percent of Haiti's ten million people live on less than two dollars per day, while an astounding half live on less than one dollar per day. Haiti also scored a poor 59 for income distribution on the 2001 Gini Index, which measures the rate of inequality in income or wealth in a given country on a descending scale of 100.[17] In Haiti, the poorest 10 percent receive 0.7 percent of national income while the richest 10 percent receive 47.7 percent.[18] In addition, Haiti ranks a dismal 161st out of 175 countries in Transparency International's Corruption by Country profile.[19] The country also holds one of the lowest literacy rates in the world at just 48.7 percent, in contrast to the global average of 84.3 percent and in contrast to the literacy rate of the Dominican Republic, which is 90 percent.[20] The child mortality rate is no better. In Haiti, more than seventy out of every one thousand newborns die—ten times more than in the United States.[21]

The economic picture is bleak. The trade deficit sits at $226 million.[22] Unemployment sits at nearly 41 percent, according to Inter-American Development Bank, while "Haiti has consistently and chronically underperformed in terms of its economic growth." More frightening than that, the economy of Haiti grew at a mere 1 percent on average between 1960 and 2005, an era that began only thirteen years after the arrival of the first NGO in Haiti.[23]

Haiti's environmental degradation is also widely known, and wood-based charcoal remains the most common source of fuel. Only 2 percent of

Haiti's forests remain. This deforestation has had a detrimental effect on agricultural production and other sectors.

Overall, Haiti's present-day situation has gotten so ugly that the country has become completely vulnerable. Haiti is so fragile, in fact, that it is ranked among the top ten countries considered as failed states, along with countries such as Somalia, Yemen, the Democratic Republic of the Congo, and Afghanistan.[24] Looking at Haiti's record of decades of political corruption, coups, and natural disasters, some think that Haiti lacks the ability to plan or deal with any national issue—no matter if it be political, economic, or natural.

Yet, just as much as the state has failed, the NGOs seeking to address the same challenges have also failed. NGO misalignment with Haiti's market-based economy has played a major role in the country's failures in a downward spiral over decades. Ultimately, the business sector has been under siege. In addition, the nonprofit models have filled voids to meet people's needs in ways that will never be self-sustaining. NGOs and aid organizations have tampered with businesses' ability and key purpose, which is to supply goods and services that satisfy customers' needs profitably through balanced transactions.

We have seen throughout this chapter that as NGOs grow in numbers and purchasing power, Haiti's misery has grown as well. Is the problem with the NGOs themselves? Or is it in the misaligned model that NGOs follow? Can organizations that have traditionally focused on aid learn instead to advocate for and participate in profitable and sustainable trade, leading to balanced transactions and a growing economy? Is there any hope that Haiti's market-based economy can regain its role as the foundation of Haiti's future? Finally, what role can NGOs play in ensuring that future? We hope to answer these important questions in the following chapters. In the next chapter we will begin to explore the ways that NGOs can partner with the private sector, make the move from aid to trade, and strengthen Haiti.

CHAPTER 5

Making the Move from Aid to Trade:

Opportunity-Based Economic Development (OBED) and the Power of Balanced Transactions

"Papa, are you going to buy some milk for me?" This is what Daniel Jean-Louis' three-year-old son, Meyer, asks when he is hungry.

His first reaction to satisfy his need for milk falls within the framework of Haiti's market-based economy in which he has been raised. He already thinks that the behavior of buying milk is normal. Before even having the ability to understand transactions, Meyer has already embraced the economic framework in which he exists by simply observing how his parents normally satisfy his needs.

No matter the political framework, the economy is an underlying current of human life, and as we outlined in chapter 3, Haiti has always had a market-based economy. Through colonization, slavery, revolution, dictatorship, and democracy, Haitian life has been shaped by small and large transactions, the lifeblood of market economies everywhere. Life in Haiti, just as life in most other places, is supported by the basic phenomenon of trade: buying and selling. Those myriad transactions shape the nation from top to bottom and bottom to top.

In spite of colonization, slavery, and dictatorship, Haitians have long purchased and produced locally to meet their needs. Although balanced transactions are needed for the Haitian economy to break even and grow sustainably, the challenges of political instability and international intervention have stood as barriers to those transactions. As mentioned prior, Haiti continues with a long list of both underlying factors preventing the healthier pace of development it needs, including key factors such as poor infrastructure, weak governance, corruption, and lack of education and job opportunities.

Yet one of the often unacknowledged challenges Haiti's market-based economy faces today has gained traction over recent decades: the strongest economic entities with the most purchasing power—NGOs—are putting negative pressure on Haitian businesses and keeping them from competing in the market. In the previous chapter, we described the way that the international community has sought, sometimes nobly, to help Haiti by attempting to apply new models of poverty reduction and growth through aid-based efforts. But the fundamental problem with those endeavors remains the same: Haiti does not need a new economic framework. Trade—not aid—is an essential factor toward long-term economic growth, job creation, poverty reduction, and the strengthening of the state.

Presently, international aid organizations have the most purchasing power in Haiti. They create the largest opportunity cost when they do not purchase from local businesses. Haiti's free-market business opportunities are threatened by the dominance of nonprofit aid models that fail to source locally. These ubiquitous aid models are incompatible with Haiti's market-based economic structure, which can only grow through balanced transactions. Instead of applying aid, NGOs need to move toward trade, aligning themselves with the local market instead of competing with it.

What Is Market Alignment?

In the simplest terms, market alignment is when business, government, and NGOs actively pursue partnerships and meet each other's needs—creating opportunity and wealth together.

International intervention in Haiti, through foreign governments and NGOs, has been a powerful economic force in the local market, and is tremendously misaligned. As we have begun to see, when organizations operate outside of the framework of a market-based economy, this misalignment can affect the economy in two potentially detrimental ways: (1) by introducing and supplying goods and services below market value, which drives down prices, and (2) by competing with a private sector that is more suited to supply those goods and services sustainably, thereby driving businesses out of the market.

When powerful economic entities do not transact locally, the market and the workforce suffer. Because resources are not being generated locally, wealth and opportunity can't be created in a sustainable way. Further, this influx of cheap, subsidized goods and services puts negative competitive pressure on the private sector.

In developed economies, governments, businesses, and NGOs grow and sustain their markets by catalyzing the private innovative business sector to meet society's needs. Further, they foster competition, ensure access to capital, and institute market regulations in order to create a stable, sustainable economic climate.

In Haiti, however, NGOs and foreign governments hold vast economic power. When they are aligned with Haiti's economy, they contribute to its growth, for example, by purchasing what they need locally. Yet misaligned practices can destabilize the market and cause it to contract. International organizations have justified their import-based procurement practices by citing the various barriers to transacting locally—including the challenges to identify local sourcing companies or to ensure timely delivery of products or services they need, as we will explore later in the book. While those barriers are real, NGOs must work to overcome those barriers in order to effect lasting change in Haiti.

NGOs can redeem their history of failure in Haiti by realigning themselves with the local economy. Humanitarian and development aid organizations have the opportunity to partner with and invest in local businesses to meet the great demand in Haiti's underdeveloped economy. Instead of pumping capital into donation and subsidy models that have proven unsuccessful, NGOs can become a real part of value chains that grow the market, create employment, and reduce poverty. As World Bank Group President Jim Yong Kim noted,

> a good job can change a person's life, and the right jobs can transform entire societies. Governments need to move jobs to center stage to

promote prosperity and fight poverty. It's critical that governments work well with the private sector, which accounts for 90 percent of all jobs. Therefore, we need to find the best ways to help small firms and farms grow. Jobs equal hope. Jobs equal peace. Jobs can make fragile countries become stable.[1]

Transactions are the lifeblood of all market-based economies. By partnering with businesses and contracting with the local private sector to supply goods and services instead of importing them, NGOs can create more transactions in Haiti. Through strategic partnership, NGOs and businesses can identify marketable opportunities and overcome barriers to transaction together, and successful partnerships will increase the number of transactions that meet needs profitably.

Through opportunity-based economic development, international NGOs, as resource distributors, can empower Haitian businesses, the country's resource generators, to grow the economy sustainably, thus combating endemic poverty.

Introducing Opportunity-Based Economic Development (OBED)

We propose opportunity-based economic development (OBED) as the key solution to develop Haiti's economy in a healthy and sustainable fashion. As a comprehensive strategy, OBED means harnessing assets and capital through entrepreneurial opportunities to increase balanced transactions, a key activity to implement OBED, thereby meeting needs profitably and generating resources. It means that needs should be met through market-based opportunities and initiatives, not through projects or programs that do not generate profit. To put it another way, OBED is the strategic pursuit of individual marketable opportunities to increase transaction so that goods are replenished, services are available, and jobs are created sustainably—thus supporting the livelihood of the citizens.

Individuals pursue these marketable opportunities to convert liabilities, assets, and resources into products and services that satisfy demand profitably. Put simply, meeting local needs creates an opportunity for a business to generate resources and meet those needs profitably. Applying OBED means that, when seeking opportunities, a resource generator develops competitive advantage in meeting demand. This leads to the development of new markets and industries that trigger innovation and expansion of the business sector, spurring balanced transactions and sustainable growth.

You may be wondering, however, how is OBED any different from basic capitalism or market-based economics?

Although the forward vision is a strong market-based economy, OBED is a particular development strategy tailored to underdeveloped or developing markets, like Haiti's; this strategy can be implemented almost immediately and seeks to realign local demand to local resource generators—especially when there is a strong presence of resource distributors such as NGOs. OBED's ultimate goal is to foster the development of individual resource generators—enterprises and entrepreneurs—to spur sustainable economic growth. This strategy is supported by sound legislative policies and development approaches that enhance a healthy economic environment, which leads to more balanced transactions and a business-supported market.

This theory is therefore practical from a few angles.

Business owners apply OBED when they pursue opportunities to provide goods and services that satisfy customer needs profitably. However, the application of OBED is as relevant for individual enterprises as it is for entire sectors and the market as a whole. As in Adam Smith's theory of the invisible hand, when combined, every single marketable opportunity pursued shapes the market as a whole. Therefore, OBED promotes the use of balanced transactions as the best way to fulfill needs in the society.

As businesses pursue opportunities, governments and NGOs also need to seek ways to support the development of those opportunities. The state can apply OBED by fostering a healthy environment through sound economic and trade policies that allow businesses to meet need on demand satisfactorily and profitably. Likewise, NGOs can realign to the growing market-based economy to ensure that private businesses become the means to generate resources and thereby facilitate transactions, not NGO distribution of resources to meet local needs.

In OBED, the more that purchasing power is aligned to businesses in the market, the more opportunities can be pursued to meet needs profitably, which leads to an overall increase in balanced transactions.

The Logic of OBED

If ...
- The strategy of OBED is the realignment of local demand to the private business sector that strategically pursues opportunities to achieve customer satisfaction and maximize profit

Then ...
- Customer satisfaction + profit maximization = balanced transactions

Therefore ...
- The outcome of OBED = increased balanced transactions that generate resources, grow businesses, create jobs, and impact an economy, which improves the well-being of individuals and society as a whole

---

We assert that in order to increase economic growth, countries need to increase balanced transactions. And, to increase balanced transactions, countries need businesses—either existing businesses able to expand or new businesses created to meet needs profitably.

Yet to have balanced transactions, you need businesses that are registered, legal, and ethical. But to have businesses, you need to have people pursuing profitable opportunities—specifically business owners and entrepreneurs—as well as a government that supports business growth through effective public policy, a strong legal system, and political stability. Actors implementing OBED must look toward a long-term goal—pursuing an optimal market framework for a society in which wealth is replenished and jobs are created. The ideal market-based system, performing at optimal capacity, pursues this strategy through entrepreneurial opportunity and innovation. Yet there would be no business opportunities if there weren't customers with needs to meet—needs such as food, lodging, healthcare, education, transportation, communication, and more. The cycle described above is predicated on customer satisfaction for that reason. OBED is particularly suited for underdeveloped economies like Haiti's because the great lack of resources creates vast needs that can be met profitably. Meeting those needs profitably will generate the revenue necessary for the government and the population to have the purchasing power to lift themselves out of poverty. When individuals and families have a stable income source, they can turn their own needs into consumer demand, whereas without an income it simply remains a need that continues the cycle of dependence on aid.

Therefore, NGOs as buyers must realign with Haiti's market-based system. By purchasing locally, NGOs can provide the market incentives that create opportunity for businesses. If the private sector can overcome barriers to transaction, balanced transactions can be created by leveraging NGO purchasing power. NGOs can also foster a business climate that creates more market opportunities. Through the application of OBED, NGOs can realign themselves with Haiti's market-based system. As the private sector meets demand profitably, NGOs will run themselves out of business, so to speak, in that they will no longer be needed.

In response to this proposal, some important questions may arise: What happens to market demand when the NGOs leave? Don't they represent a niche that, once removed, will significantly reduce the demand that the Haitian businesses depend on, thus devastating the economy that has been built on NGO demand?

If you recall, Laurent Auguste and his family business, which had operated for decades, had seen the ups and downs of market demand. Yet they had only continued to grow, since Haiti's market, and the specific need for high-quality biodegradable soap, absorbed their product supply easily. According to Auguste, "Haiti's always going to be developing," and the opportunities to meet new market demand will only grow. Consider the act of jump-starting a car after the battery has died. Currently, like a vehicle with a dead battery, Haiti's economy is not operating at full capacity. Yet, once NGOs realign with the local market-based economy, they can jump-start the natural cycle of transactions within a market-based economy, especially since this realignment will help to create more jobs in Haiti, which will increase Haitians' purchasing power, and thereby continue to grow the demands for more products and services. As you will see in the case study of Maxima S.A. in chapter 6, the businesses within Haiti also must continually innovate in order to adapt to these ever-growing market needs, compete on a national and global scale, and continue to strengthen this natural cycle of Haiti's economy.

Haiti not only has assets to develop itself into a healthy and sustainable market-based economy, but it also has immense opportunity to accomplish its goals. With its geographical proximity to the Latin American and North American markets, as well as a young, affordable labor force, the Haitian business sector needs to continue identifying its competitive advantage to grow its long-term sustainable market-based economy. To reach these long-term goals, every player in the game right now needs to be a part of pursuing those opportunities, especially NGOs who presently hold the most significant purchasing power in the country and have the leverage to change Haiti's future.

Because stories make our point more clearly than theory alone can do, throughout the rest of the book we will provide numerous case studies of NGOs that have aligned themselves with the market, partnering with local businesses in an effort to meet Haiti's many needs and also grow its economy. Together, as we shall see, these businesses and NGOs are successfully transforming aid into trade.

CASE STUDY

Information Technology Services Haiti

Every day local businesses meet the needs of the Haitian people by providing competitive goods and services. The same market-based approach is evident today as a new generation of entrepreneurs meets local needs profitably. Information Technology Services (ITS) Haiti demonstrates how businesses can serve the needs of NGOs, creating a win-win-win situation for all players: private business, NGOs, and government.

"I left my parents' house at sixteen," says Haitian entrepreneur Mendell Harryford. "I was selling T-shirts to get by and go to school." After becoming interested in graphic design in the eighth grade, Harryford graduated high school and supported himself while he studied communications through a Belgian online university before going on to study marketing. After his first business failed, Harryford remained determined and tried again. "I used the principles that I studied in communications and marketing to create strategies for clients," he says. "Now I consult with NGOs and private businesses. I'll be twenty-five tomorrow."

Mendell Harryford is a born entrepreneur. Harryford rose from severe economic hardship, sought out opportunity, developed himself professionally, and earned contracts from some of the most powerful firms in the country. His company, Information Technology Services Haiti, proves that disadvantaged entrepreneurs can establish competitive private businesses and win contracts from international organizations, creating transactions in the country.

Five months after the January 2010 earthquake, Harryford saw a growing market for high-quality digital design and printing services to create goods such as office signs, posters, and events banners as local and international organizations proactively marketed their services. When Harryford and his partner started ITS Haiti with $300, they had no office, bank account, or employees. Harryford and his associate missed clients' phone calls and struggled to find work.

One year after the company's launch, Harryford and his associate showcased their business at a trade fair and networking conference organized by Partners Worldwide, an organization that connects entrepreneurs in the developing world with a global network of experienced businesspeople who walk alongside them to provide mentoring and expertise. The theme of the conference was "Buy Haitian, Restore Haiti." The opportunity to interface with NGO clients at the conference changed everything.

ITS Haiti overhauled its entire operation. Harryford and his partner registered their enterprise with the government. They rented an office to acquire a physical address. An $800 contract for Oxfam Great Britain netted the company $400. "We bought a printer and a charger that could be used in our car's cigarette lighter," Harryford reports.

Regarding buyers they pursued early on, he says, "We started bidding for larger contracts. We tried the private sector, but they weren't as willing to pay for the work we do." The public sector also poses challenges. The Haitian government can take up to five months to confer a signed contract and requires frequent visits to its offices.

By contrast, NGO clients can afford ITS Haiti's services and are easier to do business with. "We could consult these people via internet," says Harryford, whose company has serviced USAID, the Pan American Development Foundation, Oxfam, and World Vision—multimillion-dollar aid and development organizations operating in the Haitian market. "They didn't care who we were; they only cared if we could do the job or not."

As part of a market-research intensive strategy, in less than six months, Harryford visited eighty NGOs in Port-au-Prince and its surroundings. He put up a website, bought phones, and hired four employees. In eighteen months, ITS Haiti had fourteen more employees. Harryford's application of communication and market-ing strategies and his reliance on market research before contact-ing clients reflect his innovative approach to meet market needs, and as a result he won some of the country's biggest clients.

A month before our interview, a representative from Unibank, Haiti's second largest bank, stopped by the ITS office. Harryford reports, "They said, 'Whatever project you have, bring it over and we will finance it.' So we tried it. On Monday, I told them I needed a new car. On Wednesday, the car dealership called and said I could pick up the car. Here's what happens when you're serious and dynamic: It pays off."

Between October 2011 and October 2012, the enterprise han-dled $350,000 of business and grew to twenty-two employees. "That surprised me," says Harryford.

ITS Haiti, its employees, its contractors, and every other entity Harryford and his company transact with, survive or fail by the qual-ity and quantity of the transactions they make. At the time of our interview, Harryford's company had served individuals, businesses, and over sixty NGOs. But ITS is able to win lucrative international clients because Harryford and his company are able to meet international standards, providing quality work in sufficient quantity.

While unemployment and lack of education render the Haitian workforce competitive but unskilled, the high cost of doing business in Haiti puts added pressure on private businesses to keep costs down. Beyond importing materials, "we even have to import labor," Harryford explains, forcing ITS to subcontract many jobs to firms in the Dominican Republic.

Production costs in Santo Domingo can be as low as one-fifth of those in Port-au-Prince. Harryford holds up his car key as an example: "To produce this key in Haiti ... you have to import all of the raw materials. In the DR, they already produce the metal and plastic—it's a one-stop shop. And it takes one day to assemble. In Haiti, it takes three days."

Even if some businesses are transacting with NGOs, they still need to be competitive in the market because innovation in Haiti's market-based economy will only continue to grow. How does Harryford stay ahead of his competitors? By establishing a strong business that can meet his customers' needs, which builds trust and confidence. ITS Haiti has proven its capacity to adapt to market needs, which will only prove more necessary as NGO customers, and the transactions they bring, phase out of the economy. The company will need to continue pursuing new market niches and target various sectors—such as emerging for-profit businesses—to expand its client base.

Beyond its innovative practices to ensure that its clients keep coming back—and that new clients emerge—Harryford's company values its employees, attracting better human resources and building a healthy work environment.

ITS Haiti's lowest-paid employees make a minimum of $300 a month: $10 a day or $3,600 per year. ITS pays overtime. The company takes care of the taxes. Employees get hour-long breaks, which are almost unheard of at most Haitian firms. "Other businesses start at 7:30 and don't have a closing time," says Harryford. "It's a passion for me—my employees have to be on their way home by 8 p.m. We'll drop them off wherever they live, safe or unsafe." Harryford and his partner are negotiating a partial insurance deal that the company will provide as part of their employee benefits package.

Harryford and his partner even provide small loans of a few thousand dollars to their employees at no interest. "We're not in the credit business," he says. "If it takes you eight years to pay, you can work here with no conflict. We're a family."

And, according to Harryford, that family is all about customer satisfaction. Harryford explains that his business has survived because he is available around the clock, and his loyal employees support him.

Thanks to market research, professional development, networking, and a loyal staff, ITS Haiti, through Harryford's innovative approach, has been able to meet customers' needs profitably and benefit from the presence of NGOs in Port-au-Prince. "We choose our clients," says Harryford. And clients keep choosing ITS.

Five days after our interview, Harryford attended a United Nations conference on entrepreneurship to further develop himself as a professional and to seek out even more lucrative clients for his enterprise.

When asked about his business plan for the next decade, as NGO presence in Haiti is expected to decline annually, Mendell Harryford is confident. "We are going to open the business to the general public," he says. Then "the clients will come to us." Since then, Harryford has pursued new market opportunities, and, by facilitating networking events for his peers, has helped other young entrepreneurs target new markets as Haiti's private sector emerges from the trenches of aid.

The Global Impact of Balanced Transactions

Previously in the chapter, we introduced you to the strategy of opportunity-based economic development and how balanced transactions are one of the most consistent activities that takes place when OBED is working. Yet, before we discuss the implementation of OBED, let's look at some dramatic examples of how trade—not aid—was able to lift literally billions of people out of poverty. Their stories can serve as useful illustrations of the way OBED might be applied in Haiti to achieve a similar aim.

Fifty years ago, the terms G-20 and BRICS did not exist. BRICS is the acronym for Brazil, Russia, India, China, and South Africa—five economic powerhouses and newly industrialized countries of the developing world. The G-20 is an even broader forum founded in 1999 that represents 20 major economies of the world, including all BRICS members; other emerging economies such as Indonesia, Mexico, Turkey, and Argentina; and the original G8 members, including the United States, Germany, South Korea, Japan, and the United Kingdom. These countries' national economies combined account for 85 percent of the gross world product, and BRICS as well as many members of G-20 were once underdeveloped yet are now driving forces in the global economy.

For the purpose of this section, we'll highlight the well-known BRICS countries. As of a 2012 census, the BRICS countries combined have a population of nearly three billion people, almost half of the global population. And all five BRICS countries shared some striking similarities in their approach to economic growth and poverty elimination: embracing a market-based system to increase transactions, developing new industries, and turning the unique assets their country held into viable marketable opportunities.

The first common aspect is that, no matter their political system, these governments and societies have embraced business development for the creation of new enterprises. In other words, these countries have embraced a market-based system (even though we should acknowledge that some grew with significant

Population of BRICS	
Brazil:	201 m
Russia:	144 m
India:	1,210 m
China:	1,354 m
South Africa:	53 m
TOTAL:	2.962 billion

governmental influence as you will find in the case study for both Russia and China) and have maximized existing market opportunities to spur growth, increase transactions in the country, create wealth, and reduce unemployment.

Although a market-based economy is one common factor for all of the BRICS countries, the second common factor is that each country found unique ways to develop new industries and to support new growth sectors in their countries. These efforts also led to increases in transactions across sectors and industries, which led to job creation and upward mobility across classes.

The third commonality is that the BRICS countries sustained that market-based economic growth by finding new ways to turn assets, liabilities, and equity into marketable opportunities.

BRAZIL: *Turning natural resources into opportunities for foreign direct investment*

In recent decades, Brazil has turned its vast assets into marketable opportunities, raising over 20 percent of its 197 million people from below the poverty line into the middle class.[2]

With its 7,400 kilometers of magnificent beaches, extensive rainforests, and warm weather, Brazil has a booming tourism sector, drawing vacationers and travelers from around the globe to transact in Brazil's vibrant culture and climate. In 2014, travel and tourism triggered a total impact of $209 billion, or roughly 9.6 percent of Brazil's GDP.[3] The national poverty rate fell from 21 percent in 2005 to 8.9 percent in 2013, and external debt—as a percentage of the GNI—was reduced from 47.5 percent in 2002 to an impressive 16.9 percent by 2010 amid the global economic crisis.[4] With an economy that exceeds that of all neighboring South American countries, Brazil was one of the first countries to recover from the 2008 global recession, generating a GDP growth rate of 7.5 percent through the revival of consumer and investor confidence.[5]

Brazil has also continued to expand agricultural production and mechanization, utilizing its vast land and natural resource assets to not only feed its own growing population, but also to export food to high-demand markets in South America, Africa, and Asia. Brazil's rice production has grown extensively over the last half century. In 1960, Brazil produced 4.79 million metric tons of rice. By 2003, the country became self-sufficient in rice production and began exporting 36,000 tons of milled rice the following year to countries in South America and Africa,[6] competing with rice-producer Thailand to target competitive markets in South Africa, Nigeria, and Ivory Coast, the three biggest rice importers on the continent.[7] By 2008, Brazil's rice exports climbed to more than 510,000 tons.[8] Today, Brazil continues to utilize its agricultural resources and semi-temperate climate to diversify crop production, exporting coffee, soybeans, beef, sugarcane, ethanol, and even frozen chicken.[9]

Besides agriculture, Brazil is second in the Americas in industry, which accounts for 28.5 percent of its GDP. In 1994 the Brazilian government instituted the Real Plan, an economic reform designed to help the country emerge from twenty years of authoritarian military dictatorship. As a result, national and multinational businesses invested in the production of automobiles, computers, and aircraft, and in the development of natural resources, including petrochemicals, fossil fuels, and renewable resources.

Brazil has also committed resources toward business development, and the government has implemented conditions to stabilize the macroeconomic system. The market system in Brazil has been so strong, in fact, that it increased its global market presence in agriculture, mining, manufacturing, and services, thereby increasing balanced transactions, which keep its own economy growing.

In recent decades, Brazil's development of new markets and exports has led to an increase in balanced transactions, producing significant results. The unemployment rate, which in 2001 was as high as 12 percent, dropped to around 7 percent by 2008 as more investments were made in widespread industries. Since then it has averaged around 6 percent in early 2015.[10]

According to the Brazilian delegate of the UN Economic and Social Council in 2012, "Brazilian experience suggested that tax policies that encouraged small business enterprises were a powerful job-creation tool. Over the past decade, more than 40 million Brazilians had risen out of poverty thanks to public policies aimed at ensuring sustained economic growth and social inclusion."[11]

Brazil not only turned its assets of land and natural resources into opportunities, but in 2012, became the fifth most attractive market in the world for foreign direct investment.[12] The Brazilian economy presents such low risk and so much marketable opportunity that it attracted $65 billion of foreign direct investment that year, making it the largest partner of foreign direct investment in all of Latin America.

RUSSIA: *Legislating policies for business investment*

Following the end of the USSR in 1991, Russia has made significant changes to allow people to meet their needs through transaction instead of relying on the government-run socialist economy implemented under Joseph Stalin's regime in the 1920s.

In the 1990s, new legislation was introduced to privatize various sectors and restore the free-market system. As the nation with the largest total land mass in the world, Russia has vast assets in natural resources, holds the largest reserves of mineral and energy resources, and has become one of the world's largest exporters of crude oil, petroleum products, and natural gas (which account for 68 percent of the country's exports), in addition to other commodities such as timber and metals.[13]

Besides the extraction and exportation of natural resources, Russia's industrial sector is active in arms production, aviation, space travel, automobile manufacturing, and railroads, as well as in electronics and telecommunication—all viable industries that support millions of balanced transactions each day. In addition, with a growing middle class, the service sector is the nation's leading economic sector, accounting for 58 percent of Russia's GDP.[14] Through wholesale distribution and retail trade, automotive repairs, public administration, health, education, real estate, and communication, Russia's economy and labor force rely on transactions in the service sector on a daily basis.

Some challenges to Russia's economic potential remain due to its own international diplomacy within Eurasia, and there is an ongoing concern about state interference in Russia's relatively young private sector.[15] Yet despite these factors, over the last two decades, Russia has integrated its market into the global economy. Since the collapse of the Soviet Union, and thanks to a number of significant macroeconomic policies throughout the 1990s, the Russian economy has attained stability to allow for growth in diverse sectors and industries. Today, Russia stands as the sixth largest economy in the world by purchasing power parity (PPP) calculations.[16] In this environment, vibrant private sector businesses are pursuing opportunities to produce goods and services that are exported or consumed locally, which further increases transactions and the stable average growth and development of the Russian economy.

INDIA: *Outsourcing labor in a niche market*

After India gained its independence in 1947, it became a closed, nearly autarkic economy. By the 1990s, India's economy faced imminent bankruptcy. For that reason, the Indian government eased its trade policies and lowered business taxes to promote economic growth in diverse sectors and to support the creation of new small businesses. India also opened its doors to foreign trade in order to grow its economy and create job opportunities for its rapidly growing population.

India leveraged its growing population into an opportunity to supply a vast labor force. In 1991, thanks to government policies that liberalized the economy, India's private enterprises invested in sectors ranging from production to information technology and customer service management. As a result, most readers of this book have had the experience of speaking with an Indian customer service representative several time zones away!

That year, GDP growth rate fell to 1.1 percent, but jumped to 5.5 percent within twelve months. In recent years, India's GDP reached as high as 10.5 percent in 2010—as they experienced fewer impacts of the Great Recession than other more export-reliant countries in Asia had to endure—and India's GDP has since then balanced out at 7 percent in 2013.[17] Although GDP has grown significantly since India began to open its markets to the rest of the world, as of 2014, the unemployment rate is still 8.6 percent.[18] While this figure is far lower than that of many other developing countries, it has remained relatively constant since the nation's new economic plan began. There are various ways in which unemployment rates are tracked, for example, whether the informal sector is or is not included. For this reason, the World Bank tracks as "employed" those active in the informal sector and subsistence farming, thereby recognizing an unemployment rate of 3.4 percent in 2012,[19] in comparison to other methods of tracking an estimated 8.5 percent the same year.[20]

As its population continues to grow, India must create even more jobs for its population by seeking out new opportunities to maximize transactions in new industries and markets. Beyond outsourcing services to foreign companies, India will need to find new ways to increase both profit and job opportunities throughout the entire value chain.

CHINA: Turning an overpopulation "liability" into a marketable opportunity

With over 1.3 billion people, China is the most populous country in the world. The government first saw its massive population as a burden. Hundreds of millions of rural Chinese lived in extreme poverty, and overpopulation was seen as a liability for the country.

In the late 1950s, the centralized government strategy—called the Great Leap Forward—led to rapid industrialization. Still, there was limited individual freedom to initiate and engage in innovative opportunities. Following the failure of that model—and a growing, impoverished population—in 1978 the Chinese government instigated reform to move from a centralized economy to a more market-based system,[21] permitting foreign direct investment on the nation's coastline and allowing more private-sector development.[22] In addition, in 1979 the government introduced its well-known one-child policy to prevent the country's population from growing more quickly than the economy could support, which over the last few decades has received both positive and negative review. In addition to receiving criticism for its one-child policy, China continues to undergo critique for its close monitoring of citizens, repression of civil liberties and, in some cases, human rights failures according to international standards.

While we recognize these concerns, from an overarching perspective, millions have emerged from poverty in China as the country effectively turned its overpopulation "liability" into an opportunity by supplying affordable labor to foreign companies searching for ways to cut their labor costs.

China began outsourcing its labor force by installing small production plants throughout the country. These sites became parts of various global supply chains of manufacturing, raw materials, energy, food processing, clothing, chemicals, and other industries. China tapped into global market opportunities through labor and exports. This brought new businesses into the country, which produced more transactions and thereby created new wealth.

Furthermore, the nation's tax revenue increased, which led to investments in infrastructure, education, the legal system, and the health industry. The workforce gained purchasing power through salaries and wages that provided even more domestic market opportunities for Chinese businesses. The cycle of balanced transaction and wealth creation continued. Between the early 1980s and today, over 680 million Chinese have emerged from poverty, leading to China's interior reduction of extreme poverty from 84 percent of its population three decades ago to a mere 10 percent today.[23]

SOUTH AFRICA: Sound policies to move forward as a post-apartheid economy

South Africa is best known for its achievements in human rights and its inspirational leaders, including former president Nelson Mandela and Anglican Archbishop Desmond Tutu. Dutch and English colonization along with South Africa's diverse ethnic heritage form a unique baseline of challenges and opportunities in a post-apartheid context. High rates of HIV/AIDS and persistent income inequality along racial and class lines also remain prevalent. Despite these challenges, however, South Africa has developed relative political stability compared to most other neighboring African nations and has initiated sound economic policies that contribute to its success as the newest member of the BRICS nations. South Africa has also been identified by the Fragile States Index as a nation in the "least fragile" bracket, alongside countries including Australia, the United States, Japan, Brazil, Argentina, Chile, and nations throughout Western and Eastern Europe.[24]

South Africa is renowned for its beautiful environmental features, and the country has tapped into those opportunities for its thriving tourism industry. In addition, it also has made great strides in mining and manufacturing. According to Michael Nowak of the International Monetary Fund, South Africa has laid out a number of economic policies to strengthen public finance, stabilize the interest rate, and contain inflation.[25]

Between 1998 and 2004, the average tariff on imports to South Africa decreased from 22 percent to 11 percent, creating a strong incentive for foreign companies to invest in South Africa's economy while protecting local industries such as textiles.[26] Throughout sectors nationwide, competitive imports have also led South African companies to increase the efficiency and quality of their own local production. Through these improvements, South African products are meeting consumer demand at a higher quality and a lower price, thereby triggering more transactions in the country.

The Importance of Increasing Balanced Transactions

As evidenced by the rise of the BRICS countries, market-focused initiatives—not foreign aid—contribute to the increase in balanced transactions through business development in various sectors and industries. This stands in stark contrast to Haiti and other countries in the developing world that have seen a significant increase in donation and foreign aid with fewer transactions and poor results. All of the BRICS countries share a common theme: turning assets and liabilities into market opportunities. From China to Brazil to others with newly emerging economies, countries around the globe have increased opportunities in their market-based economies for business growth and job creation.

In other words, increasing balanced transactions is the key activity to make OBED as a strategy happen. As seen in BRICS and other countries around the world, balanced transactions can increase through market-based systems that have the opportunity to increase sustainable economic growth, a reduction in poverty, and successful states. We turn now to Haiti to see how increasing balanced transactions could do far more for the nation's future than millions of dollars in aid alone could ever achieve.

CHAPTER 6

Implementing the OBED Strategy:

First Steps in Transforming Aid into Trade

In the previous chapter, we saw how the BRICS countries demonstrate the power of trade to lift people out of grinding poverty. In most cases this development was precipitated and supported by government policy. Governments provide the foundation for an increase in balanced transactions and the ensuing economic growth, but government can never be the driving or sustaining factor in that growth. Rather, economic growth requires many boots on the ground—thousands of individuals and businesses looking for goods and services to purchase and provide.

Driving and Sustaining Factors of Economic Growth

Economic growth requires a key factor to drive it, and many others to sustain it. First, economic growth is driven by marketable and viable business opportunities; we simply could not have opportunity-based economic development without opportunities to transact! Second, economic growth requires key sustaining factors, including rule of law, innovation, trade policies, infrastructure, professional development opportunities, education, environmental sustainability, and gender equality. In this chapter, we will elaborate on the first two sustaining factors, rule of law and innovation. The need for innovation will be showcased within this chapter as we highlight a wood manufacturing company in Haiti called Maxima S.A.; the impact of trade policies on Haiti's business sector will then be covered in case studies on agricultural policies found later in the book, as well as the story of solar paneling manufacturer ENERSA in the next chapter.

But first, let's look at the crucial role of marketable opportunities as the driving factor in developing an economy, and let's also look at who identifies and pursues those opportunities.

A VIABLE BUSINESS OPPORTUNITY: The Driving Factor

OBED begins when an individual or a business identifies and pursues a viable business opportunity, adds value to a resource, and transforms that resource into a marketable product or service. While governments and NGOs can sometimes identify and pursue market opportunities, that is not generally their primary role, and it is not their area of expertise (as we noted in chapter 2).

Business opportunity is the driving factor in an OBED model, and entrepreneurs and businesses are the best suited to identify and pursue those opportunities because they are the suppliers of goods and services in a true market-based economic system. Whether it is a woman selling mangoes on the street to make an income for the day, thousands of employees working in a textile plant, or a new construction firm founded to meet demand for durable construction following a natural disaster, individual entrepreneurs and businesses alike embrace the same pursuit of viable business opportunities in a market-based economic framework.

As we noted in the previous chapter, China pursued its own market opportunity when it turned one of its greatest perceived liabilities, the size and growth rate of its population, into a valuable resource: a vast, low-cost labor force that would not have been available or affordable to western markets otherwise. Taking advantage of this opportunity led China to become one of the fastest-growing economies in the world.

Haiti needs to determine and define its own business opportunities. Similar to China, Haiti could take one of its greatest liabilities—in its case, the present abundance of NGOs—and turn it into a valuable resource. For instance, cross-sector partnerships between resource distributors (NGOs and governments) and resource generators (for-profit businesses) could increase balanced transactions in Haiti and thereby spur sustainable growth. In the process, Haiti would not just break even, but would have the potential to thrive and grow beyond its break-even point.

Similar to Brazil and South Africa, Haiti could also tap into its natural resources of beaches and warm weather to promote tourism. But instead of pursuing the traditional tourist who seeks a relaxing beach resort, Haiti could also target a unique niche of travelers who are willing to spend their travel dollars to better understand the country and support its development. As we will see in a case study in chapter 8, Daniel Jean-Louis identified an opportunity to provide safe, comfortable housing to aid workers and created Trinity Lodge, now a growing enterprise.

It is important not to confuse the market-based system with government activities in that system. A country only thrives on a market-based system if the majority of demand is met by the private business sector through balanced transactions. However, in many places, governments do choose to establish government-owned enterprises to increase revenue, meet demand, or support industry. For example, in 1952 the Haitian government under President Paul Magloire launched CINA, or Cimenterie Nationale d'Haiti, a cement company. In the following decades, CINA produced cement that was distributed throughout Haiti, and the enterprise is still producing today. Its product was not distributed for free. Rather, it was sold at the market price just as any other product was. The business was not an alteration of Haiti's market-based system but rather was the property of the government, which in a market-based system simply had a different type of ownership than the typical individual private firms that own and operate businesses.

Since Magloire's time, recent administrations have privatized the enterprise, and Cementos Argos, a private company, bought a large stake in CINA and became a strategic partner.[1] Again, this business just like any business must provide customer satisfaction profitably to survive. The same can be seen in a flour company, Les Moulins D'Haiti, 30 percent of which is now owned by the Haitian government while private-sector investors in UniFinance and Continental Grain Company own the rest.[2]

As long as the pattern of balanced transaction remains the primary means to meet demand, the market system continues to exist. Balanced transactions can generate profit, and jobs will be created. Therefore, even if government or other nontraditional actors pursue marketable opportunities through registered for-profit business models on an equal playing field, OBED can still be applied.

THE RULE OF LAW: A Sustaining Factor

Business opportunities need to be coupled with supporting factors such as the rule of law and a healthy civil society. For instance, investment and economic growth will not be spurred or sustained if corruption is prevalent, as it was in the Duvalier regime of 1971–86, well known as "one of the most corrupt and repressive in modern history."[3] Without vision and accountable leadership, it is challenging to foster a healthy economic environment that harnesses opportunities to increase balanced transactions.

Some characteristics of sound rule of law include security, political stability, property rights, and justice, all of which compose a return on investment for taxpayers in a healthy society. Without these factors, no society will be able to establish an environment in which citizens have equal access to opportunity.

Governments need to enforce laws that protect equitable opportunity for all rather than allowing corruption to continue for the benefit of some. According to the World Bank, "the role of government is to ensure that the conditions are in place for strong private-sector-led growth, to understand why there are not enough good jobs for development, and to remove or mitigate the constraints that prevent the creation of more of those jobs."[4]

For instance, the poverty in South Sudan could be best explained by a lack of balanced transactions due to war, famine, and political instability, which prevents the growth of an ethical business environment and strong legal system. In Honduras, due to low levels of education, a high unemployment rate, as well as high rates of gang violence and corruption, it is a struggle for many entrepreneurs to pursue new industries and opportunities at full capacity. In Somalia, a lack of governance has led to conflict resolution at a local level, fostering civil unrest and war. This has created a framework in which businesses cannot pursue opportunities to increase balanced transactions. Currently, Somalia remains unable to generate enough jobs and resources for its citizens.

Situations like these illustrate the importance of the supporting factor of the rule of law in spurring and sustaining economic growth.

INNOVATION: *A Sustaining Factor*

When governments, NGOs, and other resource distributors apply OBED, individuals and private businesses can pursue marketable opportunities to meet customer needs profitably. However, innovation is necessary to sustain business growth and create future opportunity. In short, businesses must continue to identify new opportunities in order to thrive.

In a business cycle, and, more broadly, in an economic cycle, entrepreneurs must innovate. Well-known Austrian American economist Joseph Schumpeter defined the process of innovating as "creative destruction," which denotes a "process of industrial mutation … that incessantly revolutionizes the economic structure *from within*, incessantly destroying the old one, incessantly creating a new one."[5] Schumpeter has characterized innovation as a means to creating new goods and services, designing new methods of production, pursuing new markets, engaging new raw materials, or developing new management strategies. Innovation is the sustaining factor that achieves solutions in an ever-changing environment.

Creative destruction is at the heart of innovation. It entails an internal conflict through which the entrepreneur creatively destroys the old methods, products, or services and replaces them with an updated innovation that can achieve new opportunities. For example, new technologies and consumer habits made floppy disks obsolete rather quickly, even though they had been in use for several decades. CD-ROMs began to replace floppy disks, and USB flash drives finally eliminated them. Now, even the newest of products are being challenged by innovative cloud database systems and a consumer base that has greater internet access than ever before. Today, the floppy disk is rarely used, and soon, even USB flash drives may be obsolete.

Creative Destruction within OBED

1. Identify marketable opportunities to better meet needs profitably → **2.** Apply creative destruction methods → **3.** Innovate the products or processes toward better efficiency and effectiveness → **4.** Develop and implement these new modes of production or services[6]

In Haiti, when a business and an NGO decide to partner and transact together, the business still needs to innovate in order to increase production and sustain potential growth, as illustrated in the case study below highlighting the innovative partnership between Maxima and World Renew. However, if NGOs don't contract with businesses, but instead flood the market with similar or substitute products, businesses may never have the opportunity to innovate. In many cases, the business may have to close its doors, as Laurent Auguste's soap company did. Without the opportunity for private-sector innovation, the market is distorted and the natural process of creative destruction that grows and sustains an economy is inhibited.

As we consider applying OBED in Haiti, we cannot forget the sustaining factor of innovation. Innovation is already taking place in Haiti to a certain degree. However, more actors in the market need to implement OBED strategies so that businesses can once again be the driving force behind Haiti's economic growth.

The following case study highlights OBED alignment with the sustaining factor of innovation. Maxima, a Haitian wood-manufacturing company, and World Renew, an NGO, partnered together and leaned into the opportunity to meet new consumer demand following the January 2010 earthquake. By partnering with NGOs as the buyers—just as they would with any marketable opportunity—businesses in Haiti have innovated in order to meet new market demands. In this particular case, new market acquisitions were made as a result of a partnership between a local business and an international nonprofit organization.

Businesses may be able to get short-term contracts with NGOs; however, in the long run, businesses must also innovate in order to maintain that growth and tap into new opportunities in the market, as you will see in the following case study.

Maxima and World Renew

Opportunity-based economic development requires ongoing innovation. To pursue opportunities, businesses must constantly evolve to generate resources profitably, meet demand satisfactorily, and increase balanced transactions. Creative destruction is at the heart of innovation, and businesses that are willing to replace old models with new ideas can sustain growth and create future opportunities. By innovating to diversify product lines, maintaining high-quality standards, and diligently seeking out new markets, innovative businesses like Maxima can adapt, survive, and thrive in even the most challenging economies.

Maxima's Story

Dutch entrepreneur Kees de Gier and his wife, Evelien, have lived in Haiti for over thirty years. When they became interested in missionary efforts, de Gier says that they went into business as a mission to ensure greater "return on investment" for their efforts.

After their first enterprise failed when their mother company in the Netherlands went bankrupt, the de Giers wanted to stay in Haiti, but needed an investor to keep their small factory, along with its fifteen employees, afloat. One of their buyers in the United States met that need, and the de Giers retooled their business, Art Frame, toward manufacturing picture frames. Art Frame's products were exported to Pennsylvania and distributed in major American retail stores, including Pier 1 Imports.

In 1991, the embargo brought the Haitian economy to a standstill. While its American partner was able to attain a special permit that allowed Art Frame to continue exporting, the company was eventually forced to halt production for several months.

Still, they survived the incredible economic hardship. "After the embargo ended," says Kees de Gier, "things started booming." Production doubled and the company expanded into handicrafts.

Soon after, Art Frame separated from the handicrafts operation to pursue new opportunities, but the handicrafts company continues to employ three hundred people.

However, Art Frame's success gave way to new challenges in just a few years. De Gier explains that manufacturing picture frames was becoming less and less profitable because of rising competition from China. "You know, Haiti has no materials," he tells us. Beyond their country's vast material resources, the competing Chinese manufacturers benefit from better shipping rates due to the great volume of exports leaving the country.

Again, the de Giers had to reinvent their business model to keep their doors open and to keep employees off the street. After partnering with friend and entrepreneur Stefan Vervloet, the de Giers began manufacturing the caskets Vervloet had been importing. In 2004, the company Maxima was born.

Two years later, the business found itself struggling to find enough clients. The market for quality caskets in Haiti was small. Worse, some funeral homes would purchase only one casket for display, then sell customers a cheap imitation.

Fortunately, Maxima's owners were able to creatively adapt to market conditions. They quickly found that there was a market for quality cabinetry. Until then, most cabinetry was imported from Miami or shoddily produced by novice Haitian carpenters with limited materials.

The transition to cabinetry was simple enough. "You're still making a box," says de Gier about the production process.

Maxima began producing cabinetry to supplement its casket production, but soon moved into other markets, even manufacturing pews for some of Port-au-Prince's largest churches.

Then, in 2010, "the earthquake hit," says de Gier, "and that was the end of Maxima, really." While the factory sustained only minimal damage, the earthquake stopped most businesses in their tracks, and wiped out the majority of funeral homes that Maxima had supplied. The owners lost friends and business partners after years of contracts and building trust. "For a few days we sat at home. We didn't know what to do."

But Maxima's innovative owners began to notice something about the structures that withstood the quake: many were made of wood, including traditional gingerbread-style houses from centuries past.

Within a week, they began designing simple wooden shelters with tin roofs, designed to help house the nearly one million who had been displaced by the earthquake. After developing the design with the help of American and Canadian engineers, the company was ready to begin production. Each unit was a two-room house, made of corrugated metal roofing and prefabricated wood panels. Complete with a strong coating to repel rain and endure sunlight, hurricanes, and termites—common challenges in the tropical climate—the unit met international standards for a family of five, offering eighteen square meters in floor space.

Shortly after that, humanitarian organizations in the Netherlands began contacting Maxima. De Gier calls this the only time in his life that work came to him.

"What we thought was the end of Maxima," he says, "was a new beginning."

World Renew

After the earthquake ravaged Port-au-Prince, the small town of Léogane, and other parts of the country, Haitian families were in dire need of housing. According to Oxfam, the tremendous shortage that already stood at three hundred thousand homes was aggravated to a five-hundred-thousand-home shortage by the earthquake, and the housing sector sustained a $3 billion loss. Rapid response was needed to resettle the 1.5 million homeless people residing in hundreds of refugee camps around the city.[9]

Willys Geffrard, who has an MBA in economic development from Eastern University, believes there is "a place for NGOs, a place for governments, a place for businesses." When he joined

World Renew, Geffrard became part of an organization that emphasized local procurement in its methodology. Beginning with its alimentary-aid programs, funded in part by the Canadian Food Grains Bank, World Renew made sure that the food it distributed to communities in Haiti was purchased from local farmers and producers, which was a CFGB stipulation.

Many organizations establishing headquarters in Haiti relied on prefabricated structures shipped to the nation's ports and erected on-site, which created little employment and transaction in the local economy. World Renew took a different approach.

Maxima–World Renew Partnership

When World Renew decided to provide transitional housing units to Haitian families displaced by the earthquake, Geffrard was able to connect with Vervloet and the de Giers at Maxima through a quick connection made by Partners Worldwide, as Maxima had been a long-time member in the network. "In spring 2010," says Geffrard, "Maxima was the only contractor in Port-au-Prince that could provide a quote and was equipped … to build hundreds of houses."

Maxima was already producing structures for a Dutch organization and would complete nearly three thousand shelters for that project alone. Most of the company's employees had also lost relatives in the earthquake and many had lost their homes. After the disaster, those employees were able to count on a steady income that would allow them to rebuild, thanks to Maxima's innovation and the willingness of some NGOs to contract locally.

World Renew's leaders made the conscious decision to use a local contractor when they could have imported prefabricated shelters for less. This choice created employment opportunities throughout the country and supported hundreds of employees among the Haitian suppliers.

Geffrard estimates that hundreds of thousands of dollars were spent on materials in the city of Léogane alone. He goes on to report that at least a hundred employees at Maxima's facility worked on the order. World Renew also relied heavily on the Haitian private sector, contracting laborers, vendors, carpenters, and masons to install the homes. "At one point," says Geffrard, "we were sustaining six hundred contracted workers on a daily basis, in the field, putting those houses up."

The first year after the earthquake was a crash course. According to Kees de Gier, during the months immediately following the earthquake Maxima grew from 59 to 275 workers as the company produced thousands of transitional housing units to fulfill contracts for various organizations' housing programs. De Gier estimates that Maxima produced up to 2,500 structures for World Renew alone.

Organizations such as World Renew that prioritized contracting locally maximized their economic effect in Haiti. Employees and contractors were able to save capital and invest in durable goods as they transitioned their families back to a sense of normal life. Because of the steady income the lucrative project provided, "a lot of people who have worked for us ... have been able to build a better house," says Geffrard. Some housing recipients were even able to add rooms and enlarge the homes they received.

Evelien de Gier argues that "employment is of critical importance. There's no better sense of control and independence you can find than working for your own income."[10]

Haitian businesses supplying cinder blocks, wood, sand, and concrete were able to save and reinvest in the business thanks to the millions of dollars of business created by projects like World Renew's. "[If] they need a piece of equipment," says Geffrard, "you're going to see that they acquire that piece of equipment."

Thanks to the Direction Générale des Impôts, Haiti's tax-collection agency, every dollar that went to a registered Haitian enterprise contributed to the national budget, sustaining the government and allowing the state to expand its services, even as NGO operations declined. Tax revenues increase when there are more local transactions, and government services funded by those revenues will ideally meet the needs that NGOs in Haiti currently serve.

In partnership with Maxima and local Haitian suppliers, World Renew injected millions of dollars into the Haitian economy while building homes for vulnerable Haitian families in Port-au-Prince and Léogane. By procuring goods and services locally, NGOs that prioritized local procurement following the earthquake were able to leverage the massive increase in donations and contribute to the long-term development of the private sector. They created jobs and supported businesses through balanced transactions and partnerships, proving the success of the OBED model.

Overcoming Barriers to Transaction

Partnership is an important solution to developing vulnerable markets and is key to NGO economic realignment. But many barriers prevent NGOs and businesses from partnering to create transactions together. When World Renew partnered with Maxima, they overcame issues of quality, production capacity, and communication and were able to create wealth together. Their partnership expresses tangible ways to overcome those barriers to transaction.

Geffrard reports that Maxima communicated effectively and provided a flexible service. "If something wasn't level," says Geffrard, "we brought that to their attention and they were right on it at the factory. They sent their own carpenters and worked with our people to fix our problem. That's good service."

"We did everything in writing," Kees de Gier tells us. "For every item, there was a contract number. We respect what we say, and what we say, we write it down."

But Geffrard thinks that foreign NGOs might not contract with local businesses for another reason: "concern for employment in their own countries." With massive amounts of capital at their disposal, aid organizations from developing nations may want to create short-term jobs in their own countries, especially after a global recession that has adversely affected employment all around.

Still, Geffrard argues that NGOs need to be more adaptable to the local market-based economy, and World Renew's partnership with Maxima proved that such adaptability is possible.

"Some NGOs request delivery times that are just unreasonable," says de Gier. While Haitian businesses must pursue NGO contracts and be sensitive to their time constraints, NGOs that want to have a greater impact on the economy must work more closely with local businesses to address these conflicts.

When World Renew purchased local goods and services, partnered with local businesses, and created taxable transactions for the government, the organization aligned itself with Haiti's market-based economy, thus creating wealth and opportunity. So, how can other NGOs better align themselves with Haiti's economy?

Geffrard notes that many private enterprises are actively seeking partnerships with international NGOs. "There are Haitian local organizations and associations that have ideas as to how to create employment for their people," says Geffrard. But local businesses need support, financial and otherwise, to expand their services and hire more employees. Maxima's challenges and successes following the earthquake bear this out.

Maxima Now

Contracts for transitional housing units have dried up in the years following the initial disaster response to the earthquake, but Maxima has continued to innovate.

Kees de Gier tells us that the company had expected those contracts to decline sooner than they did, so Maxima restarted production of caskets as soon as it could, even while still filling orders for shelters. This ensured that the company would have enough business to sustain itself when NGO funds ran out.

Maxima also returned to cabinetry, but expanded its interior design services and installation to family homes and larger commercial buildings. It now produces granite countertops, another diversification of its product lines to meet the growing demand as businesses, offices, stores, hotels, and restaurants rebuild and grow throughout metro Port-au-Prince.

Leveraging the boom in contracts for shelters, Maxima purchased inventory and equipment and moved to a larger production facility. Before the earthquake, Maxima employed about fifty employees. Now it employs around a hundred.

While the conversation with NGOs has moved past transitional housing, Maxima is now the only company producing roof trusses according to US standards. De Gier hopes that NGOs seeking to provide permanent homes to Haiti's vulnerable families will take note of Maxima's superior quality.

Still, Maxima, like so many other businesses, will continue to face the systemic challenges that plague the Haitian economy.

"We are not cheap," says de Gier, "but materials are expensive." The cost of importing quality, treated lumber—along with equipment and everything else—is a resilient barrier to winning price-sensitive clients such as humanitarian NGOs.

Still, Maxima is able to offset some of that price for the consumer because of the convenience of contracting locally. Haitian customers purchasing kitchen cabinets may find them less expensive in Miami, but they will need to import them, pay customs, and then hire Haitian carpenters to install the cabinetry. Maxima can complete that process in a fraction of the time with less effort from the client.

Over the years, Maxima and their prior companies diversified production, survived staggering economic and political turmoil, and leveraged post-earthquake partnerships into future opportunities, creating jobs and continuing to produce local, value-added products.

Opportunity-based economic development means transaction, not donation—business, not aid. World Renew's emphasis on local procurement and Maxima's consistent innovation prove that solutions exist to Haiti's most resilient barriers to sustainable growth.

Applying the OBED Strategy

The implementation of OBED will take a different course in every country and context. As we have seen, each BRICS country uniquely adapted the OBED strategy to its specific situation in terms of its political structure, natural resources, economic and legal framework, international relations, population growth, and other factors. Below, we will lay out how OBED should be implemented in Haiti.

The step-by-step process to applying OBED relies on a market-based system's strategic problem-solving process. Although each context may require an adapted strategy, the following are steps that all OBED-driven actors can use to solve problems through the market-based system.

FIGURE 3: **Applying the OBED Strategy: Action Item Ecosystem**

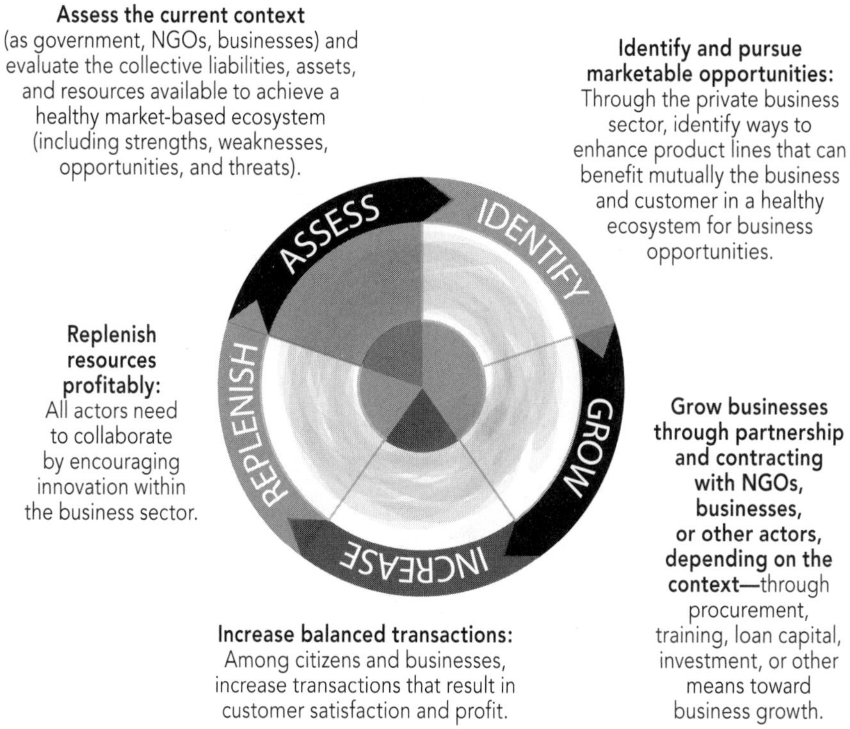

Assess the current context
(as government, NGOs, businesses) and evaluate the collective liabilities, assets, and resources available to achieve a healthy market-based ecosystem (including strengths, weaknesses, opportunities, and threats).

Identify and pursue marketable opportunities:
Through the private business sector, identify ways to enhance product lines that can benefit mutually the business and customer in a healthy ecosystem for business opportunities.

Replenish resources profitably:
All actors need to collaborate by encouraging innovation within the business sector.

Grow businesses through partnership and contracting with NGOs, businesses, or other actors, depending on the context—through procurement, training, loan capital, investment, or other means toward business growth.

Increase balanced transactions:
Among citizens and businesses, increase transactions that result in customer satisfaction and profit.

> ## OUTCOME: Impact of optimal OBED application
>
> Wealth (profit) created → customers' needs met → jobs created → increased tax revenue = better infrastructure, education, and governmental services, as well as better incomes for families, which leads to a stronger economy and state and improved lives for succeeding generations

ACTION ITEM 1: *Assess the ecosystem in its current context*

Assessing the current market-based ecosystem is the first step. To effectively apply OBED, the government, private business sector, and NGOs need to assess and evaluate their collective assets, liabilities, resources, and opportunities in order to achieve a healthy market-based ecosystem in their unique context. A business might assess new marketable opportunities to improve or grow their existing market share. An NGO might assess potential partnerships with the private sector to support business growth and transact locally. A government entity, such as a department or ministry, might evaluate trade policies that can better enhance opportunities for local businesses to grow.

This assessment and learning process is an essential first step for existing actors and, especially, new actors seeking to implement OBED.

ACTION ITEM 2: *Identify and pursue profitable market opportunities*

After the assessment is complete, businesses need to aggressively pursue any profitable market opportunity that has been identified. When businesses pursue opportunities, they respond to market demand and supply products or services that fit their own assessments, or those of NGOs, government, or other businesses in the market ecosystem.

The business strategy should be pursued at the lowest opportunity cost possible. Businesses should focus on opportunities that are guaranteed by purchasing power—that is, those that have enough market demand. Once the opportunity is pursued, the cost per unit made must be less than the cost per unit sold, providing that every unit made is sold.

The government or NGOs, as resource distributors, might identify profitable opportunities, but it will be up to the business to develop those opportunities while the government or NGO acts in a supportive role. For example, the government could decide to create policies that promote ethical tourism, and NGOs might supply training in starting up a business, but ultimately the business sector will supply the necessary services through hotels, restaurants, and tours, and by developing and managing recreational sites.

In the ideal application of OBED in a market ecosystem, for-profit businesses should pursue and develop the profitable opportunities, while governments and NGOs remain in a supportive role.

ACTION ITEM 3: Grow business through partnership and contracting with NGOs, businesses, or other actors, depending on the context

In Haiti and in many other developing countries, the strong presence of NGOs too often replaces balanced transactions with donations. Instead, NGOs need to realign their strategy to support private-sector growth in a market-based ecosystem, which can lead to sustainable development throughout the country. This does not mean that NGOs must become a chamber of commerce or convert to a social business model; rather, NGOs should seek to realign themselves with the market-based economy by partnering and contracting with businesses that can supply the products or services that the NGO needs in order to achieve its own vision and goals.

For example, Mendell Harryford, founder and owner of ITS Haiti, has been able to partner effectively with NGOs by providing the professional printing and technology services that they need (see the case study in chapter 5).

Other resource distributors, including governments, can also contract with the private sector to establish sound economic policies that support business.

ACTION ITEM 4: Increase balanced transactions

Effective realignment actions will lead to an increase in balanced transactions. As seen in the case of the BRICS countries, increased balanced transactions have led to overall economic growth in the business sector. When businesses were able to access the market, they could meet market demand profitably and could sustainably meet the needs that NGOs could not.

In addition, as businesses have grown in those countries, employment levels also rose, as did people's purchasing power across the board, which led to even more balanced transactions. And the cycle of growth continued.

Now, there are exceptions. We believe that balanced transactions should not and cannot include business or distribution practices that are an illegal or unethical means of transaction. Issues such as human trafficking and child labor must be identified and eliminated in accordance with national and international laws.

ACTION ITEM 5: *Replenish resources profitably*

An increase in balanced transactions will lead to greater profit. As businesses profit and reinvest—as economic value is added to the supply chain—initial capital grows to a higher return on investment.

When NGOs meet needs with donated revenue or free products, there is no sustainable and profitable return to reinvest. But as long as businesses are pursuing marketable opportunities, revenue and profit will continue to grow. Businesses contract with other businesses when they partner with suppliers and distributors. Businesses can also contract with other businesses. For example, when a business contracts with suppliers of raw materials used in production, or with a distributor, that increases balanced transactions and thereby has a ripple effect throughout the economy.

The government is also able to grow its functions through tax revenue that can be reinvested in the market in order to expand public services such as infrastructure and education, thereby benefiting all of society, including the business sector. This also has a ripple effect throughout the economy and resources are continually replenished.

The Ultimate Outcome

Business can be the driver of change, while every sector—including public policy, education, legislation, infrastructure, accountability, health, natural resources—needs to be equipped to embrace its role within a market-based economy and together transform society. In Haiti and in other developing countries where NGOs are prevalent, and often essential, NGOs must also realign their efforts with the existing framework and not only support, but partner with, the market's resource generators.

When OBED is appropriately implemented, the ultimate outcome is the well-being of society. You cannot have healthy citizens without jobs. And you cannot have a steady supply of jobs without wealth creation and resource generation based on balanced transactions. Furthermore, balanced transactions are predicated on the pursuit of marketable opportunities in which customers are satisfied profitably.

In the next chapter, we present three case studies of NGOs that have aligned themselves to Haiti's market economy through effective partnership and local-procurement practices. Additionally, two case studies provide examples of successful Haitian businesses that are serving NGOs and individuals and thereby meeting their customers' needs and growing the economy at the same time.

CHAPTER 7

Methods for
Supporting Business Growth

Opportunity-based economic development is a strategy particularly suited for underdeveloped and developing economies because there are vast needs throughout these societies. Opportunity-based economic development can develop an economy sustainably because it starts with meeting people's needs through for-profit models. Demand should be met increasingly through market opportunities that businesses pursue, not NGO intervention alone. Nonprofit NGO models are not designed to generate either full customer satisfaction or profit. However, NGOs can realign themselves with market-based systems and apply OBED through partnership with for-profit enterprises. In this way, NGOs can utilize the assets and capital within their power to partner with the business sector, which has the unique means to meet demand profitably and generate resources sustainably. We recognize that market-based economies are like ecosystems. Multiple actors, including governments, citizens, businesses, and NGOs, all play key roles in developing an economy and a society. Therefore, we challenge all actors, especially those in developing countries with a strong NGO presence, to apply the OBED strategy. We now turn to some specific methods—and some powerful stories of people already implementing each method—in order to apply OBED and support long-term business growth.

Four Methods for Supporting Business Growth

As you will see in the methods summarized below, there are various ways to enhance marketable opportunities for the business sector and equip businesses to achieve long-term, sustainable growth. While these methods are compatible with one another, individuals and organizations do not need to apply all of them, but may pick and choose the methods that work best for their unique situations and goals. We believe Haiti not only has the necessary assets to make these methods work, but it also has high demand and widespread needs to be met, which creates immense opportunities for NGOs and individuals to support the growth of business in order to profitably and sustainably meet the needs of the Haitian people.

METHOD 1: Buy Locally

Increase transactions by procuring what is needed locally.

METHOD 2: Create Platforms for Connecting

Facilitate communication between the aid sector and the private business sector by creating platforms for connecting.

METHOD 3: Advocate for Policy Changes

Identify government policies that need to be addressed, then advocate for those changes.

METHOD 4: Invest in a Viable Business Opportunity

Pursue viable business opportunities, establishing and promoting ethical, sustainable for-profit enterprises that meet demand profitably and create jobs.

Now let's look at these methods in more depth, including case studies that show them in action. Many of the case studies reveal individuals, businesses, and NGOs using more than one method and tailoring their efforts to the unique circumstances they encounter.

METHOD 1: Buy Locally

Because of NGOs' strong purchasing power, their procurement practices have an enormous effect on Haiti's economy. If the private sector can overcome barriers to transaction—price, quality, quantity, delivery time, and communication—balanced transactions between businesses and NGOs can be achieved. Those balanced transactions would align NGOs with the market-based system, and local procurement helps to break the cycle of poverty in a sustainable way, as the following figure illustrates.

FIGURE 4: **OBED: Breaking the Cycle of Poverty Sustainably**

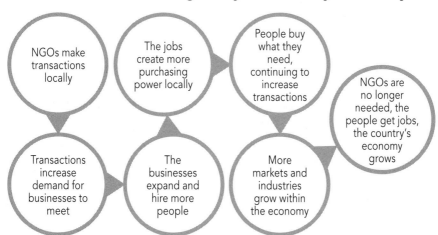

In the long run, local procurement is a win-win-win situation. NGOs can continue to serve their original clientele—often the poor who can seek support from NGOs when they don't have enough purchasing power to meet their needs, especially in cases of natural disaster, civil war, or chronic economic challenges. However, when the NGOs commit to purchase from the business sector in the country or community they serve, the businesses that supply goods and services to NGOs can grow, strengthening their own capacity to hire more people and pay them better, which thereby increases the purchasing power of employees. This has a ripple effect that grows the economy and increases overall purchasing power. Ultimately, the poor will be equipped with incomes and will eventually need fewer of the donated goods and services offered by NGOs. Last, the government and its public sector priorities can also be fulfilled through the increase in balanced transactions and the increased tax revenue these transactions and businesses and jobs can generate, ultimately leading to greater stability and sustainable growth throughout the economy and the country overall.

Therefore, when individuals, aid organizations, and NGOs partner with businesses to purchase locally, they bring themselves back into alignment with the market-based system by participating in balanced transactions. The first method is not aid; it is partnership and trade, as the case study of the FEDEPAT–Mission of Hope partnership demonstrates.

FEDEPAT–Mission of Hope Partnership

Haiti's economic woes have only worsened the nation's endemic malnutrition. Domestic food security is even further out of reach thanks to the ease of importing goods from the United States and Southeast Asia. However, humanitarian and development aid organizations can improve their alimentary-aid programs by supporting local production through buying locally. Importation and resource distribution breeds dependence. Local production creates jobs, industry, and economic growth. NGOs must seek partnerships with Haitian producers to maximize their effect, but Haitian entrepreneurs must also learn to convert those partnerships into sustainable economic growth.

Before he represented farmers in the Thomazeau region, Ken Michel was an importer. Like many entrepreneurs, he adopted the strategy of importing foodstuffs such as rice to alleviate the local market's high prices. "I used to import 6,000 tons a month—on average 60,000 tons a year," he tells us. "I did that for ten years of my life and I learned my lessons."

Michel thought that importing cheaper food would help the economy by driving prices down, but the extensive negative effect of importation on Haiti's agricultural sector, which contributed to its economic tailspin, proved disastrous as Haiti went from being a net exporter to a net importer of food.

Now Michel has a new agenda.

After attending a USAID-sponsored conference on local production in late 2010, Michel was introduced to farmers from Thomazeau, a town less than thirty kilometers from the capital. "I would say I fell in love," he says. FEDEPAT, the Federation for the Development and Growth of Agriculture in the Region of Thomazeau, is composed of thirty-two farmers associations. "I found that this community seemed to be trying to take care of its own future," says Michel.

Since then, Ken Michel has represented FEDEPAT in partnerships with Mission of Hope, Food for the Poor, the World Food Programme, and BRANA, Haiti's largest beverage company, now owned by Heineken. A Food for the Poor executive once stated that previously the majority of the rice distributed by the organization had been purchased in Vietnam instead of Haiti to keep costs down. Today, with Michel's help to bridge the gap to the market, FEDEPAT, now composed of fifty-six associations and nearly six thousand farmers, has grown its cultivation from three hundred to three thousand acres (a 900-percent increase), and has a greater readiness and ability to fulfill the contracts requested by partnering NGOs and other emerging buyers at a more competitive price.

A New Strategy for FEDEPAT's Farmers

"If you don't hear and understand what the other person has to do, you don't understand how to help," says Michel. He explains the difficulty he's faced in partnering with farmers. "I found them to be rejecting of local entrepreneurs."

Michel estimates that Haitian agriculture is five times less productive than other countries, producing 1.5 to 2 metric tons of rice per hectare while other countries produce 8 to 10. Haitian rice is also 50 to 100 percent more expensive than its foreign competitors, depending on weather conditions per season.

He also finds a lack of diversity in agricultural production, one that has rendered Haitian farmers even more vulnerable to market conditions. Without alternatives like animal husbandry, many farmers are unable to absorb losses and remain competitive.

As Michel began purchasing rice and other foodstuffs from farmers on FEDEPAT's behalf, he had to convince them to lower their prices. Farmers needed to undersell their competitors to establish their place in a market that he says is "distorted" by the surplus of cheap, imported goods. After showing farmers what their Indian, Thai, and American competitors' products looked like,

Michel asked farmers to describe the imported rice. "They always said, 'This is cleaner, whiter, dryer,'" he reports. This convinced farmers to lower prices to make their lower-quality products more competitive. Michel argues that once farmers have been educated on the realities of the international market, they can then develop a sustainable price strategy.

"I'm a firm believer in not overpaying farmers," says Michel, who thinks that programs that overpay are "subsidizing poverty." He argues that he and FEDEPAT are real partners to the farmers of Thomazeau, not merely buyers who might purchase overpriced goods today only to reject them tomorrow.

Though investment, production, and profits have increased, Michel still encounters farmers who believe his strategy of selling low to increase demand is too good to be true. "Those are hard lessons to teach people who don't have much money," he says.

Now Michel and FEDEPAT are working to improve quality by purchasing equipment such as tractors and humidimeters. He also works to establish standard trading practices for those times when farmers are unable to produce as expected due to seasonal setbacks.

In 2011, during a severe drought that adversely affected the whole of Haitian agriculture, farmers in Thomazeau began to panic, Michel says. Still, he saw a way forward and asked farmers to commit to partner the next season in order to make up on losses from the previous shortage.

He also reports that while new cultivation techniques have been slow to catch on, in 2012 "every farmer planted one plant per hole, which is a good thing."

Mission of Hope

Founded in 1998, Mission of Hope is a nonprofit educational organization that supports teachers and administrators through capacity building. Soon after its first school opened, the organization noticed something strange about the students. Children were tired, distracted, and even fainting in class from hunger. Administrators realized that they had to start feeding students if their lessons were going to stick. Beginning with local peanut butter and moving on to an array of other foods, Mission of Hope now operates a feeding program for its students and is committed to increasing local procurement.

Mission of Hope Director of Business Development Austin Holmes tells us, "Right now we're serving just under eighty-nine thousand meals a day." Most of that food is imported, yet Holmes is working to fix that.

"The total number is a combination of goods that are brought in internationally and goods that are procured and packaged domestically," says Holmes. Mission of Hope currently purchases only 5 to 10 percent of its foodstuffs locally, namely whole grain rice and beans. Holmes wants to "increase the domestic side and slowly wean off the other side," but the barriers to local procurement are resilient.

The Haitian agricultural sector is "cash-starved," says Holmes. Because the industry has poor storage capacity, refrigeration, and shelf life, the market is at the mercy of price fluctuations. Haitian agriculture has a hard time overcoming what Holmes calls the "peaks and valleys of products and commodities," and because of customs exemptions for NGOs, it remains much cheaper to import food that is then distributed below market value.

Still, if capital is the issue, why import at all? Why not purchase as much food as possible in Haiti right away? The higher prices would certainly limit the number of meals Mission of Hope could provide to students in the short term, but the ripple effect in the broader economy might be worth it.

According to Mission of Hope's website, "The World Food Program reports that food supply in Haiti only covers 55 percent of the population," "42 percent of children less than five years of age suffer from stunted growth," and "Haiti is among the worst three countries for daily caloric intake per person."[3]

This is one of the many developmental paradoxes of the Haitian economy. NGOs cannot have the most significant impact on the populations they serve unless they keep costs low to maximize their reach. Further, more local procurement will not necessarily lead to growth and stability. Initiatives that promise to purchase goods at fixed prices often fall prey to lack of incentive, stagnant production, and reduced quality (for example, see the case study on USAID and Haitian Bleu in chapter 8).

Farmers need buyers now in order to increase production and become more competitive, but Holmes believes it would be an "irresponsible use of funds" to procure everything locally today. Even if they could find the appropriate quality and quantity, Mission of Hope's purchasing would become a "private subsidy for markets that are uncompetitive."

Instead, Holmes and Mission of Hope are building the agricultural sector's capacity brick by brick, one step at a time. Mission of Hope's partnership with FEDEPAT's farmers, who are represented by Ken Michel, is informed by that long-term strategy.

FEDEPAT–Mission of Hope Partnership

Mission of Hope has a purchasing relationship with the federation Ken Michel represents, but the nonprofit also provides FEDEPAT farmers with training—from seed to harvest—and coaches them on the use of new tools and implements. In this way, Mission of Hope supports FEDEPAT both financially and through capacity building. This partnership secures revenue for farmers, improves market stability, ensures rates for the organization, and allows Mission of Hope to steadily increase local procurement as the federation is more able to meet demand and improve quality.

Since domestic food security is integral to economic stability and the kind of long-term growth that can lift a generation out of poverty, each actor involved should first prioritize local purchasing in order to help trigger growth within Haiti's local food markets, which can then lead to longer-term outcomes. Holmes believes this is a "long-term change," but that it's "the right thing to do."

When Mission of Hope began purchasing goods from FEDEPAT, Ken Michel reports that the nonprofit offered to donate a tractor to the farmers. He declined the offer. "That's awesome," says Michel, "but that's not what I want to do." Instead, Michel argued that the organization should use those funds to finance a tractor for the federation at no interest over thirty-six months.

"I can't expect Mission of Hope to finance all the tractors I need," he says, but the zero-percent financing allowed FEDEPAT to purchase the equipment it previously couldn't afford while also holding farmers responsible for their future. "The farmers agree that in three years, we can go to a bank and say, 'Listen, we borrowed so much, we paid back so much,'" Michel says. This will prove that FEDEPAT can sustain a 5-percent-per-annum business. "Today," he says, "it's a leap of faith for the bank."

As Michel cultivates partnerships between FEDEPAT and organizations such as Mission of Hope and the World Food Programme, he's seeking to leverage NGO projects and purchasing power into assets for the federation.

Michel explains that it took FEDEPAT and Mission of Hope longer to negotiate the purchase of the tractor on credit than it would have taken to simply receive a donation. But he sees both the importance of turning subsidy into opportunity and the detrimental effect of a total reliance on donated items such as food: "Every time you say 'no' to the [donated items], yet somebody still comes and gives, it's like they are enabling a drug addict who wants to get off drugs. I tell donors exactly that."

In partnership with NGO allies, Michel hopes to create a dynamic that lifts people out of their dependence. Since then, as part of a capacity-building program in Thomazeau, Mission of

Hope has also recruited farmers from the United States to teach their Haitian counterparts how best to use their equipment. "This is where the good-hearted people can actually bring their skills," says Michel. "Not 'I do it for you,' but 'Let me understand what you are doing and walk beside you.'"

Overcoming Barriers to Transaction

So, how can organizations like Mission of Hope overcome the barriers to transaction that currently restrict Haiti's economic growth?

In terms of price, Holmes explains that Mission of Hope uses the training component of its partnership with farmers as a mechanism to provide tools and even seeds, and then the organization is reimbursed with a percentage of the harvest. "What that allows," he says, "is a non-cash expense to them because it's on the back end of their production." Further, Holmes continues, "it's a non-cash expense to us. It's a portion of what we helped to create with them."

By integrating financial access into its capacity-building efforts, Mission of Hope is able to get more out of its relationship with FEDEPAT's farmers.

Holmes tells us that while "there's definitely a gap in quality" between domestic and imported rice, it has narrowed. He is also encouraged that beneficiary students "tend to like and prefer Haitian-grown products, and they tend to know them with an uncanny knack."

Although quantity still remains a challenge, when Mission of Hope purchases what it can from Haitian farmers today, it helps those farmers increase production in the next season. Mission of Hope does incur additional expenses procuring in-country, but the organization is still looking for ways to increase local procurement as prices become more competitive.

According to Holmes, delivery time and communication have

been difficult obstacles to overcome, even with FEDEPAT. When terms are not "articulated by both parties," he says, "of course there's ambiguity on the delivery." Communication is key, but so is accountability.

For organizations like Mission of Hope, truly contributing to sustainable economic development takes commitment *and* competition. By seeking out new suppliers while maintaining long-term relationships with farmers, organizations can strengthen the market at large while supporting individual producers.

Holmes says Mission of Hope is always ready to find other sellers to keep prices competitive. But he doesn't see this as a bad thing: "That's just the market maturing."

For Ken Michel, the key to creating sustainable growth in Haiti's agricultural sector is simple. While the 4,000 tons that FEDEPAT's farmers currently produce is a far cry from the 60,000 he used to import, Michel hopes to grow that figure to 40,000 tons over the next decade. Increasing local production by leveraging NGO partnerships will allow farmers to become more competitive and more self-sufficient.

He also recognizes the potential in the small amount Thomazeau's farmers currently produce. "It's no business for me," says Michel about the small production today. "But that's 4,000 tons that never existed before." And, within this partnership, production can only grow.

METHOD 2: *Create Platforms for Connecting*

Instead of distributing free or subsidized imports in Haiti, many NGOs are seeking ways to connect with local business suppliers and transact in-country. However—in addition to price, quality, quantity, and delivery time—communication between foreign NGOs and Haitian businesses is one of the most challenging barriers to partnership. Therefore, one of the best methods for encouraging local businesses is to create and support platforms that enable businesses to contact NGOs, businesses to connect with other businesses, businesses to interact with the government, and so on. The case study of Peace Dividend Trust demonstrates what can happen when the key components of communication, connection, and networking are put into place.

Peace Dividend Trust

Facilitating transaction is the basis for the sustainable development of market economies. A key component of transaction is communication. Although it is often overlooked, networking infrastructure and social platforms are crucial to business success.

Salim Loxley, former country director of Peace Dividend Trust (now called Building Markets), had spent a portion of his career in the public-sector consulting arm of PricewaterhouseCoopers, a multinational, professional services firm. "I used to work with governments on provision of infrastructure, strategy, project management," says Loxley. "When I had the chance to do that kind of work with PricewaterhouseCoopers, I jumped at it."

In 2006, a friend from university founded Peace Dividend Trust and began its first project in Afghanistan. The organization's mission was "to build markets, create jobs, and sustain peace in developing countries by championing local entrepreneurs and connecting them to new business opportunities."

Four years later, Loxley joined the Peace Dividend Trust team in Haiti, just months after the earthquake. Six months later, he was country director. Loxley didn't come to development at random. Both of his parents were expatriate development economists, and he was born in Tanzania. "I was raised in a household where there was a lot of connection to the developing world," he says. "A certain part of me felt a responsibility to help in some small way."

Today, his experience connecting Haitian businesses to agency buyers gives Loxley special insight into how NGOs can overcome structural barriers to transacting and partnering with local enterprises.

Peace Dividend Trust Haiti

The Haitian branch of Peace Dividend Trust (PDT) was founded in 2009. For three years, the Haitian team, consisting almost entirely of native Haitians, worked to connect local entrepreneurs to domestic, regional, and global supply chains. By training Haitian businesses to be more compliant with agency procurement processes and by creating an online database of local business, PDT Haiti gave NGO buyers more confidence "to go out and try to look for what they needed in the local market," says Loxley. "We knew that we needed to help to facilitate transactions, and frankly you need buyers and sellers."

Loxley credits his predecessor with creating the private-sector database, which gave the program credibility with NGOs and local businesses alike. "Nobody had really gone and done face-to-face interviews with businesses and taken them through a forty-five-minute interview to get the type of information we were getting," says Loxley.

As NGOs transacted with local businesses, thanks to efforts such as PDT Haiti's, more capital was introduced into the local economy. Local businesses that won contracts could expand operations, hire staff, save, or pursue more contracts. "It wasn't for PDT to tell businesses what to do with their money," says Loxley, "but we encouraged them by speaking about why this was important."

While he admits that not all businesses keep their capital in the market, he contends that local procurement still introduces more money into the local economy. PDT Haiti sought to make transactions easier for local suppliers and to connect them to the new opportunities afforded by NGO spending.

The organization offered a system that sent information about contracts by text messages, explains Loxley. "For every supplier listed in a category—say, transport—if a contract from an NGO came out on our site, everybody that was registered would get that SMS."

Still, it was important that PDT maintain an arm's-length relationship with NGOs and local suppliers alike. Loxley paints the organization as "a broker of information and nothing much else. We didn't get involved with respect to price or quality." Instead, PDT Haiti tried to ensure that buyers were in touch with a wide range of sellers that could meet their needs, in order that NGOs could more efficiently overcome the challenges they faced in transacting locally.

The Earthquake: Before and After

In 2010, the earthquake threw the market into crisis mode. As NGOs flocked to the country, PDT Haiti's mission to bridge the information gap between agency buyers and local sellers became even more important.

"One of the things happening [after] the earthquake was that procurement offices were extremely busy," says Loxley, "which demonstrated things that our organization underestimated."

The team at PDT Haiti soon discovered that many NGOs were in fact purchasing locally. Loxley reports that NGOs often argued that they already had suppliers, local or international, and didn't need more. However, the local transactions that were taking place weren't always balanced.

Loxley recognizes that PDT Haiti's approach added a broader market dimension to purchasing that many organizations weren't always able to address. Facing donor and institutional constraints, many NGOs couldn't afford to change their strategies and timelines to accommodate local businesses.

"There's absolutely no reason that somebody should go out and spend an exorbitant amount on products," says Loxley, "and, quite frankly, a lot of businesses took advantage of the earthquake."

He cites the real-estate market as an example of a bubble created by unbalanced transactions, namely, NGOs purchasing housing and office space at well above market value. As individuals sought to capitalize on the staggering shortages, NGOs agreed to exorbitant prices.

Still, says Loxley, "we were in an emergency situation. A lot of purchases were made for the sake of expediency." He explains: "A lot of people were struggling to get their contracts done and move things forward for their project teams. They wouldn't have had the time to go for smaller contracts."

The barriers to transaction became more difficult to overcome immediately following the earthquake. Further, NGOs' access to import goods tax-free made local procurement even less cost effective. "The emergency really changed the way buying and selling was happening between people," says Loxley. However, he argues, "it's very important not to paint all Haitian businesses with the same brush."

Ministry of Commerce Takes Over

In the aftermath of the 2010 earthquake, the Canadian International Development Agency—PDT Haiti's primary donor—wanted to shut down the program over security concerns. Loxley's team countered that due to the influx of NGOs, the post-earthquake context demanded efforts such as theirs more than ever. Nevertheless, the project under PDT was discontinued in 2013, and the database of businesses was quickly transferred to the Haitian Ministry of Commerce.

Loxley's contract ended before the transfer, but he believes the project should have been extended. PDT Haiti was forced to hand over the project in six months, which Loxley argues was not enough time to build the Ministry of Commerce's capacity, or to conduct an effective transition.

"As a team of twenty-five to forty people," says Loxley, "we were very proud of what we did. I don't think the project ended in a way that was fitting."

Lessons

Loxley worries about the security concerns that keep aid workers "in locked cars," out of markets, and away from suppliers. This distance makes it hard for NGOs to work effectively with their counterparts and contributes to the information gap that causes some organizations to exhibit behavior that can seem erratic and irresponsible, but may not be entirely their fault.

Agencies must do a better job of transacting and partnering with local business. Loxley argues that Haiti's entrepreneurial spirit needs to be valued. "In many respects, even elements of the private sector that people are keen to address and improve—the *madan saras*, the people on the road selling things—do you know what they're doing? They're selling things. They're entrepreneurs, and they are making the best with what they have."

Loxley goes on to describe Haitian farmers, who "every single day, walk down from Kenscoff with baskets of carrots on their heads. That's to be respected and supported, not disdained and criticized."

By engaging with local enterprises as viable partners in economic development, agencies can contribute to sustainable growth. "These are complex things to work out," says Loxley, "but that was one main thing we were trying to do: to get that multiplier effect."

"When I became country director," says Loxley, "we relied on people telling us if a transaction had even happened." By the end of Loxley's tenure, PDT Haiti was able to measure an increase in transactions and in revenue that flowed to Haitian business. That revenue represents nearly $30 million.

Loxley remains humble in spite of the numbers. "The bigger question is [whether] it would have happened without us," he says.

Under Loxley's direction, PDT Haiti built on the platform of local businesses that were ready to contract with NGO buyers while also improving its capabilities to measure its own impact. Peace Dividend Trust has since been renamed Building Markets. Globally, Building Markets has a staff of 150 people working in Afghanistan, Haiti, Liberia, Myanmar, and Timor-Leste. The organization has "a network of over 16,000 entrepreneurs," has "helped create or sustain over 65,000 full-time equivalent jobs," and has helped local businesses win over $1 billion in contracts.[5]

In Haiti, Building Markets reports a dollar-value impact of over $28 million, nearly four thousand verified local businesses, and over one thousand businesses trained. Its impact provides quantitative evidence of the benefits of market-based development approaches such as OBED.

Building Markets provides several key recommendations for NGOs seeking to increase local procurement. The organization argues that agencies should "prioritize prompt payment to contractors and offer advance payments to ease the credit crunch faced by local firms." Building Markets in Haiti also recommends that NGOs "unbundle large contracts to make it easier for smaller firms to compete, facilitate local bidding by producing all documents in French, and extend tender submission deadlines in order to increase the quality and quantity of local bids."

Businesses in the private sector can also improve in a variety of ways by offering information on past performance, by justifying their prices to buyers, by forming more business-to-business partnerships, and by "proactively seeking feedback when they don't win a contract in order to strengthen future bids."

Loxley recognizes that the Haitian private sector must address its systemic flaws, but he argues that Haitians' entrepreneurial spirit is a cultural advantage. "You have to leverage that," he says. "It has to be celebrated."

METHOD 3: *Advocate for Policy Change*

As NGOs, businesses, and individuals begin to work to support economic opportunity and business growth, they will inevitably encounter public policies that will either help or hinder their efforts. One of the ways, then, that they can effect change is to identify policy barriers, share information with government officials, and advocate for changes in policy to support business growth.

The results of poor government regulation of rice imports are illustrated in the case study of Hunger Relief International in the next chapter. The following case study of ENERSA further demonstrates how government procurement and policy can affect a business. At times the government supported ENERSA's efforts by purchasing from the company. But the government also undercut ENERSA's market by allowing non-restricted imports of a similar product line. ENERSA's story shows us that every effort must be made by individuals, NGOs, and businesses to share information and advocate for policy changes that support businesses.

CASE STUDY[6]

ENERSA

Despite political challenges and a repertoire of corrupt practices, the Haitian government and local institutions today have strong potential to better facilitate business development by creating favorable trade policies and tax incentives for local production. While advocacy is taking place on the ground level, as well as the international community more broadly, nationwide improvements in trade policies and access to resources are emerging, but have yet to be fully unleashed. When the government supports the efforts of private enterprises like ENERSA, they create a win-win situation: the business succeeds and the government can collect tax revenue to support its operations. For this reason, various advocacy efforts need to continue.

Jean-Ronel Noël, cofounder of Energies Renouvables S.A. (ENERSA), believes that solar energy is key to Haiti's present and future energy needs. The company he founded with partner Alex Georges is Haiti's only solar panel manufacturer. This production company purchases as much of its materials locally as possible, hires employees from Cité Soleil (Haiti's most notorious slum), brings light to the country's remotest communities, and is at the cutting edge of the nation's energy sector. Without affordable energy, both the day-to-day livelihoods and the macroeconomic growth in Haiti will remain a challenge.

"Haiti's solar potential is an estimated six peak sun hours in the dry season, about the same as that of Phoenix, Arizona, the sunniest US city. In the rainy season it's not much less," says Noël.

Even before the earthquake, Noël says, "Haiti had one of the lowest rates of electricity access in the world, with only 12.5 percent of its population connected to the grid. Diesel generators are the most popular source of electricity for most Haitians, but the rising cost of fuel continues to put electricity out of reach for most."

According to Noël, "We have a business opportunity. Solar energy is still in the dark ages in Haiti." For him, developing and distributing ENERSA's technologies is both a mission and a business model.

Beyond bringing products to underserved markets, Georges and Noël are focused on "jobs that bring added value [to] Haiti." Companies that manufacture and distribute locally create more employment than import distribution ever could, while developing the labor force and diversifying expertise in the business sector.

ENERSA's approach is paying off: the company landed a $2 million contract in 2014 with the Haitian government to install solar-powered streetlights in two of the nation's ten departments. "Today we have a fourteen-thousand-square-foot facility and thirty-eight to forty full-time people working," says Noël.

The company even partnered with another solar paneling firm in Senegal. By coaching the firm on their development philosophy and training Senegalese technicians to manufacture various products, Noël and one of their Haitian employees—who had never before left Port-au-Prince—helped the West African entrepreneurs launch production of the first "Made in Senegal" solar panels.

ENERSA's Story

In 2002, Jean-Ronel Noël and Alex Georges, having met during graduate school in Montreal, returned to Haiti to begin researching and developing alternative technologies in Haiti. At first, they sought to replace Haiti's ubiquitous kerosene lanterns with LED lamps, but the project proved unsuccessful. They retooled.

Maintaining their focus on energy, the partners used Massachusetts Institute of Technology's open-course software to learn the electrical engineering skills they needed to design simple solar implements. Thanks to a business-incubator through Haitian Partners for Christian Development, Noël and Georges were able to improve their product line for three years before moving ENERSA to a fourteen-thousand-square-foot facility.

Sustainable employment and professional development are key to ENERSA's strategy. "We wanted to create a small revolution in the way of conducting business in Haiti," says Alex Georges. From the start, ENERSA paid employees nearly four times the mandated minimum wage.

"We trained them from scratch," Noël tells us. "A lot of them don't even have a high school degree. Now they are able to do solar panels, LED, light posts, everything. They now have knowledge in electronics, electricity, and manufacturing." Today, more than half of ENERSA's employees own a home, and the company's first employee is attending a computer course at a nearby institution.

In many communities, ENERSA's solar installations are the only sources of light that allow students to study in the evenings. In a country where the sun sets just after six o'clock, access to light can make a world of difference.

"We went to the very isolated places," says Noël about various installations over the years, "places you cannot access by car, so you have to go by donkey, you have to carry things on your shoulder. We take that as a challenge." Through NGO partnerships and small contracts with various municipalities, ENERSA has brought light to communities all over the nation. Noël says that on the night after the 2010 earthquake, survivors were drawn to the solar-powered lights ENERSA had installed, and people later built camps around the streetlights (including many made by ENERSA) that remained standing throughout metropolitan Port-au-Prince.

However, soon crime skyrocketed in the other, mostly dark temporary camps due to a lack of security and inadequate lighting in the evenings.

Solar-energy firms the world over began donating streetlights, and soon thousands were pledged. This massive influx of free products decimated ENERSA's client base. The company had to compete for NGO and government contracts while the market was flooded with free imports.

Still, Georges and Noël's company was able to secure enough small contracts during the disaster-response phase to survive. By pivoting toward the temporary-housing market, ENERSA built back its client base and further developed its reputation as Haiti's only solar panel manufacturer. Soon, the national government became more interested in ENERSA's efforts.

NGO contracts proved key to the survival, growth, and development of many Haitian businesses after the earthquake, but aid and development organizations helped in other ways. Two months after the quake, ENERSA received a $15,000 emergency loan from the Appropriate Infrastructure Development Group to rebuild its damaged factory.

And ENERSA has only continued its advances in the energy sector. Since production began in 2007, the company has installed over five thousand streetlights in roughly 130 communities, generating approximately $4 million in revenue to this day.

Value-Added Manufacturing versus Importation

In 2011, Mother Jones, an American nonprofit news organization, interviewed Alex Georges about the Haitian solar-energy market following the earthquake. As international firms flooded the market with preassembled products, Georges argued that ENERSA could hire "six times as many Haitians as its competitors" by manufacturing locally.[7] Mother Jones reported that "for most of Georges' employees, ENERSA was their ticket out of the slums."[8] At the time, ENERSA employed around fifty young men from Cité Soleil, where formal jobs are nonexistent.

ENERSA seeks to purchase most of its materials in-country, but often even those materials are first imported. Haiti's importers, or "secondary retailers," as Noël calls them, create some transactions and help meet market demand, but their business models add little value to the supply chain. Most products sold in Haiti's market today are imported, then distributed by local entrepreneurs who retail the products at a marked-up price. Although Noël recognizes that importation of products and materials—such as the steel rods needed for streetlights—is necessary for businesses to function, ultimately it's the local value-added production that is essential to generate more wealth and purchasing power for Haitians through the sustainable jobs it creates.

One oft-cited example of solar energy's untapped potential to dynamize development initiatives in Haiti is the Hôpital Universitaire de Mirebalais. The structure boasts 1,800 panels from a foreign supplier. Renewable energy will keep the hospital's costs down as it serves nearly two hundred thousand Haitians. However, according to Global Risks Insights, "although 800 jobs will be created by the hospital itself, the solar roofing project only employ[s] two Haitian electricians." In addition, "while Haitians will benefit from cost savings over time, foreign suppliers and consulting firms immediately profited from the project. Solon, a German company, supplied the solar panels, and Solectria Renewables, a U.S. firm, supplied the inverters. Sullivan & McLaughlin Companies, a U.S.-based single-source electrical contracting company, sent a team to Haiti to install the system and train the Haitian electricians tasked with operating it."[9]

Partners in Health, the organization that built and sponsors the hospital, could have partnered with ENERSA and other Haitian companies to install and maintain at least some of the nearly two thousand panels. Instead, those contracts went to foreign firms while Haitian firms struggled to find enough clients.

Global Risks Insights goes on to report that, though ENERSA creates quality products, many Haitian companies just can't compete with foreign manufacturers on price. Imports are already cheaper before the NGOs that procure them bring them in tax-free. Noël estimates that imports can be "30 percent less expensive" because of customs exemptions the Haitian government provides to NGOs.

"This economy is possible only because of two things," says Noël. "You have all those NGOs getting money from abroad, and you have the Haitian diaspora sending $2 billion [a year]." These funds purchase the goods and services that support life in Haiti, but little of that capital ends up in the local economy.

Instead, "the Dominicans are benefiting more from the diaspora money," says Noël, "because we have no local production." Value-added manufacturing and agricultural production in Haiti are minimal, so most of those donations and remittances end up abroad since most people purchase imports to support their families.

Advocating Strategic Trade Policies for Haiti's Growth

For the ENERSA team, local production isn't just a matter of cost; it's a matter of conviction. According to Noël, the value of creating jobs in Haiti should outweigh shorter-term considerations of price or, what is worse, an influx of items such as solar panels offered under subsidies from foreign companies. He desires that the Haitian government incentivize local production and procurement for the economy to develop in a sustainable way. He hopes that the government will enact policies to increase custom duties on products that can be procured locally.

As amateur advocates, Noël and Georges' efforts appear never-ending. They present their products and the social impacts they have witnessed in local production through trade fairs, and they call on others from the business sector to be present and to engage the challenge with them. They regularly leverage events to present and speak to NGOs and governmental leaders on the need for change within Haiti's trade agreements. Their story has been shared through well-respected publishers including National Geographic and Mother Jones, as well as international films including the documentary *Poverty, Inc.* They have raised awareness about the need to pursue manufacturing opportunities in Haiti through partnerships with universities such as UCLA and other international institutions including Appropriate Infrastructure Development Group.

They also spend valuable time and energy advocating through the Haitian Chamber of Commerce. As active members of the chamber, Noël and Georges continue to be proactive and have helped ENERSA and other businesses secure more contracts with a shared message amid the influx of aid: local sourcing from manufacturers in Haiti is essential to achieve long-term development that can raise people out of poverty.

And in order for local sourcing companies to compete from the bottom-up, according to Noël, Haiti also needs to implement policies to ensure its own business sector is prepared to compete in the global market.

Noël points to the European solar-energy boom of 2010 as an example. At the time, Germany was one of the largest producers of solar energy in the world. Noël argues that the German government's tax incentives made solar energy more affordable and created demand. "The problem in Haiti is that there isn't that governmental leadership to intervene and initiate strategies for an increase in production and growth in local industries."

He also cites Taiwan, South Korea, and China as examples of how manufacturing in the technology sector has created important growth over the decades. "The best way to operate is to shift part of the production, part of the value-added, to Haiti," says Noël.

Although changes in this direction are not yet evident for small-business owners like Noël, the Haitian government has taken strides to improve Haiti's framework for international trade in recent years. In collaboration with World Bank, and in compliance with its rules and agreements, a new Haiti Trade Information Portal is being designed with the aim "to lower transaction costs for traders, boost interagency collaboration, and move Haiti toward greater participation in global trade." Through this online portal, traders and businesses will have access to accurate information on tariffs and non-tariff measures, more transparent practices, and a reduction in time to clear goods at the port.[10]

There has also been a promising increase in business as a focus of international diplomacy. In 2013, Haiti signed an agreement with

Vietnam to increase their cooperation in trading energy, textiles, food, and electronics, thereby building on the opportunity for healthy global market competition. Other leaders such as Gregor Avril of Haiti's main industrial association are proposing ways to make local production cheaper so that the domestic and international markets turn to Haiti as a reliable trading partner.[11]

Among these efforts, advocacy, as in any situation, must continue in order to achieve long-term development in a country that presently has some of the most liberal tariff policies in the Caribbean.

Steps Forward for ENERSA

In the midst of the challenges the company has faced—and perhaps because of them—ENERSA remains a striking example of an innovative Haitian company on the rise. Bidding against Haitian "secondary retailers," ENERSA was still able to win enough major contracts to grow its operation post-earthquake. Its $2 million deal with the government will allow the company to install 1,200 new solar streetlights around the country.

ENERSA also produces inverters, mobile cell-phone chargers, and a variety of other products. Noël believes that the company's approach will lead to the development of the sector at large, and that its partnerships with other local enterprises contributes to a stable, dynamic industry.

Noël hopes that other Haitian businesses will begin producing solar cells so that ENERSA can purchase from them instead of from the United States. He looks forward to expanding further and hiring more people in Cité Soleil who can innovate, create, and add value to solar products they manufacture in their own backyard.

"Manufacturing for me is the key word. How much added value would remain in the country? Not only money, but also expertise," he says. "When you do something, you can see the impact on the population and you can say, 'this is because of me.'"

Woman walks through downtown Port-au-Prince weeks following the earthquake, January 2010.

Two men rest on their handcart waiting for work in Port-au-Prince as a front loader sits unused on the rubble.

United Nations patrols Route de Carrefour between Port-au-Prince and Léogâne, January 2010.

Subsidized and donated imports arrive at the Toussaint Louverture International Airport in Port-au-Prince.

Vendor from the countryside sells fresh fruit in Port-au-Prince following the earthquake, January 2010.

Transactions continue at the grocery stores and bread bakeries still operating post-quake in communes such as Delmas, Port-au-Prince.

With over one million people displaced post-quake, Maxima S.A. adapted its wood manufacturing to produce thousands of transitional housing units. Co-owner Evelien de Gier showcases the frame of one unit, January 2010 (chapter 6).

By 2011, Maxima S.A. innovated again, supplying interior design services and installation to private and commercial buildings as reconstruction demand and new development investments grew in Haiti.

Panel participants express the barriers and solutions to local procurement at the first Buy Haitian, Restore Haiti event in March 2011 (chapter 9).

Sales manager of a local supplier exchanges information with an NGO buyer during networking time at Buy Haitian, Restore Haiti.

ENERSA employee applies rust-resistance to a solar panel, the company's primary product line installed as streetlights throughout Haiti (chapter 7).

Co-founder Alex Georges at ENERSA's production site near shantytown Cité Soleil, Port-au-Prince. "We wanted to create a small revolution in the way of conducting business in Haiti," says Georges.

The majority of ENERSA employees and their families reside in Cité Soleil where formal jobs are nearly nonexistent.

ENERSA employees bring light to the country through value-added production.

Laurent Auguste shares the story of his three-generation family business, Auguste Savonnerie—closed following the influx of donated soap (chapter 1).

Douglas Wiener of Café Selecto, his family's coffee company, which has operated in Haiti for over one hundred years (chapter 10).

METHOD 4: *Invest in a Viable Business Opportunity*

The most sustainable strategy for business growth is the pursuit of marketable opportunities through registered, for-profit ventures that meet needs profitably and satisfactorily, thus generating resources and creating wealth. In Haiti today, investment opportunities are endless, though challenges are vast. The manufacturing, tourism, agriculture, energy, infrastructure, and construction sectors hold strong potential to lead Haiti's economic growth, but that growth begins with local and international investment.

Yet, despite the fact that Haiti is classified as one of the poorest countries in the world and, according to some, has an unfavorable business environment, entrepreneurs and investors like Matthew Flippen are equipped to meet demand profitably and are already taking on the challenge, as the case study of TopLine Materiaux de Construction (TopLine Construction Materials) demonstrates.

CASE STUDY[12]

TopLine Materiaux de Construction

Developed market economies function because of balanced transactions, which are informed by supply and demand. When we focus on the opportunities created by demand, the vast business potential of underdeveloped markets presents itself. To be most effective, instead of distributing existing resources to meet demand, the international community and individual entrepreneurs should seek out for-profit opportunities in-country to produce goods or services that meet those demands directly within a developing market such as Haiti.

Matthew Flippen first visited Haiti on January 20, 2010. His church in Austin, Texas, asked businesspeople in the congregation to volunteer with Mission of Hope to support logistics and planning for the organization's post-earthquake emergency food relief program.

Flippen traces the process that would lead him to start a company in Haiti to a book he read years earlier: *Call of the Gospel*, by World Vision CEO Richard Stern. "I started praying every day, 'God, break my heart with what breaks your heart,'" he says. After twelve days of working in Haiti with Mission of Hope, Flippen says his heart was broken by the devastation he witnessed. During that time, he prayed for the opportunity to help. "I suspected that God's answer was going to be in a relief capacity," he says. "I was not expecting the answer to my prayer to be a business effort." After days of prayer, Flippen says that he was inspired to manufacture cinder block.

In 2004, Flippen had purchased a limestone quarry with his brother. While they approached the deal as a private-equity investment, the brothers sought to increase sales and marketing while keeping the leadership in place. Flippen says that he enjoys working in his industry because "most people in construction are real hard-working, honest people." His labor force was nearly 100 percent Hispanic and "operated like a big family," though he admits there was a "bit of a language barrier."

His prior experiences would prove a valuable tool to take on the challenge of launching a business in Haiti.

A consummate entrepreneur from an entrepreneurial family, Flippen had started his own landscaping enterprise at fourteen, a business that would eventually allow him to pay his way through college and marry his high school sweetheart.

He then worked for his father's leadership training company for four years, becoming head of business development and sales at age twenty-one. Flippen calls this his first entrepreneurial experience. Now he insists that the "CEO should always be the top promoter of the business," and says he "loves building relationships."

Later, during a two-year MBA program at Cornell, Flippen interned for a technology company and eventually gained its support in helping him launch his own venture. It failed after eleven months.

"I learned a lot of really great lessons," he says. "One of those was a large amount of humility."

The Importance of Expertise and Foreign Investment

When Flippen's volunteering trip with Mission of Hope ended, he returned the following month, and every month after that, for weeklong visits. "I know something about the block business," says Flippen, so he spent his time conducting extensive research into the Haitian market, seeking out "mission-minded investors," and developing a business plan while looking for Haitian manufacturing experts.

By April 2010, Flippen had a million dollars committed by investors "with throwaway money," he recounts, laughing. That capital, many times more accessible in the United States, gave Flippen an advantage that he recognizes is not afforded to most Haitian entrepreneurs. But Flippen also attributes his ability to build a business in Haiti to a series of miracles.

While purchasing land in Haiti can be incredibly difficult given the widespread fragmentation of ownership and the Haitian government's poor documentation of titles, within a month Flippen was able to purchase land for a limestone quarry that was owned by "fifty different families," at a price "far below what I was expecting to pay."

His operation would need water at two hundred gallons per minute, but the property had never produced a well with pressure in excess of three gallons per minute. Upon drilling the first well, Flippen's team "hit water at 150 feet, and it was ample supply for what we needed."

Just weeks before operations were scheduled to begin, Flippen's plant manager backed out of the job. That night, Flippen frantically sent e-mails to contacts in the industry and called his CFO for a breakfast meeting the following morning. At seven o'clock in the morning, Flippen received a text message from a number he did not recognize. The message contained the contact information for a Haitian plant manager who had been working in the industry in Miami for over twenty-five years. It turned out that the manager was interested in moving back to Haiti to help however he could. "He's been part of our team from the beginning," says Flippen.

After almost three years of hard work, Flippen became the founder and CEO of TopLine Materiaux de Construction. The operation sits in Source Matelas, near Cabaret, a small farming community. Nearby, Cimenterie Nationale Haiti (CINA), the nationally owned and largest cement manufacturer in the country, is the region's sole large employer.

But things may be changing for the rural municipality. The region's small harbor is being expanded into a half-million-dollar port, which should boost trade and contribute to the area's industrialization, all of which could mean windfalls for TopLine.

Responsible Local Procurement

After his initial idea to make cinder block, Flippen realized he would have to produce his own sand and gravel. However, he still had to overcome a number of infrastructure challenges, including poor roads, lack of electricity, and poor-quality diesel, a major issue given that all of his equipment is diesel powered. But Flippen considers local procurement an ethical business priority, and so he gets everything from diesel to labor in Haiti—"everything but specialized parts," he says.

Purchasing locally gets tricky when it comes to cement. "To make concrete, our raw materials are sand, water, gravel, cement," says Flippen. "We mine limestone and process and produce our own sand and gravel. We have our own water supply through wells." However, while TopLine only purchases raw materials in Haiti, most of the cement sold in the country is imported. Even companies that choose to practice responsible local procurement face structural market barriers.

According to Flippen, though CINA employs around a thousand people and sustains wholesalers and retailers, in the best-case scenario it simply packages the product in Haiti, since the company also has a large cement factory in the Dominican Republic. This is unfortunate, says Flippen, because "Haiti has the raw materials to produce cement."

Quality and Demand

In addition to the barriers to local procurement, Flippen also faces the same reluctance from NGOs to partnership that plagues the Haitian private sector. He says, "Originally I thought our business would be successful because people recognized after the earthquake that poor quality building materials contributed to many of the deaths." Betting on the country's desire to rebuild with better quality, Flippen approached the NGO community first. "Who cares more about human life than NGOs?" he asks. However, he soon found that the response he received from the humanitarian and development aid sector "turned out to be the total opposite" of what he expected.

He reports that few of the larger NGOs he sought to partner with had construction experts who valued using quality materials. Many organizations involved in building projects knew little about effective construction practices. The organizations Flippen initially targeted as potential clients often chose to purchase low-quality blocks from local masons for less money.

Flippen worries that "some of these decisions are based on marketing and fundraising," citing donor demand that can value high distribution numbers over the quality and sustainability of aid efforts. In Cabaret, near TopLine's factory, an NGO that has worked in Haiti for nearly thirty years needed to build a twelve-foot security wall. "It's probably eighty thousand blocks," says

Flippen. When he tried to get the contract, the agency chose not to purchase block from TopLine, and instead opted to purchase the blocks from five small masonries that had been producing lower-quality blocks for decades.

However, these lower-quality blocks are less resilient and less cost-effective in the long run. In reference to the mason who would build that wall, Flippen says, "If he uses our block, he uses less mortar, so it saves the customer money."

Even though TopLine products can save organizations money down the line, some NGOs are so focused on helping small informal producers that they forego a business relationship with a tax-paying, private firm. Instead, they opt to purchase materials from individuals in the informal sector, distributing donated capital directly through short-term wages, but doing little to grow the formal economy in a sustainable way.

Though Flippen can guarantee clients that his product will save them money on mortar and that his company employs an entirely Haitian labor force, he struggles to get contracts from the NGO sector. Instead, TopLine's major contracts have come from general engineering firms and contractors—other private, for-profit enterprises. Further, 30 percent of TopLine's business comes from individual homeowners.

Flippen wants TopLine to work with NGOs that are "more professionally run" and have "large teams of very qualified people." Flippen recognizes that TopLine still has to be "price competitive," but he says, "the major projects we've done in the country are quality conscious."

That emphasis on quality ensures the demand that sustains TopLine Materiaux de Construction, despite the NGO sector's reluctance to transact with local, well-established enterprises. Still, Flippen worries about the fact that, in order to support small producers, most NGOs running construction projects are purchasing poor-quality block that is unsafe for construction.

"My preference would be that all of those local corner produc-ers become distributors ... resellers of better quality block," he says. Flippen goes on to explain that many of the private engineer-ing firms he works with refuse to purchase block from the informal sector because of its poor quality. Some NGOs argue that by buy-ing from the informal sector they support individual Haitian workers directly, but if these organizations choose to work with cheaper materials, Flippen wonders what their liability may be "when another earthquake comes and destroys the homes they built."

Competition and the Importance of Investing in Labor

In spite of the challenges he has faced, Matthew Flippen remains optimistic that TopLine can have a positive impact in the market. He hopes that "by providing high quality at the market price, our competitors would have to raise their quality to stay competitive." He believes that one of Haiti's other producers of block is already working to improve its own quality for just that reason.

Before deciding to establish his own enterprise, Flippen had intended to partner with an existing local producer to support that producer's efforts and improve quality, as he and his brother had done in Texas. However, he soon found that Haitian construction materials firms "were making a lot of profit producing a low-qual-ity product," which meant they had little incentive to change strategies.

Since its grand opening in April 2013, TopLine has been able to employ forty-five people, and Flippen expects that figure to double in the next year. "We expect it to double the following year," he says, "and double one more time, so we end up with four hundred employees in four locations around Haiti."

"The impact we're having is so small, in terms of the need," he admits, "but in our region, we're having a good impact, and I'd like to have more."

In Haiti, a salary of $400 per month puts workers in the middle class. Half of TopLine's employees make at least that. Flippen hired employees slowly, ahead of production, trained the team on repairs, and licensed machine operators. Now Flippen wants to continue to develop his employees by providing training and licensing so that he can develop higher-paying jobs internally.

While concerns about security and corruption have deterred investment in Haiti, Flippen notes that neither have affected TopLine in a significant way. "Law enforcement has been our friend and an advocate of what we're doing," he says. "The government has been an advocate. We're under the Bureau of Mines. The director is a true public servant . . . an advocate."

Flippen says that the minister at the head of the agency has told him that TopLine is the only properly permitted, tax-paying business in the sector. By operating legally and ethically in Haiti's construction sector, investing in the local labor force, and raising industry standards, TopLine has gained the support of the local government and community.

Flippen believes the Martelly administration is pro-business. "I do think they're trying to limit the number of NGOs" through "small regulations increasing the cost of NGOs coming in." While these new regulations are already unpopular among some aid workers, Flippen thinks they are still not enough to stem the market distortion caused by the importation and distribution of free or subsidized goods.

When Flippen hears how much broken rice, which is produced domestically, costs when imported by the NGO sector, he is horrified. "I think it should be illegal," he says. He argues for more regulation to keep poor-quality products off of the market, but recognizes that NGOs must be made aware of the damage they can cause and of the benefit of increasing production in the formal private business sector.

The relationship between international donors, the Haitian government, and the business sector will only improve through communication. Partnering is still "the best strategy," says Flippen, because "capital is hard to come by in Haiti." Strategic partnerships allow the market to restructure its resources in a sustainable way. This requires a shifting of resources and of opportunities, and NGOs will need to take a long-term view on price. Yet, for Flippen, "starting businesses is the best way to go." Once an enterprise is profitable, it can then partner with a nonprofit to subsidize costs for low-income clients or for larger NGO projects.

TopLine's Fund-a-Home Project does just that. The program allows individuals to donate money to an American nonprofit that prepurchases materials from TopLine. The company can then subsidize NGO and community projects in Haiti "at 10 to 100 percent." One of the benefits of this model is that it sustains business growth, thus contributing to taxes and employment while supporting the needs of the vulnerable.

Though TopLine is involved in some NGO-sector projects, by working as a resource generator, it is more capable of meeting demand through balanced transactions that create wealth and opportunity in the broader economy.

At the end of the day, Flippen sees business as the only true solution to poverty and unemployment. For him, NGOs are just not designed to do that kind of work. He argues that it is "difficult for NGOs to have a positive impact in the country" because they lack the necessary skill set to build an industry that creates jobs sustainably.

However, for-profit, resource-generating enterprises that pursue opportunities to meet demand continue to prove themselves to be sustainable engines of economic growth in developing economies like Haiti's.

CONCLUSION: **The Methods at Work Together**

Although no single individual or NGO needs to implement all four of these methods, they are compatible, and Partners Worldwide is an organization that has encouraged NGOs to purchase locally, facilitated investment and access to capital, and has advocated and been a platform for connecting. With networks of thousands of local small and medium businesses around the world, including those in Haiti, Partners Worldwide facilitates partnerships that strengthen small and medium enterprises through business training, mentoring, advocacy, and access to capital.

After the 2010 earthquake, Partners Worldwide hosted four conferences in Port-au-Prince (these conferences will be discussed in more detail in chapter 9). Each conference allowed Haitian businesses and foreign and local NGOs to network and collaborate. These partnerships have already injected hundreds of thousands of dollars into the local economy by directing NGO purchasing power toward local procurement (including some of the partnerships highlighted in case studies in this book). The purchases of Haitian rice, transportation and printing services, pharmaceutical products, construction materials and labor, and even peanut butter, support local entrepreneurship.

And what has been the result of this initiative? Hundreds of jobs have been created and Haitian businesses across the country are expanding. Further, by strengthening networks of individual enterprises, Partners Worldwide is well on its way to meeting its goal of creating one hundred thousand jobs in Haiti by 2020.

CASE STUDY[13]

Partners Worldwide

Transactions are built on trust. When economic actors experience trust, they transact with each other, creating sustainable markets and value chains. The market is not a zero-sum game. Unilateral aid and trade can create dependence, but strategic partnerships create opportunity by empowering involved actors through men-

toring, training, access to capital, and advocacy. When entrepreneurs, investors, and buyers are equipped to interact on the same level, bilateral relationships develop—relationships that grow an economy and empower populations.

Doug Seebeck graduated with a degree in agribusiness in 1978. At the time, nearly 40 percent of people in the developing world were undernourished.[14] The Washington native remembers when he first learned about eighteenth-century British economist Thomas Robert Malthus, who argued that, since population grows exponentially and production grows linearly, population will be checked by lack of resources. Something about that didn't seem right to Seebeck, who saw the vast potential for growth in agricultural production through improved practices and mechanization.

Inspired to work with the poor, Seebeck moved to Bangladesh, now the world's fourth-largest rice producer, where he worked as an agricultural consultant for Bengali farmers as part of the aid efforts of World Renew (then called Christian Reformed World Relief Committee). He quickly learned that while the farmers he trained did lack some expertise, their true challenge was not their own ignorance, but access to capital and opportunity. "These farmers knew how to fish," he says. "They didn't have access to the pond."

Seebeck found that the farmers, along with his Bengali partner, knew exactly what they needed to succeed, but the fragile government and disorganized agricultural sector kept them from the small loans necessary to purchase better seeds and to mechanize production. So Seebeck and his partner began advocating on behalf of farmers to the government, to banks, and to the Bengali upper class who could finance their expansion. "When we did what the farmers said," he reports, "they flourished."

Seebeck says he learned to treat the farmers with respect, not as charity cases. Instead, his treatment of them as customers—just as he had treated the American farmers for whom he had consulted at home—led to exchange and increased opportunity.

In 1983, Seebeck and his wife moved to Kenya, where World Renew worked to combat poverty in a country with an estimated 60 percent unemployment at the time—a rate strikingly similar to Haiti's current figures. In 1997, a group of North American businesspeople visited Kenya to learn more about the organization's efforts. According to Seebeck, they wanted to contribute to the fight against poverty in a capacity beyond simply providing aid.

Recognizing the importance of strategic partnerships for empowering small farmers to increase production, Seebeck and his associates founded Partners Worldwide, an organization that connects entrepreneurs in the developing world with business professionals who serve as mentors and partners to provide their expertise and help the local businesses grow. As of 2014, Partners Worldwide had helped create or sustain over 90,500 jobs in twenty-five countries.

Partners Worldwide's first Haitian business affiliate was established in January 2000 in Port-au-Prince. Now Partners Worldwide is working to expand its network of businesses to every major city in the country and currently has affiliates in eight other cities. Dave Genzink, the Partners Worldwide regional facilitator for the Caribbean, sees a lot of potential in the trust being created in Haiti and abroad. "Transactions only happen when there's trust," he says.

According to Genzink, the relationships with long-term business mentors are an essential opportunity for Haitian entrepreneurs because the knowledge that someone else cares about their success "elevates their game." Genzink's job is to orient international businesspeople to the Haitian context. These businesspeople are most often North Americans who bring a wealth of motivational and professional resources to their Haitian counterparts. While many Haitians who run family businesses may not see themselves as entrepreneurs, the relationships they build and the mentoring they receive from successful businesspeople can help them recognize their own value as job creators. Partners Worldwide also ensures that the North American mentors visit their Haitian affiliates frequently and maintain an open dialogue. Genzink notes mentorship is about exchange, mutual learning, and personal growth.

One of the biggest challenges in the Haitian market is the difficulty of long-term planning. Genzink explains that six months to a year is considered long term in Haiti because of both political insecurity and lack of expertise. But Partners Worldwide is constantly adapting to the needs of its Haitian clients by holding business training sessions with local entrepreneurs over months instead of days. It offers more in-depth training in areas Haitian entrepreneurs need most, thereby fostering trust among Haitian trainees who share their insights, network with one another, and build on business strategies together.

As Doug Seebeck learned in Bangladesh thirty years ago, small producers can't grow production without access to capital, so Partners Worldwide also helps raise loan capital in Haiti and advocates for affordable loans for businesses within the network.

After the earthquake, Partners Worldwide even ran a short-term business recovery program that sent structural engineers down to Haiti to inspect businesses' structures so they could relaunch quickly. Immediate challenges can be overcome by tailoring the organization's efforts to the actual needs of Haitian entrepreneurs.

"Buy Haitian, Restore Haiti" was a series of conferences held by Partners Worldwide to foster communication between businesses and NGOs in the post-earthquake economy. While Haitian businesses expressed frustration that NGOs were not sourcing goods and services in-country, NGO personnel argued that the Haitian private sector lacked the production capacity, communication, and level of quality they required. This series of conferences that continue today has helped NGOs and businesses—as buyers and suppliers—bridge those gaps.

Haitian businesses that are in Partners Worldwide's network are expanding faster than their competitors because they are able to compete, thanks in large part to access to capital and expertise, in a local market that is rife with cheap imports and corruption. As exchange and dialogue are fostered, members have begun to form symbiotic business relationships. Since every business in the network must be registered, pay taxes, and operate ethically, entrepreneurs can trust each other and pursue long-term partnerships. When he is asked whether wealth is a zero-sum game in which some have to lose for others to win, Genzink answers, "I say no; wealth can be created."

Partners Worldwide's newest and perhaps most important effort in Haiti today is its 100K Jobs in Haiti initiative, which is a push to create sustainable employment in the business sector in each city by collaborating and advocating for local procurement and business strategies to create long-term jobs. The initiative calls on donors and volunteers to "publicize Haiti's advantages, not its poverty." By expanding business training and mentoring, by sharing best practices, by adapting to the actual needs of Haitian entrepreneurs, by investing in value-added business with an emphasis on agriculture, and by advocating for the Haitian private sector, Partners Worldwide provides an example of aid and development efforts that can generate sustainable results and empower Haitians to raise themselves out of poverty.

So what can other aid and development initiatives learn from Partners Worldwide's success? Doug Seebeck, president of the organization he founded almost two decades ago, argues that unilateral trade practices are plaguing developing economies.

He notes that Haiti was self-sufficient in rice before the government was pressured to lower import tariffs and the United States "dumped" rice into the economy. Dave Genzink points out that while loss of life and damage to property was catastrophic, the earthquake did far less damage to Haitian agriculture. "Why are we shipping food to a country where 60 percent of people depend on agriculture for their livelihoods?" he asks.

According to Seebeck, a unilateral power structure distorts the global economy, forcing the Global South to accept imports from the Global North, while the most powerful countries have well-enforced regulations that protect their markets. Haiti's long history of international intervention so far has had a mostly negative effect on its economy. Seebeck points out that Uganda faces many of the same challenges as Haiti, but doesn't suffer from disproportionate NGO presence—what he calls an "overwhelming flood" of "criminal intervention."

Haiti, long regarded as a humanitarian project in the United States' backyard, suffers from a power dynamic that reinforces an American savior complex while ignoring the concrete efforts Haitians are making to raise themselves out of poverty. "What gives you the right to break the law?" he asks of NGOs that operate in Haiti without a license or do not pay taxes. For Seebeck, the refusal to align with the local economy comes from a lack of respect founded in ignorance.

Dave Genzink can cite endless instances of international organizations failing to partner locally, even when the opportunity exists. He remembers less-qualified North American volunteers pushing Haitian doctors out of clinics shortly after the earthquake. He cites the example of a Dutch organization that brought four shipping containers of hand sanitizer to Haiti when Laboratoires Farmatrix, a Haitian pharmaceutical company, manufactures the product locally. Similarly, an American organization delivered three million doses of medicine for treating worms, rather than purchasing the medication from 4C, another Haitian pharmaceutical company. Furthermore, backpacks are constantly sent to Haiti and distributed to schoolchildren for free, but a Partners Worldwide business member had to lay off eighteen employees and close the doors of his backpack manufacturing company because he couldn't compete with the cheap imports.

Nevertheless, some progress has been made to stem the tide of importation and free distribution that is hurting Haitian enterprise.

Soon after the earthquake, several American pastors began an initiative to send alimentary aid to the Haitian poor. They asked their congregations to gather twenty-eight thousand jars of peanut butter, each with a quarter taped to the lid to cover the cost of shipping. When Haitian businesspeople found out about the project, they recognized the disastrous effect it could have on local producers, given that most Haitians daily consume *mamba*, the notoriously spicy peanut butter produced by local farmers. Through the efforts of Partners Worldwide, the Haitian businesspeople, along with their business mentors and advocates, successfully stopped the initiative and encouraged the churches to purchase the alimentary food locally instead.

Still, the president of Partners Worldwide argues that NGOs importing goods to Haiti and distributing them for free is only the tip of the iceberg. He wonders why NGOs are operating in Haiti at all. In fact, Seebeck believes the Haitian government needs to oust most international aid and development organizations and only allow operations that are economically responsible and sustainable.

According to Seebeck, the transactions that will grow the economy and raise the Haitian people out of poverty must connect rural villages to the value-chain within the agribusiness sector, and the emphasis must be on agriculture.

His most potent example came from a local business that produced honey. When Partners Worldwide began operations in Haiti, Seebeck was stunned to find Haitian honey being sold in recycled Heinz ketchup bottles. The lower-quality product could hardly compete against the imported American honey that lined store shelves in the capital. However, one Haitian entrepreneur, through investment in mechanization thanks to Partners Worldwide, was able to produce a high-quality product in heat-sealed bottles with an attractive label.

In 2003, Seebeck had the opportunity to present at a USAID conference in Washington, DC. At the conference, he showed the Haitian honey in a recycled Heinz bottle capped with tinfoil, a picture of the American honey being sold in Haiti, and a bottle of the competitive local honey the Partners Worldwide business member had produced.

"This is the problem with imports," he said.

But there, in Haiti's entrepreneurial spirit, was also the solution.

As seen in these case studies, when actors using the OBED strategy implemented these key methods toward sustainable business development—namely local purchasing, platforms for connecting, advocacy for policy change, and long-term investment—the outcomes enhanced marketable opportunities that businesses in Haiti could pursue. Transactions increased, viable businesses grew, and jobs were created. These methods can be adopted and replicated in other situations in order to make aid more effective through its realignment to the market-based system by which businesses can grow.

However, some people working in NGOs might interpret this realignment to the market-based system differently than what is intended, and in a valiant effort to realign, might introduce newer NGO models that are somewhat market-inclined, yet undermine the actual private business sector even further. We will present a counterargument to these efforts in the next chapter, which addresses destructive aid models.

CHAPTER 8

Destructive Aid Models:
A Response to Recent Changes in NGO Practices

While NGOs can accomplish a world of good, they can also wreak unimaginable and often unintended devastation. But what are the specific ways that NGOs cause unintended harm? Here we will start with an example of alimentary aid as a review of the traditional model of resource distribution that was identified earlier in the book. Then, we will focus on a new challenge: in a valiant response to the negative impact of alimentary aid and resource distribution, as well as the growing understanding of the need to change this traditional NGO model, there is an emerging movement of NGOs seeking to realign with the economies in which they operate. Yet, unknowingly, these NGOs are only semi-aligned and in fact continue to undermine the economy's potential for growth through the private business sector. Below, we will highlight three destructive aid models in hopes that NGOs, government officials, businesses, and individuals will recognize the actual outcomes of these emerging NGO strategies and work to change them for full realignment with Haiti's economy. We will start with a recap of the impacts of the traditional NGO model of resource distribution—in this case, through alimentary aid.

The Negative Impact of Alimentary Aid

In the wake of the 2010 earthquake, many aid organizations rushed to Haiti to provide hunger relief. But once the immediate crisis was over, many failed to make the transition from aid to trade and development. As a result, not only did many children become dependent on aid to survive, but many of their parents also fell into poverty and dependency. Yes, NGOs were feeding people. But they were also unwittingly feeding into the ongoing prevalence of poverty, as we shall see here.

Feed My Starving Children (FMSC) was founded in 1987 and is "committed to feeding God's starving children hungry in body and spirit," according to the organization's charter. This nonprofit NGO has brought 47,019,096 meals to Haiti since the earthquake in 2010. Haiti is the organization's top recipient country, with Nicaragua close behind. According to its website, FMSC practices sustainability by providing local mission partners in Haiti with donated food for long-term feeding programs.

FMSC meals contain rice with dried fruit and vegetables, supplemented by powdered vitamins. This formula is based on years of nutritional research. Along with an effective method to supply large shipments, FMSC has a recruitment and engagement process that details age requirements, amount, and location so that volunteers can come in and pack the shipments themselves—a rewarding experience for many, as volunteers have noted in online feedback.

FMSC keeps costs low by relying on volunteers. The organization has a permanent packing site and mobile sites to accommodate people volunteering under different occupations and time constraints. FMSC advertises that each of its meals costs only twenty-two cents to produce, and that 92 percent of total donations go directly toward the food program.

The donation information page presents the following donor opportunities:

- Feed five children for a month: $33
- Pay for a full box of MannaPack rice (216 meals): $50
- Feed a child for a year: $80
- Pay for one thousand meals: $220
- Feed a family of five for a year: $440
- Feed twenty-five school children for a year: $1,485
- Feed a village of one hundred people for a year: $8,030

This program is one of the largest and most well-known feeding programs in the world and has helped children in many poor countries find the food they need to survive.

The organization's operations in Haiti continue to grow. According to its post-earthquake report, "FMSC doubled meals to Haiti after its January 2010 earthquake … [and] the board stepped out in faith to commit meals beyond budget. God has blessed us with greater support and, along with greater operating efficiencies, FMSC is well-positioned to serve growing food needs around the world."[1]

FMSC and its leadership have been very generous toward Haiti, which should be applauded, but it is important to look deeper into the effects and outcomes of these kinds of initiatives.

Rice, which Haitian farmers produce, is the main ingredient in most FMSC food packs. However, FMSC rice is purchased outside of Haiti, then shipped from the United States to feed thousands of children in Haiti. The children surviving on the donated meals today will most certainly need a job in the next few years, or, for those nearing the end of the recipient age bracket, in the next few months. In the short term, this program helps many Haitian children survive, but it also undermines their futures by putting competitive pressure on Haiti's producers instead of sustaining them.

Further, FMSC is only one of many alimentary aid organizations operating in Haiti. According to its operating procedures manual, Kids Against Hunger packed and shipped more than twenty-seven million meals to Haiti in 2010, and each meal cost roughly twenty-three cents to produce.[2] In the days following the earthquake, Kids Against Hunger also worked closely with the USS *Normandy*—a 570-foot guided missile cruiser based near Haiti and preparing to deploy to the Middle East—to supply water and imported food town-by-town along the coastline nearby,[3] an essential in emergency disaster response, yet not the long-term model that Haiti needs to thrive.

Other organizations also report their involvement in daily feeding programs in Haiti. Large organizations routinely distribute imported foods such as rice, beans, flour, powdered milk, and vegetable oil to smaller NGOs, who distribute the alimentary assistance throughout the country. Schools, hospitals, orphanages, and churches depend on initiatives to carry out feeding programs or to distribute food to local families.

Another prominent organization, Stop Hunger Now, reported that in the first few weeks following the earthquake, it received over 200 tons of donated aid supplies for Haiti, including bottles of purified water and canned and ready-to-eat barbecue chicken and roast beef. It also reported that, in addition to food and water, "Stop Hunger Now is also assisting with the transportation and distribution of more than 56 tons of medical supplies and aid obtained by the North Carolina Conference of the United Methodist Church."[4]

Now that we have just a few examples of how alimentary aid initiatives are run, let's examine what opportunity cost Haiti is incurring due to this approach.

If Feed My Starving Children had purchased 47,019,096 meals in Haiti from Haitian entrepreneurs for a price of, say, twenty-five cents a meal, the deprived Artibonite region farmers and food processors would be better off with nearly $12 million in revenue. This revenue could strengthen local purchasing power and create more jobs for Haitian families, thereby triggering more opportunities for sustainable economic growth. Transportation, packaging, storage, and other parts of the value chain also represent potential income for the parents of children receiving the alimentary aid.

In addition, were FMSC to purchase the food locally, the Haitian government would draw revenue through the 10 percent sales tax—$1.2 million that could be invested in public services such as infrastructure and education. To put things in perspective, that tax revenue alone would allow the Haitian government to pay its entire police force for nearly one month. All of this could be achieved if just one nonprofit initiative sourced its aid locally.

In other words, the application of foreign aid has consequences, for better or worse. Ultimately, if Haitian farmers had greater access to market opportunities, instead of being replaced by nonprofit distributors, they might have enough purchasing power to provide their children with the meals they're currently getting elsewhere.

Three Destructive Aid Models

Having recalled the negative impact of methods such alimentary aid or resource distribution—and in light of the OBED strategy defined a few chapters ago—readers from the NGO community might be brainstorming ways that they can effectively modify their current NGO model to realign with the economy and operate more like a business.

However, this approach is dangerous. As outlined below, it has not merely been the traditional NGO model of distribution that has harmed Haiti's private business sector. Alternative development approaches are just as harmful to the economy. For this reason, we address these alternative approaches here, as ultimately, the private business sector needs to be the actor meeting demand and creating jobs for truly sustainable economic growth in Haiti. As a counterargument to this growing NGO effort to "realign" with Haiti's market-based economy, we will examine some well-intentioned development models used in Haiti today that appear to have potential for success at first. NGOs and other actors such as USAID have the best intentions to trigger Haiti's economy in some way. Yet some models only partially realign with Haiti's market-based system and the private business sector. As the case studies show, these models instead ultimately undermine opportunities for true long-term private sector business growth.

Our research has identified three emerging development approaches that are undermining Haiti's private business sector: (1) for-profit NGO operations, (2) manufactured business development, and (3) misaligned trade policies. Instead of leveraging demand (or community needs) as marketable private business opportunities, these strategies seek to meet the demand in ways that quickly evolve into causes or are not fiscally sustainable as businesses themselves. We acknowledge that various strategies—such as fair trade business development and asset-based community development— have proven effective in particular contexts. However, we argue that pursuing marketable opportunities and meeting demand through sustainable, innovative, and competitive private businesses provides the most successful outcomes through which Haiti can grow.

For-Profit NGO Operations

In order to improve sustainability, many NGOs in Haiti imitate business behavior to generate revenue. This seems like a good idea at first: organizations can rely on their pseudobusinesses to finance nonprofit operations.

However, when organizations run for-profit operations under a nonprofit charter, they can end up undermining the very private sector enterprises with which they should be partnering.

Because of their nonprofit models, NGOs don't have the same constraints and concerns—such as access to credit and maintaining customer satisfaction—that businesses do. Organizations that run for-profit operations can create large opportunity costs for the businesses they supplant, for investors, for the government, and for the broader economy. By mirroring business behavior, for-profit NGO operations block market access for the private enterprises that should be meeting that demand.

If the purpose of these operations is to generate revenue for the organization, in order to realign with the market, NGOs should register their pseudobusinesses as private enterprises, in accordance with Haitian law.

If profitable, the for-profit business could then make donations from its profits to the nonprofit organization, thereby complying with Haiti's legal requirements for private sector enterprises and nonprofit organizations. The difference here is that the business will have to be profitable on its own and will have to participate in the market on an even playing field with other enterprises, competing within the natural ecosystem of supply and demand while also paying taxes. The case study of Trinity Lodge demonstrates the deleterious effect that nonprofit "businesses" can have on a legitimately run private enterprise.

CASE STUDY

Trinity Lodge

Instead of supporting the local market economy by transacting with for-profit businesses, some NGOs choose to create a parallel structure of nonprofit pseudo-enterprises that put detrimental competitive pressure on legal, registered, tax-paying Haitian businesses. While some businesses can innovate to cope with the uneven playing field, others, sadly, will be driven out of business.

In 2009, Daniel Jean-Louis, this book's coauthor, was hired as national manager for Partners Worldwide, a global Christian network of "businesspeople faithfully pursuing a world without poverty." As a country-level manager with Partners Worldwide, Jean-Louis trained small-business owners and facilitated partnerships between Haitian business networks and businesspeople from around the globe serving as mentors.

As he trained others in the market, Jean-Louis also decided to establish his own private small business, Trinity Lodge guesthouse. The business was conceived in the same way as any other private-sector enterprise: Jean-Louis saw a market need and decided to service it.

After the January 2010 earthquake, the number of NGOs operating in Haiti grew to nearly twelve thousand organizations. Foreign personnel needing short- and long-term accommodations flooded the market. Real estate prices skyrocketed. The collapse of housing and hospitality infrastructures in the earthquake, combined with a long-running housing shortage, contributed to lack of supply. Many Haitian families rented out their own homes to capitalize on the high demand. Due to the influx of consumers, Haiti's newly revived hospitality industry experienced a boom.

After the earthquake, Partners Worldwide continued to bring pro bono business mentors to Haiti, foreign professionals who needed lodging. Jean-Louis recalls a time when one mentor was forced to stay in a $200 hotel suite, only to find out that the hot water did not work and that the air-conditioning unit turned off after midnight. The guest was even charged an additional energy fee.

As his plans for Trinity Lodge took shape, Jean-Louis scouted locations throughout Port-au-Prince and eventually found a location twenty minutes from the airport and ten minutes from Pétion-Ville, the cosmopolitan center of Port-au-Prince. One year and $6,000 in registration taxes and start-up fees later, Jean-Louis opened Trinity Lodge. To his surprise, he found himself in competition with the evangelical missionary community's own NGO "businesses," a sector he once thought would constitute his primary partners.

"Let's be blunt," says Jean-Louis. "So many mission organizations are running a guesthouse as an NGO business." Beyond housing personnel on missions, many guesthouses recruit teams of volunteers from abroad and actively market packages that include transportation, lodging, hands-on service projects, and, as Jean-Louis puts it, "praying with one or two souls." Mission trips have become commodified, particularly in the American evangelical community.

So, what's the problem? Jean-Louis estimates that a large portion of mission guesthouses operate illegally, paying no government taxes or fees. The Haitian government grants tax-free permits to nonprofit organizations for humanitarian purposes. Conversely, the state grants business permits to tax-paying enterprises operating for profit. Registered under NGO charters, missionary guesthouses can avoid paying the 5 percent of investment capital in taxes required by the Haitian tax code, as well as the roughly $5,000 business registration fee that private Haitian businesses have to pay. Under Haitian law, in accordance with international norms, nonprofit organizations are interdicted from engaging in many profit-generating transactions. Still, many unregistered guesthouses take advantage of Haiti's weak public administration and operate outside of Haitian law.

While Haitian entrepreneurs in the hospitality sector have to contract work using credit, pay interest on loans from their enterprises' revenue, and contribute annual taxes to the government, many NGO guesthouses function as pseudobusinesses—selling goods and services while collecting revenue—yet operate as nonprofit organizations, minimizing overhead and avoiding taxes. By fundraising in their home countries, NGOs are even able to raise capital without having to provide a profitable return on investment.

Now a professor of business at Quisqueya University in Port-au-Prince and a business owner himself, Jean-Louis has worked as a consultant for many NGOs over the years. Over time, he has recognized increasing tensions between the nonprofit and for-profit sectors.

Because his for-profit enterprise pays all required taxes—including payroll tax for his employees, sales taxes per transaction, income tax, and registration taxes and fees—Jean-Louis estimates that Trinity Lodge is 40 percent less competitive than NGO guesthouses in terms of price.

Coming under fire from the evangelical community over his higher prices—the same community Jean-Louis thought would constitute his major clients and partners—Jean-Louis had to reconsider his approach to avoid going under and losing his own and his partners' investment. Refocusing his business model, Jean-Louis tapped into the network of professionals employed in the private and nonprofit sectors, moving beyond a client base strictly composed of humanitarian volunteers.

Jean-Louis also raised staff wages to 200 percent of minimum wage, effectively twice the salary his guesthouse competitors were offering, and invested heavily in rare amenities such as air conditioning, hot showers, and reliable internet access. Few NGO guesthouses meet international travel standards for cleanliness, amenities, and service because of their humanitarian and volunteering model. By serving a particular niche of private and nonprofit sector professionals and by investing in personnel and amenities, Jean-Louis' guesthouse provides a level of quality and customer care that has won Trinity Lodge high ratings on TripAdvisor since its establishment in January 2011.

By 2013, Trinity Lodge had paid over $35,000 in sales taxes to the Haitian government—money that contributed to public safety, infrastructure, and education.

When faith-based or secular nonprofit operations attempt to imitate for-profit business behavior, but operate outside of the formal sector, they adversely affect formal private-sector enterprises. While Trinity Lodge was able to generate significant investment capital and find a niche market to establish a place for itself in the economy, many Haitian businesses fail due to unfair informal-sector competition from NGOs.

Putting it bluntly once again, Jean-Louis argues, "If we're about restoration, the economic system in Haiti won't be restored through illegal competition with the country's entrepreneurs."

Manufactured Business Development

In many developing countries, NGOs and foreign governments implement initiatives to develop businesses and trigger economic growth. However, many times these projects are funded by development organizations or foreign governments and often fail to collaborate with the larger value chain. Therefore, the bottom of the value chain begins to rely more fully on the initiative rather than on pursuing market opportunities directly. This approach can leave out the rest of the value chain, decreasing opportunities for local transaction and disincentivizing collaboration, further dividing producers, manufacturers, and distributors.

For example, one $2.3 million UN Development Programme project, Love N' Briquettes, sought to produce "recycled paper charcoal" briquettes, an environmentally conscious initiative meant to benefit Haiti by "turning garbage into energy" and by leading the way in "slow[ing] and revers[ing] deforestation."[5] According to an online report, the project was meant to be self-sustainable as a "low-tech and simple process" of production.[6] The initiative would distribute the briquettes to schools that were already receiving alimentary assistance from the World Food Programme. The goal was to ensure that "the revenues generated through the sales of the recycled products, compost and briquettes cover the operating costs and the salaries of the residents who make $3 and $6-a-day," according to one report. The project would also create job opportunities for retailers who would receive "training on how to market the logs that sell cheaper than charcoal"[7] and would result in a reduction in small-time crime that had been more prevalent following the earthquake due to the loss of buildings, businesses, and jobs. Briquettes were presented as a more affordable product, since by "using briquettes, the cost of cooking a meal is 22 gourdes (56c), as compared with 50 gourdes ($1.40) using charcoal."[8]

However, within two years, the plant was closed.[9] The operation was still based on a nonprofit approach, and ran out of funding. In addition, organizations partnering in the initiative became their own suppliers and consumers, creating a parallel value chain, instead of working within Haiti's larger market as viable businesses that had an innovative, competitive product.

Although this project sounds logical—and briefly employed 385 people—the project did not survive. Honorable as it may have been, it was based on a cause, not a marketable opportunity, though ideally those two factors could work together. Despite the accolades of world leaders, including former president Bill Clinton, the project failed.

While UNDP representative Laura Sheridan stated that "the agency still hopes to find a way to revive the project," journalist Amy Bracken reports that the briquette factory has shut down. According to Sheridan, the factory was turned over to the municipal government of Port-au-Prince, although the project previously had been "slow to get traction with the city." With no true local ownership or private-sector investment, $2.3 million ultimately vanished, with apparently no one to blame.[10]

Sadly, this is only one example of many manufactured business development projects in Haiti. These initiatives are not truly self-sustaining because they do not operate as for-profit businesses. While they may imitate business models, these initiatives rely on donor funding, which cannot fully create the competitive incentive that makes businesses work. Ultimately, this manufactured business model is misaligned with any transaction-based, free-market system, as you will see in the following case study of USAID and FACN's Haitian Bleu.

USAID and FACN's Haitian Bleu

True market realignment is only possible through a balanced partnership with the private sector. When the private sector can compete on price, quantity, quality, delivery time, and communication, development aid can truly lead to business development. Agencies and organizations that provide expertise, credit, and equipment help developing markets grow more competitive and sustainable. But projects and programs that subsidize costs are fundamentally misaligned with a market economy because they inject capital without creating incentive or balanced transactions, thus becoming a mechanism for an economic bubble that clogs the market's arteries.

In 1994, USAID hired an industry expert to design a high-end brand of washed coffee: Haitian Bleu. The export sold as a luxury brand for almost a decade before the unsustainability of the enterprise became apparent. Now Haitian Bleu has become a cause product with limited exposure, owing to its uneven quality and high price.[11]

Through partnerships with various regional and international agriculture and development agencies, USAID has intervened in the Haitian coffee sector since 1990. Its strategy? To capitalize on Haiti's competitive advantages—such as the low cost of labor—by seeking to strengthen the value chain between rural centers of agricultural production and roasters and retailers in specialty markets, and also by training Haitian farmers to practice more labor-intensive "washed" processing.[12]

During the first of three USAID programs intervening in the Haitian coffee sector, farmers' associations from two of Haiti's southern departments formed the National Federation of Coffee Growers or FACN. One of the program's projects was to construct a dry mill factory where the federation could process coffee to ship overseas, directly paying the associations, who then paid the individual farmers.[13]

Throughout the 1990s, Haitian Bleu's presence on the market grew, thanks to lucrative contracts with specialty roasters and retailers. Twenty-four thousand of Haiti's 250,000 coffee producers benefited from higher prices—selling their product for twice the rate of their regional competitors—while an estimated twenty million coffee producers worldwide experienced the pressure of a global crisis in coffee prices.[14]

But FACN's financial relationship with its own associations lacked incentives that would encourage quality and efficiency. The federation took on costs, and debt, to keep associations afloat, but quality and capacity diminished as farmers were guaranteed a fixed price long-term contract.[15]

The poisonous cycle of subsidy spread through the organization, but where did that infection begin?

Since the USAID program's inception, the FACN coffee producers have had to rely on assistance from expatriates like the brand's designer to select coffees and determine blends. The Center for the Facilitation of Investment, a Haitian government agency tasked with attracting investment to the country, reports that "the logistical cost and delay of sending hundreds of samples to the US was neither efficient nor a self-sufficient approach."[16]

Worse, due to the lack of organizational incentive in its financing structure, CFI reports that FACN "did not even come close to exporting enough coffee to be financially viable in any of its first five years, despite having guaranteed sales through the Haitian Bleu® program, vastly improved processing infrastructure, and extensive training."[17] In 1998, a distributor left the program amid growing complaints about FACN's production capacity and quality. Meanwhile, national coffee exports overall continued to plummet, falling 92 percent between 1984 and 2004.

In 2001, the third USAID Haitian coffee program began to

achieve modest success. USAID's technical assistance partners instituted a grant program creating organizational demand for zero-defect coffee.[18] Another revision was the institution of a new financing structure in the FACN that gave associations "fixed volume-based standard rates for dry processing and export marketing services by [FACN], rather than the actual costs incurred by [FACN]," which provided incentives for the federation to increase volume in order to break even.[19] These modifications, combined with a microcredit system for farmers and more extensive training of Haitian cuppers, allowed FACN to grow from 2 percent of Haitian coffee export by value to 12 percent, according to CFI estimates.[20]

While the Haitian government agency argues that FACN and the Haitian Bleu brand "are the driving force behind the only positive trend in the Haitian coffee sector today,"[21] the fact is that Haitian Bleu has had great difficulty integrating into the specialty market, has not achieved full self-sustainability, and has been characterized as a cause product by international roasters and retailers.

Although Haitian Bleu has survived and even become moderately profitable over the last two decades, its systemic misalignment can still be recognized.

Haitian Bleu was initially marketed as a luxury brand for a reason. Haiti's unique coffee trees combined with the region's particular mountain climate gives Haitian growers the potential to produce a truly world-class coffee, as evidenced by reports from coffee experts in publications such as *The Atlantic*.[22] But low capacity and inconsistent quality—the unintended effects of the subsidized financial structure of FACN under USAID's guidance—keep the brand incapable of competing and being successful on the specialty market without heavy borrowing and lucrative contracts from sympathetic buyers.

Instead, Haitian Bleu has become a cause product, further diluted by a variety of NGO coffee enterprises who market and distribute their own coffee product lines similar to Haitian Bleu

> and who seek to capitalize on the brand's ability to sell at above-market value in order to generate revenue to fund their humanitarian efforts.
>
> Although well-intentioned, development programs that subsidize industry, such as USAID's coffee-sector programs in Haiti, might create pockets of value, but the beneficiary enterprises can never become competitive until balanced transactions—between producers, distributors, and retailers—are achieved. Market-aligned investment, not subsidy, creates opportunity *and* incentive, instead of creating a bubble.

True economic development is based on marketable opportunities. It is a grassroots-level function, and privately owned businesses are the true engine of growth. Today, the opportunity to produce both briquettes and Haitian Bleu still exists. Entrepreneurs can still pursue these opportunities as private-sector ventures that could be both profitable for the business and satisfactory for the consumer. With this in mind, we'll now examine one more example of manufactured business development, and one entrepreneur's response to the challenge. The following case study of Oxfam Québec and Max Jean's Trash Business demonstrates both the hazards and the benefits (when done well) of individuals partnering with NGOs in the quest to develop truly profitable businesses.

CASE STUDY[23]

Oxfam Québec and Max Jean's Trash Business

The world of nongovernmental humanitarian and development aid organizations in Haiti is a vast and complex network of large and small, local and international actors applying donation-based, nonprofit models in a market economy. Employment, as a human-development metric, continues to grow in importance in development strategies, particularly after the devastating 2008 global recession. How can NGOs meet their humanitarian goals, of particular importance after the 2010 earthquake, while contributing to human development? Job creation in the NGO sector can contribute to a stronger economy, and humanitarian services that create short- and long-term employment opportunities are an important part of many NGO charters. But what happens when large international NGOs subsidize small, local organizations to create jobs and generate revenue in a dynamic market economy?

Oxfam Québec has operated in Haiti for thirty years, working on the environment, agricultural development, and humanitarian relief. During that time, the organization has been working with more civil society organizations than private enterprises. After the earthquake in 2010, Oxfam Québec's disaster relief efforts focused on the camps that sprang up all over the city.

In partnership with smaller, local organizations, particularly the many *comitées de camps* (camp committees) that formed to tackle social issues affecting the displaced, Oxfam Québec provided a variety of training programs to organizations, including financial, literacy, conflict management, and disaster/risk reduction, in hopes that those services would be duplicated and made available to the most vulnerable. The organization also provided latrines and other hygiene and sanitation services.

"From a development perspective," says our confidential source at Oxfam Québec in Haiti, "I thought, 'We can't just give access to funds.... We want to see your business plan.'" Our source reports that Oxfam Québec supported some revenue-generating organizations whose statuses as nonprofit organizations remain unclear.

While many organizations partner with private business, which this book encourages, some emergency relief programs, such as Oxfam Québec's, are not allowed to support private enterprise with their funds, because they operate under humanitarian rather than development mandates.

Nouvelle Vision pour les Enfants Démunis d'Haïti (NOVEDEMH), a camp committee established in Delmas after the earthquake, works to provide sanitation and environmental education services to its community while striving for social inclusion of young people without jobs. While it carries an organizational status with the Haitian government, post-earthquake, the organization operated revenue-generating programs with the support of Oxfam subsidiaries, including Oxfam Québec.

According to Max Jean, NOVEDEMH's general coordinator, "An enterprise and an organization have different aims. We aim to provide a service and create jobs, but not primarily to generate revenue."

As NOVEDEMH assessed its community's specific vulnerabilities, Jean explains that the organization recognized that access to electricity was a significant problem, compounded by the fact that the state was losing revenue because of illegal connections. "So our first project was electrifying Delmas 69," the name of the street where most of the committee members and families were based. With around 235 subscribers, NOVEDEMH created collective subscriptions to regularize access to electricity. Sixty percent of the revenue went to Electricité d'Haïti (EDH), while 40 percent went to NOVEDEMH to pay staff and expand services.

"This is how we got into profit-generating activities," says Jean. "We saw a need and we filled a service. Then we began a project called Management of Solid Wastes."

Timeline of Oxfam Québec–NOVEDEMH Relationship

Oxfam Québec and NOVEDEMH have partnered together on over fifty small projects, according to Jean. Using its own funds along with funds from sister organizations such as Oxfam Holland,

Oxfam Québec provided various training services to NOVEDEMH, and NOVEDEMH was a preferred partner.

As NOVEDEMH sought to expand its services, in hopes of achieving financial autonomy and sustainability, the Haitian organization sought funding for its waste-management project from Oxfam Québec. "We wrote the project [manager] to ask for capacity reinforcement because we didn't have materials," says Jean. "The project was for $150,000 but [Oxfam Québec] saw that we didn't have the capacity to absorb that capital."

After declining NOVEDEMH's proposal for the $150,000 figure, Jean reports that Oxfam Québec conducted a preliminary study. "[Oxfam] thought it was a very good program and they duplicated the project with several other organizations and separated the funds. Our portion came to $35,000."

The full nature of Oxfam's partnership with NOVEDEMH and the seven other community organizations remains unclear at best, but both Jean and our confidential source report that the organizations signed a contract for a four-month pilot program.

Beyond subsidizing waste collection bins for low-income subscribers, Oxfam's $35,000 budget also subsidized NOVEDEMH's employees, and the organization had nearly 150 staff members at the height of its services. Soon, however, the subsidy model began to show its cracks.

Many subscribers joined the program to purchase subsidized trash bins, but then used them to collect water or to resell at a markup. Jean reports that many households signed up under different names, instead of just one per household as had been planned. After clients had purchased the bin for a fraction of its real price, many also canceled their subscriptions to the waste-collection service.

He goes on to report that, while NOVEDEMH had nearly three thousand people signed up for its service, the actual number of households with valid subscriptions was closer to five hundred.

What is worse, Jean says that Oxfam Québec admonished NOVE-DEMH not to retrieve its waste-collection bins, though a clause in the subscriber contract gave it the right to do so.

According to both sources, Oxfam Québec conducted a report to create a strategy for NOVEDEMH's waste-collection program to become self-sustaining. According to the study, with Oxfam Québec's support over two years, NOVEDEMH needed one thousand customers to be able to sustain itself.

When financing for the four-month pilot program ended, NOVEDEMH planned to reduce personnel, but, according to Jean, Oxfam Québec required the Haitian organization to maintain its personnel.

Our confidential source contests that claim: "No, we did not encourage him to keep all of his employees, but to keep a record."

After two more months, as NOVEDEMH continued to spend its revenue on payroll, the Haitian organization learned that Oxfam Québec did not intend to continue its financial support. This came as a surprise to Jean, who claims that NOVEDEMH had at least a verbal agreement with Oxfam Québec that the subsidy would restart. According to him, the Canadian organization simply gave NOVEDEMH twenty-five more waste-collection bins, then discontinued its support.

Over the next several months, NOVEDEMH reduced personnel until services declined and eventually ended. According to Jean, the other organizations involved in the Oxfam Québec–subsidized waste management program have failed as well.

In a surprising twist, our Oxfam source claims not to have known that the project had failed until our interview.

Forward strides as a private waste management business

After NOVEDEMH's waste-collection service failed, Jean and his wife sought to continue providing services, but this time, as a business separate from the community organization.

Samaritan's Purse, a Christian international relief organization working in Haiti, provided a vastly different partnership model. Working alongside NOVEDEMH in the area of sanitation and waste management, Samaritan's Purse sought to partner with individuals rather than organizations to ensure accountability.

"Samaritan's Purse wanted to work with my wife and me," Jean reports. In 2011, the international development organization provided Jean and his wife, Roseline, a compactor for recycling plastics on credit, which he then paid back over time with the profit generated.

His business today, Dynamic Waste Collection Services, a for-profit enterprise, is made up of four staff and one hundred contractors who collect plastic bottles. The contractors are paid not through a payroll subsidy, but based on the amount of recyclable plastic they bring in.

Jean explains that the new business project "is a franchise. Samaritan's Purse gave it to us to respect it that way. Like Coca-Cola."

Collectors and the middlemen who operate compactors, as Jean does, add value to the product chain of recycled plastics. Dynamic Waste sells their collected bundles to Haiti Recycling, a larger company that then sells the plastics to companies in the United States and China.

The for-profit enterprise is expanding tentatively after NOVEDEMH's waste collection program's failure. Jean's wife reports that the couple had to rebrand their service to regain consumer confidence after the poor services the NOVEDEMH project rendered.

According to Jean, "The difference is, now we are operating on a budget."

Subsidy-based partnerships operating in market-based economies are destined for failure because true sustainability cannot develop in a subsidy model. While Oxfam Québec's aim to create employment while providing sanitation services is commendable, its goals were not in line with those of its partner, NOVEDEMH, who intended to create a sustainable, revenue-generating pro-gram within the community organization.

NOVEDEMH's intention to establish an enterprise within an NGO structure also failed to recognize the realities of doing busi-ness. "We didn't see right," says Jean. "We were still waiting for aid. We didn't understand that we needed a business. Because if we had seen it that way, with the small money Oxfam gave us, we would have already been doing marvelous things."

Misaligned Trade Policies

In addition to the two destructive models of for-profit NGO opera-tions and manufactured business development, there is a third destructive practice: misaligned trade policies. Misaligned trade policies create chal-lenges for the local market. Trade policies are most clearly misaligned when they bypass private sector production in favor of importation, especially when a well-intentioned importation policy is nearly forced on the receiv-ing country.

Many developing countries suffer from the enormous pressure of international interests on their economies. While foreign aid may be well-intentioned, we must examine the economic, social, and political motives of donor countries to understand why well-intentioned policies can have such disastrous effects.

Our research has found that, historically, both the Haitian government and foreign governments including the United States have not only closed their eyes to the misalignment of many of their trade policies with Haiti's market-based economy, but have promoted this very misalignment them-selves. Much research has been conducted and published in recent years arguing that failing to realign with Haiti's market-based economy, and in particular, restoring the potential capacity of its agricultural production, is of grave concern.

The case study below looks in more detail at the mutual decision of the American and Haitian governments to forge an importation quota that the

Haitian market was not yet ready to bear. It was a coerced decision: Haiti had to agree to import US rice in order to receive USAID and International Monetary Fund (IMF) support. As a result, Haiti soon became the third largest *importer* of rice from the US, although rice is a product Haiti used to *export*. The decision was so devastating for Haiti's agricultural market that Haitian leadership, recognizing the impacts, tried to move their low-wage labor force into manufacturing industries in order to replace the jobs that were lost in agricultural production and trade.

Perhaps the most surprising discovery of our research has been the transparent and systematic dismantling of the Haitian agricultural sector's productive mechanisms through a process of ostensibly well-intentioned international intervention—and all with the general approval of the Haitian state. The dismantling is transparent in that the problem has been documented by dozens of studies over the last thirty years. These studies have been commissioned, conducted, and reviewed by the world's foremost humanitarian and development organizations, and these studies are readily accessible through cursory internet research. It is systematic in that these studies, instead of being a catalyst to correcting the problems they identified, have simply been ignored. Some of the very same organizations (including the UN and US agencies) that conducted the research continued to implement those destructive policies with the tacit approval of the developed world—and of the Haitian government itself. What makes this discovery fundamentally shocking is that this process has failed so absolutely in generating wealth, employment, and development in the Haitian agricultural sector, yet continues to run its course with little visible resistance from the agencies, organizations, and governments that should be most interested in its actual outcomes.

In this case study, we will review how this process of dismantling has specifically affected the Haitian rice industry in order to understand why it has failed and how it has been allowed to continue. We will also examine the Haitian government's role in the perpetuation of failed economic development strategies.

Haitian Agriculture Under Siege

"It may have been good for some of my farmers in Arkansas, but it has not worked. It was a mistake ... I had to live every day with the consequences of the loss of capacity to produce a rice crop in Haiti to feed those people because of what I did."
—*Former president Bill Clinton, March 10, 2010*[24]

HAITIAN AGRICULTURE AT A GLANCE: Structural Adjustments

Haiti has long been an agriculture-based economy. In the colonial era, Saint-Domingue produced 60 percent of the world's coffee and 40 percent of the world's sugar, and proving itself to be the "Pearl of the Antilles," was one of the richest colonies in the world during the French empire. Production and exportation have dropped precipitously since then.

In the early part of the twentieth century, American intervention, in the form of the American Occupation of 1915 and the Haitian-American Sugar Company, adversely affected production, perpetuating a transfer of the ownership of Haiti's means of agricultural production from the small farmer to large enterprises, many of which were foreign owned.

Under the Duvalier regime, the Haitian government began to exchange lowered import tariffs and a new emphasis on low-wage manufacturing in urban centers for military and political support from the United States and other international powers such as Canada and France. According to Alex Dupuy, "although the Duvalier dictatorship embraced the assembly industry, it resisted demands to remove the 50 percent tariffs on food, especially rice, and thereby enabled Haitian farmers to continue producing all of the rice consumed in Haiti while limiting other food imports to about 19 percent."[25]

However, after the overthrow of Jean-Claude Duvalier in 1986,

General Henri Namphy, who led Haiti's interim government, was pressured to liberalize the Haitian market by further reducing import tariffs and agricultural subsidies.[26]

During his first short term as president, Jean-Bertrand Aristide's attempts to reverse these policies were resisted by the Haitian Chamber of Commerce, the IMF, and USAID, until he was ousted by the Haitian military later in 1991. When Aristide returned to power in 1994 with the support of the Clinton administration, he lowered tariffs on food imports, including rice, to 3 percent.

The economic impacts of this one trade policy were enormous. Prior to the policy, in the 1970s, only 19 percent of Haiti's demand for food was imported, as opposed to 51 percent today, including 80 percent of rice.[27] Haiti "went from being self-sufficient in the production of rice, sugar, poultry, and pork to becoming the fourth-largest importer of subsidized US rice in the world and the largest importer of foodstuffs from the United States in the Caribbean."[28]

Now Haitian agriculture is in a catastrophic state of affairs with most farming taking place on small plots of land averaging 1.8 hectares and "only 12 percent of arable land being irrigated."[29]

What has made matters worse, as evidenced above, is that international financial and political support for the Haitian government, since the 1970s, has come with conditions—most notably "structural adjustments"—changes in foreign trade policy that opened up Haiti's struggling economy to the global market before it was ready.

For the Haitian government to borrow capital to build roads, schools, and other essential infrastructure, it has been pressured to accede to international donor requirements that have, up to this point, demanded that the Haitian government reduce import tariffs—to the benefit of major international agricultural exporters such as the United States—and reduce government expenditure in local agriculture.[30] This has had a detrimental effect on the small

Haitian farmers with limited access to capital who make up the backbone of the Haitian agricultural system.

Here, the Haitian government's alignment with the international community's demands has proven disastrous for the Haitian agricultural sector.

Rice Production

The Artibonite Valley, epicenter of Haitian agricultural production, produces up to 80,000 tons of rice each year. However, statistics indicate that in 2013–14, Haiti required 490,000 tons of rice to feed its population,[31] despite the evident decreases of Haitian production since the 1980s[32] and the fluctuations ever since.[33] Now, nearly 80 percent of all rice consumed in Haiti is imported.[34] In large part, the Haitian government's answer to this local production shortage is to rely on the importation of rice to meet demand rather than investing in domestic production.

According to Yasmine Shamsie, the first implementation of lower import tariffs on rice "was a disturbing policy prescription given that in 1995, a USAID report had concluded that tariff reductions of between 3 and 10 percent would threaten the very existence of the Haitian rice farmer." She goes on to report that "as far back as 1987, authors of another USAID report had warned that these policies would most likely bring a loss of income to rice-growing peasants of about US$15 million a year, further reducing their already poor standard of living."[35]

Due to the rapid turnover of trade policies, thousands of Haitian farmers could not compete with the price of imported rice. In April 2000, rice growers and their spouses and children tried to escape Haiti and reach the Turks and Caicos islands by a makeshift boat. Tragically, all sixty of them died when the boat capsized halfway through the journey.

In 2012, the Martelly-Lamothe administration agreed to purchase 300,000 tons of rice from Vietnam per year to address periodic food shortages. These shortages are one of the detrimental effects of the very same import-focused trade policies. Prime Minister Lamothe argued that "the principal goal of the agreements we have signed with Vietnam is to find innovative ways to ensure food security for all our citizens." In 2013, Haitians saw a 33 percent reduction in the price of rice from the previous year.[36]

There is nothing innovative about these strategies. The fundamental issue remains the same: The importation of subsidized foodstuffs has never led to an increase in domestic production and thereby stable employment made possible through balanced transactions—and how could it? Rather, cheap imports put negative competitive pressure on an already fragile industry, driving down prices, profits, and exports.

Still, the Haitian government continues to rely on the same failed development strategies to this day.

Replacing Agriculture with Manufacturing

Haiti's abundant low-wage labor force makes it an obvious candidate for investment in manufacturing, particularly in the garment industry.

Under Duvalier, Haitian factories produced garments and other goods, such as baseballs, but working conditions were dire and the wages could not support employees' upward mobility or the country's economic growth. Worse, manufacturing jobs in urban centers drew workers from the provinces toward the cities, contributing to the debilitating centralization Haiti now faces. Port-au-Prince grew exponentially as agriculture stagnated and new job creation was concentrated in the cities. The preference for development in urban rather than rural areas only accelerated this process of centralization.[37]

After Aristide raised the daily minimum wage in 1995, against opposition from the World Bank, which thought the move would drive away investors, the international community had to face the

fact that "despite all the advantages of the export-assembly strategy it advocated, the strategy did not create the conditions for a
more sustainable development of the Haitian economy." Worse,
according to Dupuy, "even at the height of its operation in the
mid-1980s, the assembly industry never employed more than 7%
of Haitian workers and did not contribute significantly to reducing
the underestimated 38% unemployment rate of the active urban
labor force."[38]

The dominant thought was that the Haitian economy could be
developed through the establishment of a manufacturing base,
whose livelihoods would be supported by lower food prices,
thanks to the importation of agricultural goods. This is why policies
that were known to have a detrimental effect on the agricultural
sector were allowed to continue.

Today, these development models have failed by every significant metric of economic development. Why then does the Haitian
government continue to employ these strategies?

A Missed Opportunity for Change

Following the 2008 food crisis, agricultural and rural development came to the forefront in Haitian policy documents as domestic and imported food supply could not meet market demand.
Political instability threatened the economy at large.

While the Haitian government's trade policies have been ineffective, its support of domestic production has also been limited.

"The sector has received a disproportionately small part of
national budgets and outside dollars," argues Shamsie. "Budget
support to agriculture decreased from almost 10 percent in 2000–
2001 to less than 3 percent in 2002–2003."[39]

The Préval government reacted to the food crisis by allocat-
ing more funds to the Ministry of Agriculture's efforts to build
infrastructure and provide training and access to capital, raising

support for agriculture to 7 percent of its budget for 2009–10, "a lower figure than experts recommended."[40]

After the 2010 earthquake, the Martelly-Lamothe administration made agricultural and rural development a top priority in national reconstruction. The administration rolled out a key policy document, the 2010 National Agriculture and Investment Plan (NAIP), to support agriculture and rural development. However, "the much-heralded increase in assistance to rural development is likely to fall short of expectations because it comes with a superficial rebranding of a not very useful approach."[41]

The Haitian government's NAIP is funded by groups such as the International Development Bank, the United States, the European Union, France, the World Bank, Canada, and the Inter-American Institute for Cooperation on Agriculture—all of whom helped develop the plan based on strategies that have had detrimental effects on Haitian agriculture and on the Haitian farmer's livelihood. The government's "new" plan is based on prescriptions from organizations and donors that still embrace "a liberal, trade-based approach."[42]

Dupuy sums up the issue clearly: "In the contemporary era, neoliberal policies imposed on Haiti in the last three decades cemented the country's political and economic dependence. This was achieved by a dual strategy pursued by international financial institutions (IFIs) and the US government to promote urban sweatshop garment production, on the one hand, and laissez-faire agricultural policies, on the other."[43]

The opportunity for true agricultural development—which would create jobs, benefit the environment, and address the nation's crippling centralization—has been paid lip service by the international community and by the Haitian government, but the current post-food crisis and post-earthquake strategies remain largely the same.

Even after formally apologizing for the disastrous effects of tariff reduction on Haiti's agricultural sector, which he supported as US president, UN Special Envoy to Haiti Bill Clinton "is now spearheading the very same failed strategy that he repudiated in his mea culpa before the US Senate."[44]

This failed approach is evident in USAID's still-floundering Haitian Bleu coffee program, which relies on a subsidized, top-down approach that does not address the larger value chain.

Ultimately, succumbing to international pressure, the Haitian government has failed to promote sustainable growth in agriculture by not effectively supporting the Haitian agricultural sector in such a way that would increase local transactions.

Instead, the Haitian government has acceded to trade policies that have allowed foreign interests and ineffective development models to stand in the way of real economic growth, further dismantling the livelihood of the millions who rely on Haiti's agricultural sector.

In light of these challenges, some tangible solutions for realignment of the agricultural sector have emerged. According to "Using Food Aid to Support, Not Harm, Haitian Agriculture," a 2010 report of the Center for Economic and Policy Research,

> although there is much that can and should be done to support Haitian agriculture and the rebuilding of the economy, it is most important to immediately reduce the harm caused by imported, subsidized rice. This can be done by having the international community immediately commit to buying Haitian rice for the next two years. (There are two planting seasons and harvests per year.) Since food aid was 13 percent of the total rice supply last year, and Haitian rice production is about 15 percent of total supply, buying up all of Haiti's rice should be close to the amount of food aid—for rice—that the international community would be expected to provide this year.

The report continues:

> There would have to be a commitment to buying the rice at a price that is high enough to encourage local production. This price should

be somewhat higher than an average of past years' market prices, since these prices—driven down by imports—have not allowed for sustainable production.[45]

The Opportunity Cost of Destructive Aid Models

Considering Haiti's present situation from an economic standpoint, if opportunity cost is "the loss of potential gain from other alternatives when one alternative is chosen,"[46] then Haiti has missed out tremendously thanks to the misguided and even destructive aid models implemented by governments and NGOs. In most cases, the private sector has been left to fend for itself, with fewer opportunities and more significant barriers to transaction.

Various development models have been attempted in Haiti, yet instead of partnering with the local business sector, too many NGOs have simply chosen to become distributors, as seen with Feed My Starving Children and hundreds of other international nonprofit organizations.

Haiti's NGOs, which represent enormous purchasing power in the market, have not grown the country's economy by distributing resources. Why? Because, as we have seen, nonprofit resource distribution can never create what businesses create: new cycles of profit that can increase jobs, generate more tax revenue, and provide long-term investment opportunities. Haiti can't break even and grow today because aid has replaced the natural pattern of transaction. For-profit NGO operations, manufactured business development, and misaligned trade policies have created significant opportunity costs for Haiti's economy and haven't provided the solutions the country so desperately needs.

We are not asking NGOs to quit. Rather, let's embrace and strengthen Haiti's economy by partnering with the private sector. According to a Chinese proverb, "The best time to plant a tree was twenty years ago; the second best time is now." Although Haiti's fragile economy has been damaged by wrong-headed approaches, there still remain tremendous opportunities for NGOs to redeem themselves through partnering with businesses and realigning with Haiti's market-based economy.

CHAPTER 9

Buy Haitian, Restore Haiti:
Bringing NGOs and Businesses Together

Partnerships between Haitian businesses and NGOs are key to helping NGOs realign with Haiti's market-based economy. This first step toward realignment has potential to transform the market so that businesses can play their natural and essential role as resource generators, adding value and meeting needs profitably and thereby creating employment and triggering economic growth. Through partnerships, the NGO sector can do what it's supposed to do—serve the people of Haiti by addressing the underlying causes of hunger, suffering, and poverty long-term through sustainable growth, instead of treating the symptoms only.

But how can NGOs and businesses achieve truly successful partnerships that increase balanced transactions in the economy? The "Buy Haitian, Restore Haiti" series of conferences sought to answer that very question.

First Conference

In March 2011, Partners Worldwide hosted the first "Buy Haitian, Restore Haiti" event in Port-au-Prince in collaboration with Building Markets (then called Peace Dividend Trust). The event was a business conference and trade fair designed to connect the NGO sector to local businesses in response to the need for increased local procurement one year after the earthquake. The alarming fact that in 2010 only 1.6 percent of the USAID post-disaster budget was spent in Haiti informed this response.

During the day-long event, a panel discussion on local procurement included four representatives from medium to large NGOs working in Haiti with significant financial resources: Salim Loxley of Peace Dividend Trust, Michael Dytynyshyn of Samaritan's Purse, Neel Stratton of World Vision, and Willys Geffrard of Christian Reformed World Relief Committee (now called World Renew). Speaking to over 250 NGO representatives and Haitian business owners, the panelists discussed the many barriers they had faced so far in seeking local procurement in Haiti.

Though there was a strong recognition that partnership isn't the simplest approach, the post-conference survey still confirmed a shared goal to overcome those barriers through networking and partnership. When asked, "How important was the conference to you?" 36 percent of attendees responded that it was somewhat important, and 43 percent indicated that it was very important. In particular, the attendees valued the opportunity to be a part of the discussion and have new opportunities to connect with buyers or suppliers. Another question asked, "Do you plan to follow up or have you obtained a contract from networking?" In response, the overwhelming majority, 91 percent, reported that they did. Many indicated that they saw potential in opportunities to contract across the nonprofit and for-profit sectors.

When asked, "Would you participate in a similar conference next year?" 74 percent responded positively. Many attendees expressed interest in more frequent networking opportunities in the coming months.

The question, "What can Partners Worldwide change to improve the conference next time?" elicited the following open-ended responses:

- "It would be good to find a way to connect NGOs with needs in the production sector to entrepreneurs in production who otherwise do not know who to meet."
- "Many more contacts between NGOs and businesses."
- "Have a match-making system between foreign companies and Haitian companies."

In the survey data and responses above, there was a strong demand, particularly from Haitian businesses, for professional networking. Prior to the conference, the leaders of Partners Worldwide suspected that there were bottlenecks preventing local procurement, yet the top four barriers of price, quality and quantity, delivery time, and communication were identified by the end of the day-long networking conference. And, as seen in participant comments below, the local-procurement movement began:

- "Congratulations to you. This meeting will allow contractors to be in contact with NGOs."

- "The initiative is excellent and allows SMEs [small and medium enterprises] to expand their sphere of activities and opportunities."

- "I think this is a good move for my company and for the country."

- "This new approach will make a real difference between companies and NGOs and especially the Haitian people."

- "It allows businesses to connect with other businesses and particularly with NGOs."

- "I think this meeting was very beneficial for many enterprises, and I hope there will be many more forums like this."

Second Conference

The second "Buy Haitian, Restore Haiti" conference was held ten months later in January 2012. A panel of NGOs expressed similar goals and challenges as the panel from the previous year. The panel consisted of Austin Holmes from Mission of Hope; Jason Burger from CSS International Holdings; Willys Geffrard from World Renew; Anne Hastings, then director of the Fonkoze lending institution; Didier Louis, director of Hunger Relief International; Sabine Cordele, logistics manager for Concern Worldwide; Segolene d'Herlincourt from Peace Dividend Trust; and Marie Lievre from Acted Haiti.

In addition, many Haitian business owners reported their progress after improving strategies and implementing best practices to overcome the barriers to partnership—price, quality and quantity, delivery time, and communication—as were identified in the first conference. The business representatives included Rob Waddell, CEO of JobPaw.com; Alex Georges, co-owner of solar-panel manufacturer ENERSA; Lawrence Alexander from Haiti Broilers S.A.; Paul Ducarmel of peanut butter producer Doucot Chocolat; and Evelien de Gier, co-owner of the wood manufacturing and interior design firm Maxima S.A.

However, all of the NGO representatives confirmed that the barriers identified in the first conference still remained, making it a challenge for organizations to increase local procurement. According to one representative: "Many suppliers are still ignoring basic purchasing principles and procedures, for instance, to send a price quote when they submit their offer. And sometimes buyers are poorly welcomed to their store fronts. Other handicaps are that some of the offers are poorly formulated and, even after they get the contract, they still don't respect the delivery time."

Furthermore, some NGOs and businesses agreed that there remained a lack of expertise—whether in the business sector, or among NGO staff, some of whom were unable to identify quality products at a good price. Businesses also reported a lack of affordable credit, preventing them from fulfilling larger contracts with quick turnover, especially since many NGOs would not pay for contracts until they were fulfilled.

The panel discussions also recognized a lack of local procurement incentives in the trade policies of the Haitian government. The government did not have trade policies requiring NGOs to transact locally, instead permitting NGOs to import products with low fees and little regulation—and according to local companies present, gave NGO imports first priority for entry into the country over the materials that Haitian businesses needed in order to produce and supply goods and services efficiently and effectively.

Many of the issues identified in the earlier conference remained, but this conference allowed NGOs and businesses to further develop their understanding of these issues and to posit solutions.

Following the second conference, Partners Worldwide and a number of businesses and organizations in the network formed the 100K Jobs in Haiti coalition. The alliance sought to converge their efforts toward job creation through local procurement practices, advocating for Haiti's emerging business sector, business training, and improved access to financial resources such as loan capital and investment.

Ninety days after the second conference, Partners Worldwide and the newly established 100K Jobs coalition distributed post-conference surveys to determine the conference's effectiveness in connecting NGOs and businesses. The survey findings indicated positive outcomes.

Fifty percent of business respondents reported successful transactions as a result of connections made during the conference. One company increased sales by 25 percent, while another increased sales by 75 percent. For the print and design company ITS Haiti, entrepreneur Mendell Harryford reported over $50,000 in new contracts from connections made at the conference. Three months after the conference, ITS had doubled its number of employees.

Among NGOs, 71 percent of respondents reported a greater than 10 percent increase in local purchasing from suppliers they had met at the conference. One NGO reported securing a contract with a local supplier valued at over $250,000 thanks to a connection formed at the conference.

In spite of the remaining barriers, the needs of NGOs and their clients were beginning to be met profitably by Haitian businesses, thus leading to job creation within the business network.

According to Austin Holmes, "At Mission of Hope, we are continuing to network with others to aggregate our local purchasing and invest in local companies through secure purchasing contracts. We believe that we can marshal substantial resources to the private sector and bring transparency to the social sector by measuring both ourselves and partner NGOs on domestic purchases and competency building of local staff. The Partners Worldwide conference was a great encouragement to this and will be a significant part of doing this."

Another NGO leader commented anonymously, "I have lived in Haiti for thirty-one years. Sourcing has always been a nightmare. This has changed a lot over the last few years. In many sectors (e.g., building supplies), you can buy cheaper in Haiti than abroad, never mind the freight and customs. In addition, you can now find high-quality items."

A Haitian business owner also commented on the potential for partnership, stating that, "We valued our presence at the conference, as it established us as a company that 'needs to be there' and gave us the chance to showcase our professionalism."

Opportunities for local procurement continued to come into focus.

According to the same post-conference survey, NGOs and local businesses not only better understood their role in Haiti's broader market economy, but they also saw the value of partnership across sectors. They saw the need to adapt strategies and seek shared solutions to the barriers of price, quality and quantity, delivery time, and communication in order to increase transactions.

The movement for local procurement grew. As the following case study of Hunger Relief International shows, visionary NGO leaders such as Didier Louis can create enormously beneficial ripple effects when they choose to source their organization's needs locally.

CASE STUDY[1]

Hunger Relief International

As humanitarian and development aid organizations spend money to improve the lives of the Haitian people, organizations that seek to align themselves to the economy can maximize their effect by creating more sustainable transactions. As the economy becomes more sustainable, the public and the private sector should take the place of those organizations in meeting the population's needs, and responsible nongovernmental organizations will be freed to help in other areas of the world.

Didier Hérold Louis started working as country director for Hunger Relief International (HRI) in 2010, shortly after the earthquake. Trained as a medical doctor in the Haiti State University's Faculty of Medicine, Louis practiced for only two years before transitioning into public health.

"It was actually my dream to become a medical doctor," he says. "I come from a very poor family." Louis's grandmother, a street vendor, sent all seven of her children to school. "We made it up the social ladder," he explains.

While working for the Haitian Group for the Study of Kaposi's Sarcoma and Opportunistic Infections, in partnership with New York's Cornell University, Louis provided care for patients living with HIV/AIDS. After seizing an opportunity to attend the National Institute of Health in Bethesda, Maryland, for training in public health and clinical research, Louis continued to develop his expertise by training as a program manager in Haiti. Although he had achieved his dream of practicing as a medical doctor, Louis wanted to reach more people. "I had the feeling that I could do more," he says. This need for interaction with the population led him to public health management.

When Rachel Zelon, executive director of HRI, arrived in Port-au-Prince for a weeklong visit less than a month after the catastrophic January 2010 earthquake, Louis was working for another international organization managing a clinic in Carrefour. As earthquake victims gathered on empty lots, soccer fields, and wherever else they could erect temporary structures for their families, many organizations were working to improve living conditions for the displaced. When Zelon arrived, Louis helped her assess the damage and determine what HRI could do to help.

"When [Zelon] told me that she wanted to start Hunger Relief International in Haiti, I was like 'What? Why should you or another individual start another NGO in Haiti? What will be the difference?'" Louis recounts.

When HRI's executive director explained that the organization planned to provide food to orphans and vulnerable children in Haiti, that it wanted to hire Louis as country director, and that it was willing to buy locally, Louis recognized an opportunity to contribute to a stable market for Haitian farmers. "I do believe that this is exactly what we need to do," he says. "We need to get people to work in Haiti.... That's how we can expect this country to develop."

Louis has been working for humanitarian organizations in Haiti since 2001, and many NGOs run feeding programs in the country. Still, he says, "I didn't know of any NGOs or local organizations that were buying local food in Haiti."

Hunger Relief International in Haiti

HRI in Haiti partners with twenty-five orphanages around Port-au-Prince to provide alimentary aid to some of the nation's most vulnerable children. "Food is a door opener," says Louis.

In partnership with C3 Global, a charismatic Christian outreach network, HRI assesses local orphanages and C3 Global finds US churches willing to sponsor them. C3 Global passes the churches' funds on to HRI, and HRI uses those funds to purchase food from farmers associations in the Artibonite Valley, an epicenter of Haitian rice production.[2]

With three employees in the Artibonite—an agronomist, an administrator, and a security guard—HRI in Haiti also hires between ten and twelve short-term employees ten days a month to process and package food destined for children in the capital. Every two months, a local transporter in the Artibonite is hired to get the food to Port-au-Prince before the goods are distributed to orphanages over three days.

"I do believe that we are impacting hundreds of farmers from different farmers associations," says Louis. Because HRI is a repeating client that operates in their region, representatives from local farmers associations can compete for HRI's business without some of the transportation costs associated with bringing their product to the capital. Further, "they understand that we are buying the food to provide to the children in orphanages in Port-au-Prince," says Louis, who explains that while producers still make a profit, the farmers often lower their prices to accommodate the organization's humanitarian efforts.

Louis recalls the first time he went to the Artibonite Valley to meet with some of their suppliers. "They were very skeptical," he says. "It's pretty much normal that people are skeptical about NGOs, because we have so many NGOs that just show up like that, and make promises to people—promises that they usually do not keep."

Still, Louis found farmers receptive, once he made their goals and strategy clear. "I strongly believe that when you share information with people, and you give them a way to check on the information that *you* gave them, it creates credibility," says Louis. Under his guidance, HRI in Haiti shares with farmers and potential suppliers the names of orphanages, the number of children living at these orphanages, and the organization's budgeting and accounting practices.

How Can Humanitarian Organizations Do Better?

Louis believes the country needs more humanitarian and development aid organizations to apply the local-procurement strategy implemented by HRI in order to create an economic sustainability that will benefit the population as a whole. When NGOs provide imported food to vulnerable orphans, they help them. When NGOs provide locally purchased food to vulnerable orphans, they help not only the orphans but also local farmers, vendors, and transporters.

HRI feeds 1,300 children with three tons of food each year, but far vaster feeding programs exist. The World Food Programme provides alimentary assistance to nearly 1.4 million people, including the children it serves through school feeding programs across the country.[3] The Haitian government's Programme Nationale de Cantine Scolaire (National School Canteen Program) feeds nearly four hundred thousand.[4] Save the Children and Compassion International also operate school feeding programs. Although in 2011 World Food Programme purchased over 3,000 metric tons of Haitian rice for use in school meals,[5] according to Louis, it is just a starting point, and even more of these enormous alimentary aid programs need to begin purchasing locally.

National statistics indicate that Haiti requires nearly 500,000 tons of rice to feed its population,[6] even as the Haitian agricultural sector and farmers' livelihoods continue to shrink. When NGOs spend massive amounts of capital to distribute imported foodstuffs in Haiti, their funds have a limited, if not detrimental, effect on the broader Haitian economy. Responsible organizations must aim to address development metrics such as trade balance and agricultural revival, unless they intend to provide services indefinitely.

Louis believes that a "total absence of regulation" on imports allows well-meaning organizations to bring in hundreds of thousands of tons of "free stuff," forcing Haitian producers to lower prices to untenable levels. In 1995, Haitian import tariffs fell from 35 to 3 percent.[7] Now 51 percent of food and 80 percent of rice consumed in Haiti is imported.[8] Because importers face such low tariffs, and because the agricultural sector has been rendered incapable of meeting market demand, NGOs can justify importation, for now.

But HRI in Haiti is thinking long term. Louis explains how his organization decided to provide four goats to sixteen farmers, which boosted their productive capacity and helped them become more sustainable. After providing one male and three female goats to each family, HRI is repaid with one goat from every litter, providing meat to the children living in the partnered orphanages in the capital. In two years, farmers can expect to have as many as twenty-two goats, significantly improving their financial standing and helping them better feed their own children.

Hunger Relief International's local-procurement practice maximizes the effect of its funding, and feeds vulnerable children in the capital while supporting farmers, laborers, and transporters in the Artibonite Valley. By sharing information with farmers and by investing in their productive capacities, HRI is developing a transaction partnership between orphanages and their food suppliers—a partnership that can be sustained even after HRI's role has ended.

Haitian Responsibility

"It takes vision and leadership to do every single thing," says Louis, and vision and leadership are things he believes the nation severely lacks. "I have a feeling that most of the people we have in charge in this country—they are acting like foreigners. They are acting like people who have no binding to this country or to the people of this country. And it's sad. Time is passing by, and to me, everyone seems asleep at the wheel. Sometimes we move, and it makes people think that maybe we're waking up. But we're just changing positions."

Louis points to the nearly $2 billion that USAID spent in Haiti in the year after the earthquake as an example of the fundamental errors in how Haitians and the international community have approached the nation's development.[9] "How much has that amount impacted Haitians' lives?" he asks. "I don't think it did much." Louis argues that Haitians must own Haiti's development process and must work to orient efforts undertaken by the government and the international community toward practices that make a real difference, such as local procurement.

One potentially surprising statistic is that two-thirds of Haitian children living in orphanages have one or more living parents. "And pretty often," says Louis, "those parents take their children home on summer vacations for a week or two." With unemployment hovering around a staggering 40 percent—not even including the underemployed or those seeking jobs in the formal sector[10]—many parents are unable to ensure their children's livelihoods. Among children living in orphanages, 10 to 15 percent have reached the age of eighteen and should, by law, no longer reside in those institutions. But many orphanages still take care of these young men and women, allowing them to stay on at the orphanage to help with the cooking and cleaning.

In such dire circumstances, some orphanages have understood the need for sustainability and are actively working to feed the children in their care without the support of foreign donations. By doing so they are taking ownership of their conditions and their futures. One of the orphanages that is partnered with HRI leases a six-acre property on which they grow several crops, including various vegetables, beans, and nine thousand banana trees.

By diversifying their own supply source internally and providing a model of productivity for the kids to learn through, the partnering orphanage is working to become self-sustaining.

"The good thing for me about this right now is that these people want to do *business*," says Louis about future goals. "These people understand that they will not have HRI, an NGO, providing food to these children someday. They won't have HRI to provide backpacks, notebooks, and pencils.... They won't have US churches to send down boxes of shoes and stuff like that. At a certain point, they need to get away and be on their own. They need to become sustainable and to provide for themselves."

If NGOs maximize the effect of their capital by purchasing locally, and if Haitian institutions like this orphanage can meet the needs of the people in their care, Haiti has a chance at establishing a model of productivity for its young people who represent the emerging generation of entrepreneurs. A prospect Louis finds "very, very encouraging."

Third Conference

In September 2012, just eight months after the previous conference, the third conference invited even more NGOs and businesses to join in the vision for restoring Haiti through local procurement. Businesses came with a stronger voice, reaffirming their capacity to source NGO demand.

Two respected business owners—Jean Marc Ewald from Haiti's largest peanut butter and coffee production company, REBO S.A., and Evelien de Gier from Maxima S.A.—advocated for local procurement on behalf of the business sector. The audience of over three hundred NGOs and businesses raised many significant questions, particularly about overcoming the four major barriers that restricted partnership: price, quality and quantity, delivery time, and communication.

Price

Regarding the issue of price, many NGOs committed to paying more, if needed, to source locally. They understood that Haitian businesses, unlike NGOs, cannot import materials duty-free. Some of the NGOs that couldn't find local products within their budget continued to import foreign goods as before.

A significant lack of competition also influences price. Some Haitian companies have been accused of creating monopolies through their exclusive distribution rights with foreign manufacturers, thereby eliminating price competition for certain brands. Vehicles, generators, batteries, and many other technologies not produced in Haiti fall into this category. Because demand for these products is very high, prices can further inflate. For some NGOs, the response is often to seek out imports they can bring in themselves.

On the other hand, many medium to large businesses reported that they were seeking contracts to meet market demand through local production. However, variables such as high manufacturing costs, local taxes, and expensive credit at times drive the price of local products up further.

The conference participants brought a variety of perspectives to the situation. Some argued that despite the higher prices for local products, in order for the business sector to grow, new trade policies and regulations would be needed to encourage NGOs to increase local procurement.

Some NGOs were able to find affordable local products, but for most, price was still a concern. Still, many NGOs committed to purchasing more products locally in order to contribute to job creation and strengthen the business sector, in spite of price. However, for other NGOs, purchasing large quantities abroad still made more financial sense, since it would allow them to provide their services to the most clients.

Quality and Quantity

Some attendees shared best practices regarding the healthy procurement process they had achieved. One NGO and its business partners had learned to overcome the barrier of quality and quantity by designating a specific individual from each party—such as a bilingual purchasing manager and a sales representative—to connect on a regular basis. They could meet at any time to review the process as necessary, which built trust while monitoring quality and quantity more openly. Then the two counterparts would report back to their employers and work to find efficient solutions to issues that arose.

The NGO buyer was also encouraged to make regular and unannounced visits to the manufacturing site. Feedback was welcomed and corrections were offered. The NGO felt more confident in the relationship and agreed to make more up-front payments for its contracts, providing the businesses with the capital they needed to purchase raw materials in advance and thereby to have sufficient supplies to produce the desired quantity. This process established trust and helped both parties avoid miscommunication and anticipate issues before they arose.

Other attendees reiterated the same findings. Many participants believed that NGOs should commit to purchasing locally in order to help businesses increase their revenue stream. With that increase in revenue, business could then make more purchases and have the necessary materials to pursue larger contracts in the future. According to one participant, if NGOs were to realign their purchasing power with the local economy, businesses and producers—such as farmers—could expand production and distribution so much that it could reverse the effects of the Haitian government's 1995 trade policy that lowered import tariffs from 35 to 3 percent.

Other avenues to partnership emerged in the discussion. Some participants argued that NGOs should provide more of the technical assistance that businesses and producers lack.

One attendee suggested that more farmers could become part of self-owned and self-directed federations in order to reduce waste and better connect to the rest of the value chain; Ken Michel's partnering federation and its work with Mission of Hope exemplifies this strategy (see the case study of FEDEPAT–Mission of Hope in chapter 7).

Delivery Time

When asked about improvements in delivery time, one NGO representative shared that both delivery time and communication improved when the organization was able to make frequent visits to production sites.

Regarding the relationship between payment and delivery, many attendees suggested that NGOs purchase further in advance, rather than seeking orders at the last minute, in order to give businesses the lead time needed to ensure that raw materials, factory space, and other essential elements of production were available.

Communication

According to one business participant, many enterprises still faced the challenge of communication when NGOs announced tenders in English. This practice disqualified many Haitian entrepreneurs from the start, and the practice had persisted since the first post-earthquake conference. Further, many tenders were being published in foreign media well before they were published locally, which gave foreign firms an advantage over Haitian companies.

Conversely, one NGO representative explained that NGOs have limited time to meet distribution deadlines. It can take too much effort to meet with local companies individually, or even for a purchasing manager to initiate contact with potential suppliers. According to him, timely communication between NGOs and local businesses often does not seem achievable since most NGO executives speak English or other foreign languages, and only lower-level staff speak Creole or French.

At the second conference, panelist Evelien de Gier had expressed that, ultimately, both NGOs and businesses need to work to overcome communication challenges. NGOs need to find ways to publish tenders in both national languages, but businesses also need to develop bilingual staff in order to secure contracts and grow.

By the third conference, many participants emphasized the importance of establishing trust between NGOs and businesses, two sectors which, until that point, had very rarely interacted with each other. As a result, NGOs strengthened ties and increased postings of their calls for tenders in French and Creole in the national newspaper. Online networks such as the Haiti Business Directory and Building Markets also continue to showcase businesses' viability in their various sectors, allowing NGOs to make more informed purchasing decisions.

In addition, the businesspeople better understood the need to accommodate the English language and numerous other international languages in order to pursue opportunities and increase their likelihood of winning a contract.

The case study of HEJEC below demonstrates the importance of price, quality and quantity, delivery time, and communication in order for NGO-business partnerships to succeed. In addition, it exemplifies another factor: the importance of competition in spurring businesses to meet their customers' needs in an accurate, timely, and professional manner.

The outcomes of the third conference were encouraging. Challenges were further clarified, but solutions were also found. While the number of NGOs in attendance decreased, business-to-business networking increased. In particular, more medium to large businesses attended the conference and saw the importance of networking across sectors to build relationships with other businesses as well as NGOs. This time many businesses helped sponsor the event, which kept costs low and encouraged small-business owners to attend. Additionally, job creation became a shared goal for the businesses and NGOs in attendance. The vision for the fourth conference emerged.

CASE STUDY[11]

HEJEC

In order for NGO-business partnerships to succeed, it is necessary to address the challenges of price, quality and quantity, delivery time, and communication. Furthermore, competition is a crucial factor in spurring local producers and suppliers to meet customers' needs and improve quality.

In spite of the global economic recession, Haitian American Jerry Jean-Louis flew to Port-au-Prince in 2010 after he completed a US Army tour in Afghanistan. He sought a viable business opportunity in a market that, according to Minister of Finance Wilson Laleau, will not attain emerging status until 2030. Having specialized in languages, logistics, and transportation, Jean-Louis sought to apply his new skill set on the Haitian market. "Because I was really new in business—I didn't have any [other] ideas," he says.

In late 2010, Jean-Louis spent $617 to register HEJEC Security Transportation with the Haitian government. In 2013, Jean-Louis reported that the company is worth half a million dollars. HEJEC is a dynamic business model that moves local and foreign business-people, aid workers, VIPs, and goods by car, truck, boat, cow, or donkey. Staffed by ex-military and police personnel and managed by specialists whom Jean-Louis refers to as his "MBA people," HEJEC advertises advanced GPS systems, security expertise, interpretation, and digital communications services as a must-have package for travelers seeking a customized, efficient, and effective transportation service.

With five to ten of their employees involved per contract, mainly composed of business and security personnel, HEJEC absorbs many costs upfront by producing detailed analysis before bidding on contracts or approaching potential clients with pro-posals for HEJEC's translation, shipping, transportation, and con-sulting services.

Within the first two years, HEJEC contracted with over two hundred individuals and organizations. The company's client base for shipping and transportation includes over thirty customers, including NGOs, governments, and Haitian and foreign compa-nies. Nearly a hundred individuals have contracted their personal transportation services, 75 percent of whom were foreigners, according to Jean-Louis.

By paying rent and taxes, making payroll, and purchasing goods and services locally, businesses such as HEJEC spend much of their revenue on the local market, creating the all-important transactions that sustain market economies.

"Avis is not my plan," says Jean-Louis, referring to the American car rental company. HEJEC provides a far broader service. From arrival to departure, Jean-Louis promises to "solve headaches and issues" that can arise on business trips, official visits, or tourist holidays. By pursuing lucrative foreign clients with premium services, HEJEC directly attracts foreign capital to the Haitian economy.

But how does HEJEC make a profit competing with other rental and transportation companies that offer more basic packages at half the price?

Premium-service companies staffed by qualified professionals can thrive on the Haitian market, but the weak private sector —whose failure to deliver services on time, lack of quality and quantity, and poor communication practices are the norm—lowers standards all around. Bad businesses may lack expertise, but they also lack the competition that would drive them out of the market.

"Competition is what I will lay out, what another company will lay out, and what the client will choose for himself," says Jean-Louis. "And if you sell the best service, you get to keep the client. The client will get to make the choice." Time and again, subjects report that NGOs, local or foreign, are looking to award jobs to the best candidate—regardless of personal connections or status—a dynamic that, for better or worse, compels Haitian businesses to improve their products or services as they pursue existing and new clients.

HEJEC has been able to develop a high-paying, loyal client base, composed mostly of foreign leaders and professionals, because it has earned its clients' trust by overcoming the professional challenges many of its Haitian competitors cannot. Jean-Louis and his company have raised the bar for transportation services in terms of quality, communication, and services, which has attracted increasingly larger contracts.

Partnering with Population Services International

Founded in 1970, Population Services International (PSI) is a global health organization seeking measurable impacts. Only 1 percent of its staff are expatriates because PSI has a policy of doing business and hiring staff locally as much as possible. According to the organization's website, "PSI-Haiti began programs in 1989 to ensure access to affordable health products and services." Twenty years later, PSI is at the forefront of the fight against malaria in Haiti.

When Jean-Louis read about PSI's goal to distribute 3.5 million mosquito nets throughout the country—even to the remotest mountain villages that are unreachable except by cow and donkey—he saw an opportunity. According to the HEJEC head, "We felt, as a company, that we needed to take it to heart. Because if people were going to spend millions of dollars on these nets, the middleman would have to do a great job."

The key to Jean-Louis's success may be the fact that he understood both the scale of the commitment of the various actors involved and the "national need as Haitians to be part of it." These were grand ideas for a private business, perhaps, but this big-picture perspective, along with HEJEC's understanding of the level of dedication needed to complete the task, helped the company put forth a significant first effort before approaching the lucrative contract.

After producing a timeline and infrastructure analysis and reviewing potential issues that could compromise the project, HEJEC approached PSI with a bid—and lost to a competitor. But two weeks later, PSI contacted Jean-Louis to award his company the $500,000 contract after all. According to Jean-Louis, the first company that had been awarded the contract "did not take what [PSI] said into consideration" and "weren't respecting the delivery time."

Over the course of four months, HEJEC delivered 3.5 million mosquito nets to remote areas in all ten departments of Haiti. "It was never routine," says Jean-Louis. "Every day we would need to plan how many trucks we would need for the day, how many donkeys, and how much personnel."

While contracting can have negative consequences for labor—

such as poor remuneration and inconsistent employment—HEJEC's use of short-term labor allowed them to hire employees throughout Haiti's provincial departments instead of relying on a single team from the capital that would have to be mobile. By cutting travel expenses for its own personnel, HEJEC was able to keep operational costs in check while creating thousands of local transactions throughout the country.

So how did each mosquito net get where it needed to go? Jean-Louis explains that since the product wasn't available domestically at the scalability needed for the buyer, the nets were transported from overseas into Haiti via containers on cargo ships with a company called NATRANS. From there, they would be stored, then transported by HEJEC via trucks. "We would go wherever we could reach in trucks, and then the rest we would use the appropriate way to get there," he says about the donkeys and cows they used to transport the nets. Once there, HEJEC distributed the nets to villages and communities that PSI serves.

Population Services International's lucrative partnership with HEJEC served its humanitarian function, supported a legal and professional private-sector operation, and created thousands of transactions between HEJEC, local transporters, interpreters, coordinators, and more. PSI needed to partner with a company that could meet its needs to achieve its humanitarian goals, but the organization's determination to contract with a Haitian business—and its willingness to give Jean-Louis's company an opportunity even after the first Haitian transportation company had failed to meet expectations—speaks to the organization's understanding of the importance of doing business locally.

When customers enter a market with high expectations and clear demands, they force providers to compete more aggressively for their business. Even companies that do not win the contracts gain invaluable experience by competing for clients, which incrementally raises the collective standard of quality. By actively seeking private-sector partnerships, organizations such as PSI legitimize and develop the private sector by creating competition. The mere presence of economic opportunity has a dynamizing effect on the private sector.

Finally, the transactions created by partnerships between international organizations and private enterprises have a ripple effect throughout the host economy in myriad instances. HEJEC paid employees and paid its taxes. The company paid utilities bills and bought supplies on the local market. Contractors spent their paychecks on their families—buying food, paying their rent, or providing tuition for their children.

While the Haitian private sector has the responsibility of earning customers' trust, forward-thinking international organizations are already seeking partnerships with private enterprises, which creates jobs and healthy competition.

Fourth Conference

In previous conferences, partnership was identified as the key framework to helping businesses and communities successfully recover from the devastating economic effects of the 2010 earthquake in sustainable ways. However, the need for new tools to reach higher levels of partnership emerged. Therefore, the fourth conference, held in January 2014 and appropriately titled "Restore Haiti: Explore Business Opportunities," focused on connecting Haitian and foreign businesspeople and investors to explore market opportunities together.

NGO-business partnership gave way to business-to-business partnership. Together, investors and businesspeople discussed their goals to more effectively resource local businesses, expand production, meet local contract demands, and create employment.

After presentations from Haitian businesspeople, government representatives, and a representative from the US embassy, some of Haiti's premier entrepreneurs had a chance to discuss the capacity and potential of the private sector. Several companies—including Maxima, ENERSA, Laboratoire Farmatrix, TopLine Materiaux de Construction, and Café Selecto—showcased their innovative product lines.

Another Port-au-Prince company, Surtab, had begun producing touch-screen Android tablets in October 2013. By January 2014, Surtab was producing four thousand units per month. Under the leadership of Maarten Boute, former CEO of the leading mobile services company Digicel Haiti, the operation sought not only to create jobs, but also to show that high-tech electronics assembly in Haiti is possible and to encourage others to follow in its path.

In addition, after meeting at the conference, Surtab partnered with a Haitian entrepreneur to furnish its tablets with locally produced leather cases.

More than two hundred people attended the fourth conference, and over 90 percent responded to the post-conference survey. Seventy-seven percent indicated that they somewhat agreed or completely agreed that private investment could trigger growth in their business. Sixty-one percent of businesses attending reported that they had contracted with and supplied NGOs prior to the conference. One hundred percent of business respondents agreed that the growth of their business could trigger growth in Haiti's economy.

Through these conferences, the key methods of the OBED strategy were implemented to increase market realignment, and this realignment became a shared commitment and a top priority among participants. As businesses and NGOs connected through this series of conferences, more opportunities for transactions emerged for local purchasing, a platform to connect was implemented, a new voice for advocacy was found, and there were opportunities to network in order to increase investment. This market realignment helped spur growth within the businesses seeking to meet needs through balanced transactions in Haiti.

CHAPTER 10

Advocating for Haiti's Future:
A Final Call for Change

During our interview with Salim Loxley, former director of Peace Dividend Trust (PDT) in Haiti, he recounted a phone call he received at his office in October 2010, following the outbreak of the cholera epidemic.

"We need 4.5 million bars of soap by Friday," said a representative of the United Nations Development Program (UNDP). Eager to seize the opportunity, Loxley began searching through PDT's directory of Haitian businesses. Within an hour, he identified Carribex, a local soap producer. The company was able to fill the UNDP's order in less than seventy-two hours. The partnership went so well, in fact, that Carribex secured a $600,000 contract for soap through UNICEF, another branch of the United Nations.[1]

For his article "The Multiplier Effect," Jacob Kushner interviewed Carribex's owner, Fritz Brandt, and reported that this contract "marked the first time in seven years of operating his factory that one of the foreign NGOs or international bodies that spend billions of aid dollars annually on supplies and equipment had ever contracted with him."[2]

Companies such as Carribex were able to continue operating after the earthquake because their growth wasn't impeded by an influx of foreign goods in the market—which was precisely what led to the demise of Auguste Savonnerie, as seen in chapter 1. Had the UNDP and UNICEF imported that enormous quantity of soap and distributed it for free—rather than purchase locally through Carribex—the company, and the hundreds of people Carribex employs, might also not have survived the competition.

Local procurement is possible and barriers to transaction can be overcome. In the contract with Carribex, both the agencies and the enterprise were able to agree on a price. Carribex's quality, quantity, and delivery time exceeded buyer expectations.

Unfortunately, most Haitian companies never get this phone call. Instead, they find themselves competing against nonprofit organizations and agencies with vast donor resources. When these organizations import products tax-free, then distribute them for free or at subsidized costs, they decimate the very client base that Haitian manufacturers and producers rely on. However, particular departments of the United Nations—in addition to organizations such as World Renew, Hunger Relief International, and Mission of Hope—have chosen to realign with Haiti's market-based system by contracting with local enterprises to satisfy the needs of the people they serve.

According to the Inter-American Development Bank, Haiti lost between $8 and $14 billion of gross domestic product during the earthquake due to damage of buildings and real estate and the direct loss of inventory and production capacity.[3] Yet, just by realigning their programs with the Haitian market, humanitarian aid and development organizations have a unique opportunity to redress the catastrophic economic effects of the earthquake. Through agency and NGO contracts, Haitian companies can restore and increase production, replenishing what was lost and creating the employment that is so critically needed beyond the disaster-response phase.

Thanks to agency and NGO market realignment, increases in foreign-direct investment, an increase in purchasing power of Haitians through remittances from the large Haitian diaspora, and increased political stability, GDP grew at 1.8 percent in 2005, fell to -5.4 percent in 2010 due to the earthquake, then grew back to an even higher rate of 5.6 percent in 2011,[4] before stabilizing at a more sustainable growth rate of 3.8 percent in 2014.[5]

Furthermore, according to data from the US embassy's commercial representative in Port-au-Prince, indicators show that while private investment was increasing, foreign aid was decreasing from 2010 to 2013.[6] As more investment took place, less aid was needed, or vice versa—as less aid was implemented, more businesses sought opportunities to meet the needs of the Haitian people.

FIGURE 5: Foreign Aid vs. Private Investment in Haiti, 2005–2013[7]

(in billions of USD)

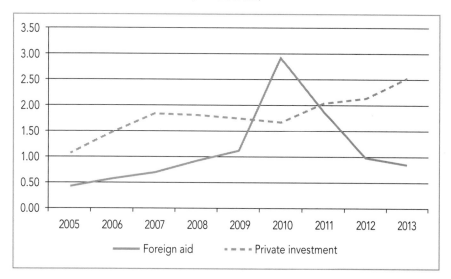

Haiti's market-based economy has begun to produce promising results. It is fair to say that as humanitarian aid and development initiatives continue to realign with the Haitian private sector, the country will continue to grow at a healthy rate and create more jobs for its hard-working people. With a strong business sector filling a greater role to satisfy demand—as any market-based economy requires—Haiti's future could be bright.

The potential for NGOs to realign themselves with Haiti's market-based system might be unique, but the market economy is currently the most prevalent system in the world. Developing that system is the natural choice for many emerging economies such as India, Kenya, Bangladesh, Brazil, and other developing nations. In fact, any poverty reduction has not been a miraculous act, but a careful, intentional strategy to equip emerging markets to meet national and global demands profitably.

For instance, to achieve the UN's Millennium Development Goals, the world's richest countries agreed to increase their annual commitment to Official Development Assistance (ODA) to 0.7 percent of their GNP.

However, several nations with large, impoverished populations have seen rapid economic development and a reduction of extreme poverty sooner than anticipated. This was not because of increased ODA. Rather, those advances are due to globalization's potential to increase trade by opening up emerging economies. Cross-border trade policies have proven particularly effective in East Asia and South Asia.

Four hundred million people in China alone have emerged from poverty in line with the nation's meteoric economic growth over the last three decades, during which time it has leveraged its labor force to turn over-population into a marketable opportunity. Beyond economic powerhouses such as China and India, other neighboring economies such as Bangladesh and Uzbekistan, previously known for their extreme poverty, have also made strides. According to a *Yale Global* report, "never before have so many people been lifted out of poverty over such a brief period of time."[8]

The Economist reports that, "China (which has never shown any interest in [Millennium Development Goals]) is responsible for three-quarters of the achievement. Its economy has been growing so fast that, even though inequality is rising fast, extreme poverty is disappearing." *The Economist* goes on to report that "China pulled 680m people out of misery in 1981–2010, and reduced its extreme-poverty rate from 84% in 1980 to 10% now."[9] Nearly a billion people have risen out of poverty and the rate of poverty has decreased from 25.7 percent in 2005, to 15.8 percent by 2010, and is projected to have decreased to an astounding 9.9 percent by the end of 2015.[10]

The *Yale Global* article points to various reasons why many emerging nations have been able to develop so quickly:

Already one can point to a number of probable sources emerging or accelerating around the turn of the century: an investment boom triggered by rising commodity prices; high growth spillovers originating from large open emerging economies that utilize cross-border supply chains; diversification into novel export markets from cut flowers to call centers; spread of new technologies, in particular rapid adoption of cell phones; increased public and private investment in infrastructure; the cessation of a number of conflicts and improved political stability; and the abandonment of inferior growth strategies such as import substitution for a focus on macroeconomic health and improved competitiveness. These factors are manifestations of a set of broader trends—the rise of globalization, the spread of capitalism and the improving quality of economic governance—which together have enabled the developing world to begin converging on advanced economy incomes after centuries of divergence. The poor countries that display the greatest success today are those that are engaging with the global economy, allowing market prices to balance supply and demand and to allocate scarce resources, and pursuing sensible and strategic economic policies to spur investment, trade and job creation.[11]

Thus developing nations have been able to reverse weak economic growth and combat endemic poverty.

If humanitarian and development aid organizations working in Haiti have distorted the market through the importation of free and subsidized goods, the Haitian government should be held equally accountable for allowing and even encouraging that process. While NGOs, as resource distributors, have failed to meet demand sustainably and have put unfair competitive pressure on tax-paying resource generators, the Haitian government, itself a resource distributor, has been aligned to the will of the international community rather than to the needs of the local economy. So far, the Haitian government's decisions, informed and influenced by the international community's demands, have ultimately prevented balanced transactions from gaining traction. This misalignment increases the burden foisted on for-profit enterprises, who find themselves in competition with cheap imports and with the government itself.

In a healthy market economy, consumers can choose to make the best transaction for themselves, purchasing the best product at the best price. Government trade policies should not allow foreign interests to make economic conditions more difficult for local businesses. Policy changes are needed to build a structure in which businesses can grow in Haiti. The government must take the following conscious steps to build a framework and favorable environment in which businesses can grow: revisiting and adapting the customs and taxes on imports, requiring NGOs to procure locally, and working closely with the business sector to strategically grow emerging sectors, such as tourism, production, infrastructure, and agronomy.

Through legal structures and sound policies, the Haitian government could ensure opportunities for economic growth, better equipping the business sector and thereby sustaining and increasing transactions in the country. By following this course the Haitian government has the potential to turn Haiti around—instead of perpetuating a failed state through poor governance.

Economies cannot break even or progress when resource distributors—the government and NGOs—have greater purchasing power than resource generators, and do not use that power in a way that aligns with the economy. Resources will run out if they are just distributed by NGOs and not created by local businesses. A real engagement with Haiti as a market-based system will empower its enterprises and entrepreneurs to play a lead role in the nation's economic future. Haiti is a country with immense potential to generate employment and growth in industries such as agriculture, construction, energy, manufacturing, textiles, and tourism. Local purchasing by NGOs, donors, agencies, and ministries, which leads to increased production and business development, is essential. Even more, when local businesses can practice market-driven innovation, this plays a positive psychological role in restoring Haiti's culture—one of entrepreneurship, independence, dignity, and ownership of one's destiny.

Even in the midst of unfair trade policies, failed development initiatives, and a flood of foreign aid, the Haitian economy has grown. It is critical, however, for international and domestic nonprofit organizations to partner with Haiti's for-profit businesses—as have Mission of Hope and World Renew—but also to advocate for more local, balanced transactions that generate customer satisfaction profitably.

Failure to support and partner with local businesses only perpetuates already deep problems. When local businesses are not viewed as worthy—or even capable—of meeting demand, the floodgate for misguided, misaligned aid opens wide.

Here are some ways for individuals, NGOs, and their supporters to advocate for Haiti's sustainable development and for the well-being of its people:

- Advocate on behalf of Haiti's "orphans." An estimated 80 percent of "orphaned" children in Haiti have at least one living parent, but these parents simply can't provide for their families because they are unemployed or underemployed. However, jobs can radically change the lives of Haitian families. Find and share the stories of parents who were able to secure a job and support their own children through private sector businesses that are sustainable within Haiti's market-based economy.

- Advocate for—and alongside—the local business sector. For example, share the story of the Haitian peanut farmers and local *mamba* businesses that couldn't compete with the alimentary-aid programs that distribute donated or subsidized imports. This dynamic occurred over and over again after the earthquake and undermined many entrepreneurs' livelihoods and various industries in Haiti's business sector. Instead, people need to make a profit to keep their businesses running, and to employ others from their community. Advocate that NGOs commit to local procurement from Haitian businesses, even if they might still distribute those goods for free to those in need.

- Advocate for trade as an essential element for economic growth and poverty reduction—and seek after trade policies that strengthen the Haitian economy and its opportunities in the global market.

- Advocate for sustainable policies and procedures. Aid dumping undermines local purchasing, and did so in 2010. Most NGOs in Haiti pay no taxes on imports. They also face no restrictions on the quantities they distribute. Because of these policies, many nonprofits flooded Haiti's economy with assistance but prevented local businesses from satisfying those same needs, thus disrupting their essential client base.

- Advocate for sustainability to your donors, ministry partners, or the NGOs you support. Advocating can be as simple as communicating your concerns to the organizations and charities you respect. Write a letter to the organization that supports the child you sponsor. Encourage them to purchase locally, and share the issue through your social media network. Don't cancel your support, but challenge NGOs to realign the support you're providing with the local market-based economy.

Whether or not you have funds or expertise to offer Haiti, you can be an advocate for the local economy. You can help more ministries and organizations understand the importance of developing the local business sector.

Through market realignment and the application of opportunity-based economic development, Haiti can someday reach the point where local businesses meet the needs of its people, which will thereby release NGOs to help elsewhere and will equip the Haitians to take the lead once again in their country's future.

Our final case study demonstrates the strength and resilience of Haitian private enterprise. For over one hundred years, Café Selecto has profitably supplied local coffee drinkers with their morning brew. Our hope is that, for many years to come, this company's success will be mirrored and multiplied in thousands of businesses across Haiti.

CASE STUDY[12]

Café Selecto

In spite of the vast amounts of aid poured into the country over the last twenty years, Haiti remains a market-based economy in which businesses have met consumer demand with quality products. Coffee, ubiquitous in Haiti since the colonial era, provides one of the most potent examples of how Haitian enterprise has addressed demand while creating the transactions that keep market-based economies alive.

Douglas Wiener represents the fourth generation of the family that owns Café Selecto, a coffee company that has operated in Haiti for over a hundred years. "Haiti used to be a big producer, just like Brazil," he explains. "All of the Haitian economy relied on coffee. Taxes were paid by coffee exports. We paid our debt of independence with coffee."

Wiener proudly recounts the story of his Polish and Austrian ancestors who immigrated to Haiti in the 1820s. "The state invested in coffee then. The money that came out of the taxes went to building infrastructure. That's how all the schools in Haiti were built."

From the end of the colonial era through the industrial revolution, and over the last century, Café Selecto has evolved from a network of plantations to a centralized exporter in Port-au-Prince, to a brand that supplies both foreign and local markets. To stay afloat when most of Haiti's ports closed during the Duvalier era—and to compete with Columbian, Brazilian, and Jamaican production—Café Selecto now adds value to its product by roasting and packaging the beans itself.

"Three generations ago, we exported mostly to Europe," Wiener explains. "We sold two hundred to three hundred containers of coffee a year to Italy alone." Now that Haitian coffee production is at an all-time low, companies like Café Selecto have had to change strategies. The family now invests in its supply chain and focuses on producers and the local market. Last year, Café Selecto planted four hundred thousand coffee trees in farmers' gardens to ensure supply. "Farmers love to get new trees," says Wiener. "And as long as value is added, the local market is profitable."

Perhaps surprisingly, Wiener estimates that micro-business and informal-sector artisan suppliers, collectively known as *Madan Sara*, buy and sell more volume than major producers—including Café Selecto and Rebo Café—combined. And even as informal-sector suppliers continue to collectively outsell companies like his, the market for Haitian beans has changed as well.

While the Dominican Republic forbids the importation of coffee, much of Haiti's production is sold across the border illegally. "They have four million tourists and they need a lot of coffee," Wiener explains. The Dominican Republic's high demand allows importers to pay Haitian farmers more for their crops, but the illegal market does not encourage a higher-quality product. "So," says Wiener, "it deteriorates the plantation."

The coffee industry in Haiti supports a vast network of businesses and individuals—producers, wholesalers, and retailers—whose myriad transactions help keep the country's market-based economy alive. "Who profits from the coffee?" Wiener asks. "The farmer profits," he answers. "He hires help in the field, and they profit. Then the person who rents out the donkeys profits. You have people drying the coffee here, sorting the coffee there, at the plant. Then you have the roasting master. And after that, you have the marketing people; you have the drivers; you have the people making the drinks. There is a whole economy around coffee." And that economy has existed in Haiti since before the Haitian Republic's founding.

Two hundred thousand Haitian families produce coffee. Informal-sector sales keep the industry alive, and those transactions throughout the value chain feed hundreds of thousands (if not millions) of families every day. However, that same informality restricts investment and contributes to the product's deterioration, even as global coffee prices continue to rise.

The most alarming failure of Haitian producers to capitalize on the country's long history of coffee production occurred when the Haitian coffee industry lost a $200 million Japanese investment to its more-structured Jamaican competitor because of Haiti's political instability and the informality of its private sector.

During that same period, in the mid-1990s, USAID and its investment partners helped Haitian coffee farmers create an association in hopes of establishing a unified brand capable of competing on the international market. The initiative was somewhat successful in offsetting a steep decline in coffee prices that marked the decade, but over ten years later, Haitian Bleu has yet to find its footing on the market. "Haitian Bleu is like a bison," says Wiener, commenting on the brand's scarcity. "Have you ever seen a bison? Have you seen Haitian Bleu coffee? Money was pumped into marketing, but the existing supply chain was not modernized."

Wiener blames mistrust of the private sector for the USAID initiative's failure to engage companies like Café Selecto—and its failure to produce a viable Haitian brand. "They considered the private sector as people who take advantage of the farmer. And then everybody had that image." Wiener argues that the industry has grown more inclusive, explaining that the younger generation of Haitian entrepreneurs understands that in order to have a sustainable supply chain, everyone has to profit. "We're all in the same boat. We need to reinvest and reinvest and reinvest."

While the Café Selecto brand and the coffee industry at large have suffered from Haiti's political instability as much as from foreign misperception, Wiener still sees vast potential in the niche coffee product Haiti can produce. "Haitian coffee is very valuable. We have the only old species left, called the Tipika tree. I am trying to capitalize on this in the fourth generation." Indeed, in spite of low production, Haitian coffee continues to sell at a price several percentage points higher than coffee from other countries.

When asked about adding even more value to his product through fair-trade certification, Wiener is more skeptical. "It's a market," he says, "but I think there is something beyond fair-trade now." Third-party fair-trade certification is difficult to maintain because of cost and local-market constraints, but social media technologies such as Facebook allow consumers to connect more fully with producers than ever before, potentially eliminating the need for fair-trade certification. "As a business, to get fair-trade certified is at least $4,000 per year," Wiener explains. "That's an extra cost before you get your production out. And for the farmers that group themselves together and sell coffee, they do a little fair trade, but it's not 100 percent of their trade." Of course, farmers associations that struggle to remain competitive would have great difficulty maintaining fair-trade certification.

What then can the international community do to contribute to a sustainable and growing Haitian economy in terms of the coffee industry? Wiener calls out NGOs for branding Haitian exports as cause products and for contributing to a misperception of Haitian industry. "I want these guys—since they have all this power getting donations, getting supplies—I want these guys to come and meet us," says Wiener. "I've studied in the United States. We have the same education. Haitians are not different. Haitian companies are not different from any other companies. I wish they would try to get their orders from local companies first." This failure to recognize Haitian private-sector expertise and production capacity further delegitimizes producers and hinders their competitiveness abroad, and this is in addition to the problematic importation of locally available goods.

Still, international perceptions are slow to change after years of negative portrayals of Haitian business owners—who provide most of the country's few jobs—as exploitative and untrustworthy. The same systematic importation of agricultural products for aid, development, and general operations continues to restrict the positive impact NGOs could have on the Haitian economy, and on developing economies more broadly. Donation-based aid contributes to investment misalignment and does little to create more transactions, which are the lifeblood of all market-based economies.

In Wiener's opinion, NGOs that truly aim to develop Haitian industry should do specific things—such as holding focus groups— to better understand how they can positively impact the economy. If aid is meant to improve the economy in a sustainable way, the international community *must* begin buying agricultural products locally, starting with products such as coffee.

By effectively marketing Haitian coffee as unique and continuing to add value locally, Haitian coffee producers might once again compete on the global commodities market, but as long as the international community and the Haitian private sector are at odds, NGOs will continue to have limited or adverse effects on Haitian industry. Haiti's economic resources have yet to be replenished through donation-based aid. Realigning aid to spur transactions is key to the economic survival and health of industry in the developing world.

Although distribution quotas may be the common measurement by which organizations attempt to justify their work in developing nations, what would happen if the measure of an organization's impact was linked to its contribution to the growth and sustainability of a particular industry? This question is particularly poignant given the huge number of people that a simple product such as coffee can affect.

"Getting the economy sustainable—is that something that sells?" asks Wiener. "I hope it does."

NGOs in Haiti and Around the World:
An Overview

The main way to sustain and grow a market-based economy like Haiti's is to promote transaction. These essential transactions are made possible through entrepreneurship and private business ventures, which are the resource generators of market-based economies that create employment and income by meeting needs profitably. However, there has been a rise and expansion of NGOs around the globe throughout history, including in Haiti, where NGOs hold significant power and influence for Haiti's present and future. According to the UN Office of the Special Envoy for Haiti, 99 percent of post-earthquake foreign aid to Haiti was disbursed through NGOs and private contractors.[1] In this appendix, we will outline the overarching characteristics of NGOs and the relationship that NGOs have with Haiti's market-based system.

Aid Models and Their Priorities

Official developmental assistance (ODA) is funded by donor countries and can come in two forms: bilateral and multilateral. Bilateral ODA includes support provided by a donor government to a recipient country, and is provided by entities such as the United States Agency for International Development (USAID). Through official aid and development agencies, donor governments might administer emergency aid intended to assist recipient governments in short-term disaster relief. Through multilateral

ODA, donor countries can work together to provide financial support or subsidized loans to recipient countries through international institutions such as the World Bank or International Monetary Fund.

Private aid is another important form of aid that is distinct from ODA because it is funded by private individuals and institutions. Compared to ODA, which typically consists of governmental assistance, private aid is administered by NGOs, such as Oxfam, the Red Cross, or the Salvation Army.

The Many Definitions of "Nongovernmental Organization"

The term "nongovernmental organization" is defined in various ways. According to the World Bank, NGOs are "private organizations that pursue activities to relieve suffering, promote the interests of the poor, protect the environment, provide basic social services, or undertake community development."[2] The United Nations further states that the role of NGOs is to advocate for and promote the interests of the poor. The UN goes on to define an NGO as "any non-profit, voluntary citizens' group which is organized on a local, national or international level. Task-oriented and driven by people with a common interest, NGOs perform a variety of services and humanitarian functions, bring citizens' concerns to governments, monitor policies, and encourage political participation at the community level."[3]

USAID provides a simpler definition: "an NGO will be defined broadly to include a wide range of local organizations in countries which are recipients of U.S. foreign assistance."[4] This definition is specifically tailored to describe entities working directly with USAID.

NGOs address a wide range of issues throughout the globe—from Africa to Asia, the Americas to Europe. NGOs are more common in the developing world, where many seek solutions to persistent challenges in sectors such as health, the environment, or politics. NGOs are as diverse as the communities in which they operate, and even the leading global institutions do not agree on one definition.

NGOs can be categorized according to their various orientations (charitable, service, participatory, or empowering) and according to their levels of cooperation (community-based, citywide, national, or international). All NGOs, no matter their level of cooperation, are typically not-for-profit—in contrast to for-profit enterprises—and are also not part of any government. They also address social issues that governments and local institutions may not have the capacity to address, and they address these issues in ways that they deem most beneficial and effective. Finally, since most NGOs operate under a not-for-profit model, they work to procure and distribute preexisting resources instead of generating new resources or profits.

NGOs have been present in Haiti since the mid-1940s, and their numbers have increased ever since. The Haitian Constitution defines an NGO as a "private, apolitical, not-for-profit institution or organization that pursues the objectives of development at the national, departmental, or communal level, and uses resources to realize them."[5]

Although multilateral and bilateral aid have had a significant presence in Haiti over the years, the intervention of private NGOs has consistently increased. Since most donor policies and practices fund NGOs instead of the Haitian government, nearly all aid funds, even government funds, are disbursed through the many NGOs that exist in Haiti.[6]

Understanding NGOs and NPOs[7]

According to the United Nations Environment Programme, types of NGOs and NPOs (nonprofit organizations) can be understood by their orientation and level of operation.

Orientation

Charitable orientation often involves a top-down model effort with little participation by the beneficiaries. It includes NGOs/NPOs with activities directed toward meeting the needs of the poor through activities such as distributing food, clothing, or medicine or providing housing, transportation, and education. These NGOs/NPOs may also undertake relief activities during a natural or manmade disaster.

Service orientation includes NGOs/NPOs designed to foster beneficiary participation in the implementation of programs and services. These NGOs/NPOs might be involved in health services, family planning, or education.

Participatory orientation is characterized by self-help projects where local people are involved in the implementation of a project by contributing cash, tools, land, materials, or labor. In the classic community-development project, participation begins with the definition of the need and continues into the planning and implementation stages. Cooperatives often have a participatory orientation.

Empowering orientation includes NGOs/NPOs that aim to help poor people develop a clearer understanding of the social, political, and economic factors affecting their lives, and to strengthen their awareness of their own potential for self-determination. Sometimes, these groups develop locally and spontaneously around a problem or an issue; at other times, outside help from NGOs plays a facilitating role in their development. In any case, this orientation represents the maximum involvement of the local people, with NGOs serving as facilitators.

Level of Operation

Community-based organizations (CBOs) arise out of people's own initiatives. These can include sports clubs, women's organizations, neighborhood organizations, and religious or educational organizations. There are a wide variety of these organizations, and they can be supported by national or international NGOs, bilateral or multilateral agencies, or they can be independent from outside help. Some are devoted to raising the consciousness of the urban poor or helping them to understand their rights in gaining access to needed services, while others are involved in providing such services.

Citywide organizations include organizations such as the Rotary or Lion's Club, chambers of commerce and industry, coalitions of business, ethnic or educational groups, and associations of community organizations. Some exist for other purposes, and become involved in helping the poor as one of their many activities, while others are created for the specific purpose of helping the poor.

National organizations include those such as the Red Cross, YMCA/YWCA, and professional organizations. Some of these have state and city branches and assist local NGOs.

International organizations range from religious groups to secular agencies such as Redda Barna, Save the Children, Oxfam, CARE, and the Ford and Rockefeller Foundations. Their activities vary from funding local NGOs, institutions, and projects, to implementing the projects themselves.

The Rise of NGOs as Resource Distributors

In the United States, nongovernmental organizations arose during the growth of the antislavery and women's suffrage movements in the late 1800s through the early 1900s, and at that time more than one thousand were registered.[8] NGOs grew rapidly in the 1930s while many nations were addressing the need for disarmament prior to World War II.[9] Following the war, the term "nongovernmental organization" became officially recognized by the United Nations. Through the implementation of the United Nations Charter, the newly established ECOSOC (United Nations Economic and Social Council) was granted the role to "make or initiate studies and reports with respect to international economic, social, cultural, educational, health, and related matters" and to make recommendations to the UN, "promoting respect for, and observance of, human rights and fundamental freedoms for all." Later in the charter, NGOs that held General Consultative Status are described as national or international organizations that are neither governmental nor member states and that work within ECOSOC to advise it in its research and recommendations to the UN. Some of the earliest NGOs in this group were well-known entities such as the International Chamber of Commerce and World Federation of Trade Unions.[10]

NGOs are founded, developed, and managed by civilians. A guidebook from the US Department of Defense outlines some important characteristics of NGOs:

- "NGOs have major global procurement capabilities for relief supplies, technical and capital assets, vehicles, and other material that can be used to respond to humanitarian emergencies. NGOs can be not-for-profit (nonprofit)."

- "NGOs require funding from external sources to design, implement, and manage their programming."

- "NGOs obtain funding from numerous sources including government agencies, private foundation grants, and private contributions or gifts-in-kind from companies and other organizations."

- "Donations of cash, material, or even services (legal, technological, and the like) to NGOs normally qualify as charitable gifts and can be used to lower tax liability for the donor."[11]

As television, radio, and internet coverage of world conflicts has expanded in recent decades, the exposure of social issues around the world provided a new opportunity for NGOs to offer services in a wide range of regions, locally and globally. Also, highly pronounced humanitarian crises such as civil wars in Darfur, Eastern Europe and Central Africa; famines, natural disasters, and tsunamis in countries including Ethiopia, Haiti, and Japan, respectively; and chronic poverty throughout many parts of the developing world have provided much of the basis for NGOs to multiply in size and scope.

As the US Department of Defense guidebook recounts, "in June 1997, the vital role of NGOs and other major groups in sustainable development was recognized" by the United Nations, "leading to intense arrangements for a consultative relationship between the United Nations and nongovernmental organizations. Globalization throughout the twentieth century heightened the importance of NGOs, which have since developed to emphasize humanitarian issues, developmental aid, and sustainable development."[12] These needs have been embraced as an invitation for NGOs to provide goods and services through their own structures.

In the twenty-first century, the presence of NGOs worldwide has grown to an unprecedented level: "More than 90 percent of aid coordinated by the United Nations is provided by NGOs, 95 percent of which is provided by only 35 to 40 major American and European organizations," and within the NGO community "faith-based organizations are the largest growing group of NGOs and accounted for 10.5 percent of USAID dollars to nongovernmental aid organizations in fiscal 2001, and 19.9 percent in 2005."[13]

Around the globe, the total number of NGOs has increased. In the United States alone there are approximately 1.5 million NGOs,[14] whereas Russia has 277,000,[15] and India nearly 3.3 million—approximately one NGO per four hundred Indians.[16]

NGOs in Haiti

In Haiti, a country with a population of only ten million, respected sources estimate that there are between ten and twenty thousand NGOs total, roughly one NGO for every five hundred to one thousand people.

However, the Haitian Ministry of Planning only recorded a total of 134 legally registered NGOs between 1947 and 1994—the year in which a coup d'état overturned President Aristide. From that year until 2005, the same ministry reported an increase to 343 registered NGOs—a growth of 156 percent in a decade.[17]

In October 2013, the Haitian government reported just six hundred formally registered NGOs, which is a far cry from the true number of organizations operating in Haiti. Even on the conservative estimate of ten thousand NGOs in Haiti, an overwhelming majority of these organizations operate illegally, even though many have made appropriate steps and applied to become legally registered.[18]

NGOs play such a crucial role in Haitian society that they have a place in the Haitian Constitution. The Haitian government's Ministry of Planning has the right to recognize or deny an NGO's legal status; in addition, among the key characteristics required for an NGO to have legal status in Haiti are that it must be private, not-for-profit, "engaged in development," and "apolitical."[19] Furthermore, "smaller groups—grassroots organizations and sometimes missionary groups—are supposed to register directly with the appropriate ministry" such as the Ministry of Women's Condition, Agriculture and Natural Resources, or Social Affairs and Labor. According to Mark Schuller, "NGOs follow a complex process whereby they submit their paperwork to the [Ministry of Planning and External Cooperation], which conducts 'reconnaissance' visits and then forwards the application to an inter-sectorial group that reviews materials such as workplans and budgets." As many NGOs have experienced, the application process can be lengthy and, at times, confusing.[20]

Governmental Programs and Their Support for NGOs

Many institutions that provide humanitarian and development aid are not NGOs; rather, they are government corporations that support other countries in disaster response and development through grants, subsidized loans, and nonfinancial partnerships. The most prominent foreign agencies in Haiti are the United States Agency for International Development (USAID), the European Commission's Humanitarian Aid and Civil Protection Department (ECHO), and the Organization for Economic Co-operation and Development (OECD). These institutions provide support for environmental care, economic development, political stability, disaster relief, and social issues, and they tend to provide support to their political allies bilaterally.

Let's take a closer look at the four largest governmental programs (USAID, ECHO, and OECD) and the ongoing role of official developmental assistance.

United States Agency for International Development (USAID)

Of the State Department's $51.6 billion annual budget, USAID received approximately $3.8 billion in 2011. USAID's stated purpose is to "advance the national security interests of the United States through global engagement, partnerships with nations and their people, and the promotion of universal values." The agency invests in diplomacy and development to foster national security, "[open] new markets for US businesses," and "[increase] trade."[21]

USAID considers NGOs "critical change agents in promoting economic growth, human rights and social progress." The organization often partners with NGOs across projects and programs to "strengthen their capacity to achieve their missions."[22]

European Commission's Humanitarian Aid and Civil Protection Department (ECHO)

Formerly known as the European Community Humanitarian Aid Office, ECHO is another governmental organization that directly funds and supports NGOs. Based in Brussels, Belgium, ECHO is now a department of the European Union's executive commission and has over two hundred staff based at its headquarters and four hundred more around the globe. They provide emergency response after natural disasters or manmade crises in over 140 countries. Since 1992, ECHO has worked closely with NGOs by performing needs assessments, monitoring the implementation of crisis response, and evaluating results.

According to ECHO's website, "nongovernmental organizations (NGOs) have become essential actors in the social field, particularly in the fight against poverty and social exclusion. They engage in regular dialogue with public authorities with a view to ensuring better implementation of EU initiatives and policies in the EU countries."[23]

Since its inception, ECHO has provided €14 billion (approximately $18.6 billion) of humanitarian assistance and has an annual budget of over €1 billion. In 2011, ECHO assisted 117 million of the world's most vulnerable people in over ninety countries outside of the European Union.[24]

Organization for Economic Co-operation and Development (OECD)

Other governments around the globe, including Japan, South Korea, Venezuela, Brazil, and Cuba, are involved in international development, humanitarian work, and crisis response. These governmental organizations partner with foreign governments and provide direct support to infrastructure. They also provide support to international and local NGOs, through in-kind assistance and financial grants. The OECD was formed in 1960,[25] representing the donor countries Belgium, Canada, France, Germany, Italy, Portugal, United Kingdom, and the United States. Within months, Japan and the Netherlands joined.

The Ongoing Role of Official Developmental Assistance (ODA)

The phrase "official developmental assistance" (ODA) was first established by the OECD. The Development Assistance Committee of the OECD provides soft loans to poorer developing countries starting at $900 million. Since its establishment, OECD member countries have committed an average of 0.7 percent of their own GNP annually, which is then administered by the World Bank.[26] According to the OECD, ODA financing is "administered with the promotion of the economic development and welfare of developing countries as the main objective," and is "concessional in character." In addition, at least 25 percent of ODA financing must be provided as a grant. Further, "ODA flows comprise contributions of donor government agencies, at all levels, to developing countries ('bilateral ODA') and to multilateral institutions."[27]

According to the OECD, African countries have received $28 billion, the largest amount of ODA in 2009, including $25 billion to sub-Saharan countries, with Sudan and Ethiopia leading in ODA received. The second largest amount, $24 billion, was designated to developing countries in Asia. Afghanistan alone received $5.1 billion, and Iraq received $2.6 billion for recovery. As described by Global Humanitarian Assistance, "between 2003 and 2012 Haiti received US$10.6 billion in official development assistance (ODA), making it the 20th largest recipient. In the same 10-year period the proportion of ODA given as humanitarian assistance averaged 19%, ranging from 55% in 2010 to 5% in 2003. Haiti received the equivalent of 17% of its gross national income (GNI) as aid (ODA) in 2012."[28] In addition to the ODA, in 2012 Haiti also received other forms of private aid, together totaling $1.3 billion in assistance;[29] that same year, they generate a GDP of $7.89 billion, a mere $775 per person.[30]

Although total ODA represents a significant figure, it only accounted for 7 percent of the estimated $1.7 trillion of international aid that flows to developing countries. In fact, ODA grew by 63 percent over a decade, reaching a peak of $128.5 billion in 2010.

The United States is the largest source of ODA with an average of $30 billion annually from 2009 through 2011, despite the 2008 recession. Five countries—the United States, Germany, the United Kingdom, France, and Japan—provide almost two-thirds of ODA.[31] Today, more than three-quarters of ODA is administered through the United Nations, World Bank, and European Union. The governments of developing countries can use ODA to support a wide variety of activities, most commonly infrastructure, governance, agricultural production, education, health, water and sanitation, conflict and emergency relief, food security, and social protection. The well-known Millennium Development Goals were initiated in 2000 by the United Nations to eliminate extreme poverty by 2015. Part of the UN's strategy is a commitment from donor countries to increase ODA by $50 billion to a total of $154.5 billion by 2010.[32]

Conclusion

Despite these massive efforts and generous contributions, these resources are still channeled through resource distributors instead of resource generators, and as this appendix shows, NGOs and countries contributing through ODA continue to have a strong foothold in determining Haiti's future. Looking forward, the challenge is to move from aid to trade and to align all actors with Haiti's market-based economy. We are at a crucial point to make these changes toward trade. Case in point: Of the $148 billion of ODA disbursed in 2010, only 1.35 percent of ODA was utilized as equity investment, which was most often directed to fund activities such as agricultural development, health, and education.[33] Had more ODA funds been utilized to support businesses, nations like Haiti might by now be further along the development curve. In fact, the Millennium Development Goal to eliminate extreme poverty by 2015 could have been reached already, not through generous ODA aid, but through strategies that equip and catalyze local businesses to enter the global market and increase trade so that individuals and families can raise *themselves* out of poverty.[34] With this background on the presence of NGOs in Haiti and the use of significant contributions being made through ODA, it would appear that moving forward there is only room for improvements.

Notes

CHAPTER 1: The Tragedy of Auguste Savonnerie: How International Donations Killed a Successful Haitian Business

1. "MINUSTAH Fact Sheet," United Nations Stabilization Mission in Haiti, Jan. 2012, http://www.minustah.org/pdfs/fact_sheet/FactSheetMINUSTAH_2012_jan_Report_EN.pdf.

2. Daniele Lantagne, G. Balakrish Nair, Claudio F. Lanata, and Alejandro Cravioto, "The Cholera Outbreak in Haiti: Where and How Did It Begin?," *Current Topics in Microbiology and Immunology* 379 (2014): 145–64, doi:10.1007/82_2013_331.

3. *Cholera in Haiti. An End in Sight* (United Nations in Haiti, 2013), 23, http://www.humanitarianresponse.info/system/files/documents/files/UNhaitiCholeraBrochure20131216low.pdf.

CHAPTER 2: Business, Government, and NGOs: The Major Players in Haiti's Economic System

1. "The World's Next Great Leap Forward: Towards the End of Poverty," *The Economist*, June 1, 2013, http://www.economist.com/news/leaders/21578665-nearly-1-billion-people-have-been-taken-out-extreme-poverty-20-years-world-should-aim.

CHAPTER 3: The History of Haiti's Market-Based Economy from the Precolonial Years to the Present

1. Franklin W. Knight, "Regional Overview," in *Islands of the Commonwealth Caribbean: A Regional Study*, ed. Sandra W. Meditz and Dennis M. Hanratty (Washington, DC: Federal Research Division, Library of Congress, 1989), 1–23, http://www.loc.gov/item/88600483/.

2. Mats Lundahl, *The Political Economy of Disaster: Destitution, Plunder and Earthquake in Haiti* (Abingdon, UK: Routledge, 2013), 6–12.

3. Mats Lundahl, "Haiti," in *History of World Trade Since 1450*, ed. John J. McCusker, vol. 1 (Farmington Hills, MI: Macmillan Reference USA, 2006), 345.

4. Robert I. Rotberg, *Haiti: The Politics of Squalor* (Boston: Houghton Mifflin, 1971), 25–29.

5. See T. S. Ashton, *The Industrial Revolution (1760–1830)* (London: Oxford University Press, 1948).

6. Franklin W. Knight, "The Haitian Revolution and the Notion of Human Rights," *The Journal of the Historical Society* 5, no. 3 (2005): 396–97, doi:10.1111/j.1540-5923.2005 .00136.x.

7. Jack R. Censer and Lynn Hunt, *Liberty, Equality, Fraternity: Exploring the French Revolution* (University Park: Pennsylvania State University Press, 2001), 123–24.

8. Censer and Hunt, *Liberty, Equality, Fraternity*, 124–26.

9. "Haitian Constitution of 1801," http://college.cengage.com/history/world/keen/ latin_america/8e/assets/students/sources/pdfs/33_haitian_constitution_1801.pdf.

10. Censer and Hunt, *Liberty, Equality, Fraternity*, 127–28.

11. Lundahl, "Haiti," 345.

12. See C. L. R. James, *The Black Jacobins: Toussaint L'Ouverture and the San Domingo Revolution*, 2nd ed. (N.p.: Vintage, n.d.), 293–321.

13. William Loren Katz, "Toussaint L'Ouverture and the Haitian Revolution," http:// people.hofstra.edu/alan_j_singer/CoursePacks/ToussaintLOuvertureandtheHaitian Revolution.pdf.

14. Robert K. Lacerte, "Xenophobia and Economic Decline: The Haitian Case, 1820–1843," *The Americas* 37, no. 4 (1981): 499, http://www.jstor.org/stable/980837.

15. Lacerte, "Xenophobia and Economic Decline," 505–6.

16. Lacerte, "Xenophobia and Economic Decline," 504.

17. Brown, *Toussaint's Clause*, 292–95; "The United States and the Haitian Revolution, 1791–1804," US Department of State, Office of the Historian, https://history.state.gov/ milestones/1784-1800/haitian-rev.

18. Robert Debs Heinl and Nancy Gordon Heinl, *Written in Blood: The Story of the Haitian People 1492–1995*, Rev. ed. (Lanham, MD: University Press of America, 2005), 323–75

19. Brenda Gayle Plummer, "Race, Nationality, and Trade in the Caribbean: The Syrians in Haiti, 1903–1934," *The International History Review* 3, no. 4 (1981): 521, http://www .jstor.org/stable/40105175.

20. Patricia Schutt-Ainé, ed., *Haiti: A Basic Reference Book: General Information on Haiti* (Miami: Librairie Au Service de la Culture, 1994), 44.

21. Brian Weinstein and Aaron Segal, *Haiti: The Failure of Politics* (New York: Praeger, 1992), 25–28.

22. Weinstein and Segal, *Haiti*, 63, 40; Chantal Hudicourt Ewald, "The Legal System of Haiti," in *Modern Legal Systems Cyclopedia*, ed. Kenneth R. Redden and William E. Brock, vol. 7, pt. 1 (Buffalo, NY: W. S. Hein, 1989), 7.210.7, 7.210.9.

23. Nick Davis, "The Massacre that Marked Haiti–Dominican Republic Ties," BBC News, Oct. 13, 2012, http://www.bbc.com/news/world-latin-america-19880967; Lundahl, "Haiti," 346; Michele Wucker, "Race & Massacre in Hispaniola," *Tikkun* 13, no. 6 (1998): 61, http://www.tikkun.org/article.php/nov1998_wucker.

24. Lundahl, "Haiti," 346.

25. Anne Green, "Haiti: Historical Setting," in *Dominican Republic and Haiti: Country Studies*, ed. Helen Chapin Metz, 3rd ed. (Washington, DC: Federal Research Division, Library of Congress, 2001), 286–87, http://www.loc.gov/item/2001023524/.

26. Anne Green, "Haiti: Historical Setting," 288.

27. Derek E. Hemenway, Faranak Rohani, and F. J. King, *Cuban, Haitian, and Bosnian Refugees in Florida: Problems and Obstacles in Resettlement* (Florida Department of Children and Families, Refugee Programs Administration, June 1999), 30–31, http://www.cala.fsu .edu/files/refugee_lit_review.pdf.

28. Fred Doura, *Haïti: histoire et analyse d'une extraversion dépendante organisée* (Montreal: Éditions DAMI, 2010), 101–8.

29. Lundahl, "Haiti," 346.

30. Rémy Montas, ed., *La Pauvrete en Haïti: situation, causes et politiques de sortie* (Commission Economique pour l'Amérique Latine et les Caraïbes [United Nations ECLAC], Aug. 2005), http://www.cepal.org/fr/publicaciones/25746-la-pauvrete-en-haiti -situation-causes-et-politiques-de-sortie.

31. Garry Pierre-Pierre, "Haiti is Suffering Under Oil Embargo," *The New York Times*, Nov. 3, 1993, http://www.nytimes.com/1993/11/03/world/haiti-is-suffering-under-oil -embargo.html.

32. Paul Altidor, "Impacts of Trade Liberalization Policies on Rice Production in Haiti" (master's thesis, MIT, 2004), 21, http://dspace.mit.edu/bitstream/handle/1721.1/28350/ 56025477.pdf?sequence=1.

33. Celine Charveriat and Penny Fowler, "Rice Dumping in Haiti and the Development Box Proposal," Institute for Agriculture and Trade Policy, Mar. 2002, http://www.iatp.org/ files/Rice_Dumping_in_Haiti_and_the_Development_Box_.htm.

34. Mark Weisbrot, Jake Johnston, and Rebecca Ray, *Using Food Aid to Support, Not Harm, Haitian Agriculture* (Center for Economic and Policy Research, Apr. 2010), 2, http:// www.cepr.net/documents/publications/haiti-2010-04.pdf.

35. Lundahl, "Haiti," 346.

36. Pascal Fletcher, "Food Dependency Is Poverty Trap for Quake-Hit Haiti," Reuters, Mar. 26, 2010, http://www.reuters.com/article/2010/03/26/us-quake-haiti-food-idUSTRE 62P2EU20100326.

37. Fletcher, "Food Dependency Is Poverty Trap."

38. "Rebuilding Haiti: Open for Business," *The Economist*, Jan. 5, 2012, http://www .economist.com/node/21542407.

39. "Key Sectors: Telecommunications," Centre for Facilitation of Investments, http:// cfihaiti.com/sectorspdf/Telecommunications.pdf (site no longer available).

40. "Key Sectors: Tourism," Centre for Facilitation of Investments, http://cfihaiti.com/ sectorspdf/Tourism.pdf (site no longer available).

41. "Table 6.14: World Development Indicators: Travel and Tourism," World Bank, http://wdi.worldbank.org/table/6.14.

42. "Key Sectors: Manufacturing," Centre for Facilitation of Investments, http://cfihaiti .com/sectorspdf/manu.pdf (site no longer available).

43. "Key Sectors: Manufacturing," Centre for Facilitation of Investments, http://cfihaiti .com/sectorspdf/manu.pdf (site no longer available).

44. "Caracol Industrial Park," USAID, Jan. 28, 2015, http://www.usaid.gov/haiti/caracol -industrial-park.

CHAPTER 4: An Abundance of NGOs: How International Aid Contributed to a Failed State

1. Unni Karunakara, "Haiti: Where Aid Failed," *The Guardian*, Dec. 28, 2010, http://www.theguardian.com/commentisfree/2010/dec/28/haiti-cholera-earthquake-aid-agencies-failure.

2. "Nobody Remembers Us," Human Rights Watch, Aug. 30, 2011, http://www.hrw.org:8080/es/node/101165/section/2.

3. Mark Schuller, "Invasion or Infusion? Understanding the Role of NGOs in Contemporary Haiti," *The Journal of Haitian Studies* 13, no. 2 (2007): 103–5, http://www.hrdf.org/files/schuller-invasion-or-infusion.pdf.

4. Vijaya Ramachandran and Julie Walz, "Haiti: Where Has All the Money Gone?," CGD Policy Paper 004 (Washington, DC: Center for Global Development, 2012), 5, 7, http://www.cgdev.org/files/1426185_file_Ramachandran_Walz_haiti_FINAL.pdf.

5. Ramachandran and Walz, "Haiti: Where Has All the Money Gone?," 6.

6. "Haiti - Economy: The Draft Amending Budget 2011–2012 Criticized," *Haiti Libre*, Jan. 25, 2012, http://www.haitilibre.com/en/news-4802-haiti-economy-the-draft-amending-budget-2011-2012-criticized.html.

7. "GDP (current US$)," World Bank, http://data.worldbank.org/indicator/NY.GDP.MKTP.CD.

8. Ramachandran and Walz, "Haiti: Where Has All the Money Gone?," 7.

9. "Haiti Received Record-High Foreign Direct Investment in 2011: Report," *Caribbean Journal*, May 7, 2012, http://www.caribjournal.com/2012/05/07/haiti-received-record-high-foreign-direct-investment-in-2011-report/.

10. "Haitian Companies Still Sidelined from Reconstruction Contracts," Center for Economic and Policy Research, Apr. 19, 2011, http://www.cepr.net/index.php/blogs/relief-and-reconstruction-watch/haitian-companies-still-sidelined-from-reconstruction-contracts.

11. Martha Mendoza, "Would-be Haitian Contractors Miss Out on Aid," *Boston Haitian Reporter*, Jan. 14, 2011, http://www.bostonhaitian.com/2011/would-be-haitian-contractors-miss-out-aid.

12. Ramachandran and Walz, "Haiti: Where Has All the Money Gone?," 13.

13. Paul Farmer, "Testimonial to the Congressional Black Caucus: Focus on Haiti" (Office of the Secretary-General's Special Adviser on Community-Based Medicine & Lessons from Haiti, July 27, 2010), http://www.lessonsfromhaiti.org/press-and-media/transcripts/farmer-caucus/.

14. Jake Johnston and Alexander Main, *Breaking Open the Black Box: Increasing Aid Transparency and Accountability in Haiti* (Center for Economic and Policy Research, Apr. 2013), 3–11, http://www.cepr.net/documents/publications/haiti-aid-accountability-2013-04.pdf.

15. Johnston and Main, *Breaking Open the Black Box*, 3.

16. "GDP per capita (2005 PPP$)," United Nations Development Programme, https://data.undp.org/dataset/GDP-per-capita-2005-PPP-/navj-mda7.

17. *Haiti: Country Strategy* (Inter-American Development Bank), I.1.2, http://idbdocs

.iadb.org/wsdocs/getdocument.aspx?docnum=36600159; "Table 2.9: World Development Indicators: Distribution of Income or Consumption," World Bank, http://data.worldbank .org/indicator/SI.POV.GINI?page=2, and http://wdi.worldbank.org/table/2.9. The most recent Gini Index survey in Haiti was conducted in 2001.

18. *Haiti: Country Strategy*, I.1.2.

19. "Corruption by Country/Territory," Transparency International, 2014, http://www .transparency.org/country#HTI.

20. "The World Factbook," Central Intelligence Agency, Apr. 10, 2015, https://www.cia .gov/library/publications/the-world-factbook/geos/ha.html.

21. "World Development Indicators," World Bank, http://data.worldbank.org/country/ haiti, and http://databank.worldbank.org/data/views/reports/tableview.aspx.

22. "Haiti Balance of Trade," Trading Economics, 2014, http://www.tradingeconomics .com/haiti/balance-of-trade.

23. *Haiti: Country Strategy*, I.1.2–3.

24. "The Fragile States Index Rankings 2014," The Fund for Peace, http://library.fund forpeace.org/library/cfsir1423-fragilestatesindex2014-06d.pdf.

CHAPTER 5: Making the Move from Aid to Trade: Opportunity-Based Economic Development (OBED) and the Power of Balanced Transactions

1. "Jobs Are a Cornerstone of Development, Says World Development Report 2013," World Bank, Oct. 1, 2012, http://www.worldbank.org/en/news/press-release/2012/10/01/ jobs-cornerstone-development-says-world-development-report.

2. "Enabling Poor Rural People to Overcome Poverty in Brazil," International Fund for Agricultural Development, Nov. 2011, http://www.ifad.org/operations/projects/regions/ PL/factsheet/brazil_e.pdf.

3. World Travel & Tourism Council, "Benchmark Report - Brazil," May 2015, 1, http:// www.wttc.org/-/media/files/reports/benchmark%20reports/country%20reports%202015/ brazil%20%20benchmarking%20report%202015.pdf.

4. "Poverty headcount ratio at national poverty lines (% of population)," World Bank, http://data.worldbank.org/indicator/SI.POV.NAHC/countries/BR?display=graph.

5. "The World Factbook," Central Intelligence Agency, Apr. 10, 2015, https://www.cia .gov/library/publications/the-world-factbook/geos/br.html.

6. "Ricepedia: Brazil," Global Rice Science Partnership, http://ricepedia.org/brazil.

7. Antony Sguazzin, "Brazil Starts Rice Exports to S. Africa, Competes with Thailand," Bloomberg, July 28, 2011, http://www.bloomberg.com/news/articles/2011-07-28/brazil -competes-with-thailand-with-start-of-rice-exports-to-south-africa.

8. "Ricepedia: Brazil."

9. "Brazil Agriculture," http://www.brazil.org.za/agriculture.html#.VPEv1vmUePU.

10. "Brazil Unemployment Rate," Trading Economics, http://www.tradingeconomics .com/brazil/unemployment-rate.

11. "Global Economic Woes Threaten Efforts to Eradicate Poverty through Decent, Productive Work, Commission for Social Development Told," UN Commission for Social

Development, Economic and Social Council, Feb. 2, 2012, http://www.un.org/News/Press/docs/2012/soc4789.doc.htm.

12. "2013 Investment Climate Statement - Brazil," US Department of State, Feb. 2013, http://www.state.gov/e/eb/rls/othr/ics/2013/204608.htm.

13. "Russia Exports," Trading Economics, http://www.tradingeconomics.com/russia/exports.

14. "World Factbook," Central Intelligence Agency, https://www.cia.gov/library/publications/the-world-factbook/geos/rs.html.

15. "World Factbook," Central Intelligence Agency, https://www.cia.gov/library/publications/the-world-factbook/geos/rs.html.

16. "World Factbook," Central Intelligence Agency, https://www.cia.gov/library/publications/the-world-factbook/rankorder/2001rank.html.

17. "GDP Growth (annual %)," World Bank, http://data.worldbank.org/indicator/NY.GDP.MKTP.KD.ZG?order=wbapi_data_value_1984%20wbapi_data_value%20wbapi_data_value-first&sort=asc.

18. "India: Unemployment rate from 2010 to 2014," Statista, http://www.statista.com/statistics/271330/unemployment-rate-in-india/.

19. "Unemployment, total (% of total labor force) (modeled ILO estimate)," World Bank, http://data.worldbank.org/indicator/SL.UEM.TOTL.ZS.

20. "India: Unemployment rate from 2010 to 2014," Statista, http://www.statista.com/statistics/271330/unemployment-rate-in-india/.

21. Elizabeth J. Perry and Christine Wong, "The Political Economy of Reform in Post-Mao China: Causes, Content, and Consequences," in *The Political Economy of Reform in Post-Mao China*, ed. Elizabeth J. Perry and Christine Wong (Cambridge, MA: Harvard University Press, 1985), 1–10.

22. On this era of economic development in China, see the essays in Y. C. Jao and C. K. Leung, eds., *China's Special Economic Zones: Policies, Problems and Prospects* (New York: Oxford University Press, 1986).

23. "The World's Next Great Leap Forward: Towards the End of Poverty," *The Economist*, June 1, 2013, http://www.economist.com/news/leaders/21578665-nearly-1-billion-people-have-been-taken-out-extreme-poverty-20-years-world-should-aim.

24. "Fragile States Index," *Foreign Policy*, http://foreignpolicy.com/fragile-states-2014/#rankings.

25. Michael Nowak, "The First Ten Years After Apartheid: An Overview of the South African Economy," in *Post-Apartheid South Africa: The First Ten Years*, ed. Michael Nowak and Luca Antonio Ricci (Washington, DC: International Monetary Fund, 2005), 1–10, http://www.imf.org/external/pubs/nft/2006/soafrica/eng/pasoafr/pasoafr.pdf.

26. Nowak, "The First Ten Years After Apartheid," 8.

CHAPTER 6: **Implementing the OBED Strategy: First Steps in Transforming Aid into Trade**

1. "History," Cimenterie Nationale Haiti, http://www.cina.com.ht/about-us/history.

2. "Groupe Financier National (GFN)," Unibank, https://www.unibankhaiti.com/a -propos/groupe-financier-national-gfn/unifinance.

3. Jon Henley, "Haiti: A Long Descent to Hell," *The Guardian*, Jan. 14, 2010, http:// www.theguardian.com/world/2010/jan/14/haiti-history-earthquake-disaster.

4. "Three Distinct Layers of Policies Are Needed," World Bank, http://go.worldbank .org/ULGUQGKUM0.

5. Joseph Schumpeter, *Capitalism, Socialism, and Democracy* (New York: Harper Colophon, 1976), 83.

6. Schumpeter, *Capitalism, Socialism, and Democracy*, 82–83.

7. Willys Geffrard (Country Director, World Renew), in discussion with the authors, Dec. 22, 2012.

8. Kees de Gier (Co-owner, Maxima S.A.), in discussion with the authors, May 5, 2014.

9. Duong Huynh, Janaki Kibe, Josie McVitty, Delphine Sangodeyi, Surili Sheth, Paul-Emile Simon, and David Smith, *Housing Delivery and Housing Finance in Haiti: Operationalizing the National Housing Policy* (Oxfam America Research Backgrounder Series, 2013), 62, http://www.oxfamamerica.org/static/media/files/housing-delivery-and -housing-finance-in-haiti.pdf.

10. Jacqueline Klamer, "New Hope for Haiti's Recovery," *UrbanFaith*, Feb. 26, 2010, http://www.urbanfaith.com/2010/02/new-hope-for-haitis-recovery.html/.

CHAPTER 7: Methods for Supporting Business Growth

1. Ken Michel, in discussion with the authors, Dec. 22, 2012.

2. Austin Holmes (Director of Business Development, Mission of Hope), in discussion with the authors, May 15, 2014.

3. "About Haiti," Mission of Hope Haiti, http://www.mohhaiti.org/about_haiti#.VO6 WbfmUePU.

4. Salim Loxley (Country Director, Peace Dividend Trust), in discussion with the authors, Feb. 19, 2014.

5. "Our Impact," Building Markets, http://www.buildingmarkets.org/our-impact.

6. Jean-Ronel Noël (Co-Owner, ENERSA), in discussion with the authors, May 8, 2014.

7. Jaeah Lee, "Haiti Searches for a Solar Future," Mother Jones, Jan. 28, 2011, http:// www.motherjones.com/environment/2011/01/haiti-searches-solar-future.

8. Lee, "Haiti Searches for a Solar Future."

9. Alissa Orlando, "Developing Haiti's Domestic Solar Industries," Global Risk Insights, June 21, 2013, http://globalriskinsights.com/2013/06/developing-haitis-domestic-solar -industries/.

10. "Design and Implementation of Haiti Trade Information Portal (HTIP), 2014–2015," Nathan Associates, Inc., http://www.nathaninc.com/projects-and-cases/ design-and-implementation-haiti-trade-information-portal-htip-2014%E2%80%932015.

11. "Trade in Haiti: Chicken and Eggs," *The Economist*, Aug. 24, 2013, http://www .economist.com/news/americas/21584012-haitis-government-tries-risky-experiment -industrial-policy-chickens-and-eggs.

12. Matthew Flippen (CEO, TopLine Materiaux de Construction), in discussion with the authors, Nov. 10, 2013.

13. Doug Seebeck (President, Partners Worldwide), in discussion with interviewer Christopher Cartright, Sept. 20, 2013; Dave Genzink (Regional Facilitator of the Caribbean, Partners Worldwide), in discussion with Christopher Cartright, Sept. 29, 2013. Special thanks to Christopher Cartright for interviewing Seebeck and Genzink and for assisting in the writing of this case study.

14. *The State of Food Insecurity in the World 2006* (Rome: Food and Agriculture Organization, 2006), ftp://ftp.fao.org/docrep/fao/009/a0750e/a0750e00.pdf.

CHAPTER 8: **Destructive Aid Models: A Response to Recent Changes in NGO Practices**

1. "History of Feed My Starving Children," Feed My Starving Children, http://www.fmsc.org/aboutus/history-of-fmsc.

2. *Kids Against Hunger: Satellite Operating Procedures Manual* (Kids Against Hunger Coalition, 2012), 26, http://www.illinifightinghunger.org/wp-content/uploads/2012/08/Sat_Ops_Manual_Part1.pdf.

3. Steve Pardo, "USS Normandy Diverted from Middle East to Help Haitians," *The Detroit News*, Feb. 4, 2010, http://www.kidsagainsthungercoalition.com/index.php?option=com_content&view=article&id=112:steve-pardo&catid=1:latest-news&Itemid=71.

4. Chessney Barrick Pullen, "Thank You for Your Continued Response to the Crisis in Haiti," https://www.causes.com/posts/299741-thank-you-for-your-continued-response-to-the-crisis-in-haiti.

5. Jacqueline Charles, "Haiti Learning to Burn Trash Briquettes, Instead of Trees," McClatchey-Tribune News Service, Dec. 21, 2009, http://www.cleveland.com/world/index.ssf/2009/12/haiti_learning_to_burn_trash_b.html.

6. Gemma Pitcher, "Clearing Haiti's Streets of Rubbish Means Clearing Crime Too," Environment News Service, June 7, 2010, http://www.ens-newswire.com/ens/jun2010/2010-06-07-03.html.

7. Bryan Schaaf, "Haiti Turning Garbage Into Energy," Haiti Innovation, Dec. 18, 2009, http://haitiinnovation.org/en/2009/12/18/haiti-turning-garbage-energy.

8. Pitcher, "Clearing Haiti's Streets of Rubbish."

9. Amy Bracken, "In Haiti, Success Isn't Enough to Keep Innovative Energy Program Alive," Public Radio International, Nov. 2, 2012, http://www.pri.org/stories/2012-11-02/haiti-success-isnt-enough-keep-innovative-energy-program-alive.

10. Bracken, "In Haiti, Success Isn't Enough."

11. Mats Lundahl, *The Political Economy of Disaster: Destitution, Plunder and Earthquake in Haiti* (Abingdon, UK: Routledge, 2013), 166–68.

12. Lundahl, *The Political Economy of Disaster, 166–68.*

13. Lundahl, *The Political Economy of Disaster, 166–68.*

14. Luke Dunnington and Tom Lenaghan, "A Case Study in Brand Creation with Small Holders - Haitian Bleu®," Center for Facilitation of Investments, http://cfihaiti.net/pdf/coffee-industry.pdf.

15. Dunnington and Lenaghan, "A Case Study in Brand Creation."

16. Dunnington and Lenaghan, "A Case Study in Brand Creation."

17. Dunnington and Lenaghan, "A Case Study in Brand Creation."

18. Dunnington and Lenaghan, "A Case Study in Brand Creation."

19. Dunnington and Lenaghan, "A Case Study in Brand Creation."

20. Dunnington and Lenaghan, "A Case Study in Brand Creation."

21. Dunnington and Lenaghan, "A Case Study in Brand Creation."

22. Jennifer Ward Barber, "Haiti's Coffee: Will It Come Back?" *The Atlantic*, Jan. 27, 2010, http://www.theatlantic.com/health/archive/2010/01/haitis-coffee-will-it-come-back/34264/.

23. Anonymous source (Oxfam Québec), in discussion with the authors, Dec. 21, 2012; Max Jean (General Coordinator, NOVEDEHM), in discussion with the authors, Dec. 15, 2012.

24. Quoted in Weisbrot, Johnston, and Ray, *Using Food Aid, 1.*

25. Alex Dupuy, "Disaster Capitalism to the Rescue: The International Community and Haiti after the Earthquake," *NACLA Report on the Americas* 43, no. 4 (2010): n.p., https://nacla.org/article/disaster-capitalism-rescue-international-community-and-haiti-after-earthquake.

26. Dupuy, "Disaster Capitalism to the Rescue."

27. Dupuy, "Disaster Capitalism to the Rescue"; Jonathan M. Katz, "With Cheap Food Imports, Haiti Can't Feed Itself," *The Huffington Post*, May 20, 2010, http://www.huffingtonpost.com/2010/03/20/with-cheap-food-imports-h_n_507228.html.

28. Dupuy, "Disaster Capitalism to the Rescue."

29. Yasmine Shamsie, "Haiti's Post-Earthquake Transformation: What of Agriculture and Rural Development?," *Latin American Politics and Society* 54, no. 2 (2012): 135, doi:*10.1111/j.1548-2456.2012.00156.x.*

30. Dupuy, "Disaster Capitalism to the Rescue."

31. Rachel Trego, *Rice Production and Trade Update* (USDA Foreign Agricultural Service, GAIN Report, Nov. 7, 2013), 3, http://gain.fas.usda.gov/Recent%20GAIN%20Publications/Rice%20Production%20and%20Trade%20Update_Santo%20Domingo_Haiti_11-7-2013.pdf.

32. Josiane Georges, "Trade and the Disappearance of Haitian Rice" *Ted Case Studies*, no. 725 (June 2004), http://www1.american.edu/ted/*haitirice.htm.*

33. "USDA GAIN: Haiti Rice Production and Trade Update," The Crop Site, Nov. 14, 2013, http://www.thecropsite.com/reports/?id=3048.

34. Dupuy, "Disaster Capitalism to the Rescue."

35. Shamsie, "Haiti's Post-Earthquake Transformation," 136.

36. "Haiti Welcomes 2013 with Bold Strategic Alliance with Vietnam," PR Newswire, Jan. 2, 2013, http://www.prnewswire.com/news-releases/haiti-welcomes-2013-with-bold-strategic-alliance-with-vietnam-185465712.html.

37. Shamsie, "Haiti's Post-Earthquake Transformation," 134–35.

38. Alex Dupuy, "The Neoliberal Legacy in Haiti," in *Tectonic Shifts: Haiti Since the Earthquake*, ed. Mark Schuller and Pablo Morales (Sterling, VA: Kumarian, 2012), 25.

39. Shamsie, "Haiti's Post-Earthquake Transformation," 134, 136.

40. Shamsie, "Haiti's Post-Earthquake Transformation," 137.

41. Shamsie, "Haiti's Post-Earthquake Transformation," 133.

42. Shamsie, "Haiti's Post-Earthquake Transformation," 134.

43. Dupuy, "Disaster Capitalism to the Rescue."

44. Dupuy, "Disaster Capitalism to the Rescue."

45. Mark Weisbrot, Jake Johnston, and Rebecca Ray, *Using Food Aid to Support, Not Harm, Haitian Agriculture* (Center for Economic and Policy Research, Apr. 2010), 3, http://www.cepr.net/documents/publications/haiti-2010-04.pdf.

46. Oxford Dictionaries (US), s.v. "opportunity cost," http://www.oxforddictionaries.com/us/definition/american_english/opportunity-cost.

CHAPTER 9: Buy Haitian, Restore Haiti: Bringing NGOs and Businesses Together

1. Didier Hérold Louis (Haiti Country Director, Hunger Relief International), in discussion with the authors, Dec. 20, 2012.

2. Celine Charveriat and Penny Fowler, "Rice Dumping in Haiti and the Development Box Proposal," Institute for Agriculture and Trade Policy, March 2002, http://www.iatp.org/files/Rice_Dumping_in_Haiti_and_the_Development_Box_.htm.

3. "Haiti: Overview," World Food Programme, http://www.wfp.org/countries/haiti/overview.

4. "Profil de projet: Appui au programme de cantines scolaires," Gouvernement du Canada, http://www.acdi-cida.gc.ca/cidaweb/çpo.nsf/projfr/A035146001.

5. Alexis Masciarelli, "Haiti: School Kids Eat Haitian Rice for Lunch," World Food Programme, Jan. 9, 2012, http://www.wfp.org/stories/haiti-school-kids-eat-haitian-rice-lunch.

6. Rachel Trego, *Rice Production and Trade Update* (USDA Foreign Agricultural Service, GAIN Report, Nov. 7, 2013), 3, http://gain.fas.usda.gov/Recent%20GAIN%20Publications/Rice%20Production%20and%20Trade%20Update_Santo%20Domingo_Haiti_11-7-2013.pdf.

7. Paul Altidor, "Impacts of Trade Liberalization Policies on Rice Production in Haiti" (master's thesis, MIT, 2004), 21, http://dspace.mit.edu/bitstream/handle/1721.1/28350/56025477.pdf?sequence=1.

8. Jonathan M. Katz, "With Cheap Food Imports, Haiti Can't Feed Itself," *The Huffington Post*, May 20, 2010, http://www.huffingtonpost.com/2010/03/20/with-cheap-food-imports-h_n_507228.html.

9. Vijaya Ramachandran and Julie Walz, "Haiti: Where Has All the Money Gone?," CGD Policy Paper 004 (Washington, DC: Center for Global Development, 2012), 6, http://www.cgdev.org/files/1426185_file_Ramachandran_Walz_haiti_FINAL.pdf.

10. "World Factbook," Central Intelligence Agency, https://www.cia.gov/library/publications/the-world-factbook/geos/ha.html.

11. Jerry Jean-Louis (Owner, HEJEC), in discussion with the authors, Dec. 15, 2012.

CHAPTER 10: Advocating for Haiti's Future: A Final Call for Change

1. Jacob Kushner, "The Multiplier Effect: Driving Haiti's Recovery by Spending Aid Dollars Locally," *Global Post*, May 11, 2012, http://www.globalpost.com/dispatch/news/regions/americas/haiti/120510/haiti-aid-economy-private-enterprise?page=full.

2. Kushner, "The Multiplier Effect."

3. "Haiti Reconstruction Cost May Near $14 billion, IDB Study Shows," Inter-American Development Bank, Feb. 16, 2010, http://www.iadb.org/en/news/webstories/2010-02-16/haiti-earthquake-reconstruction-could-hit-14-billion-idb,6528.html.

4. "Haiti Overview," World Bank, http://www.worldbank.org/en/country/haiti/overview.

5. "The World Factbook," Central Intelligence Agency, Apr. 10, 2015, https://www.cia.gov/library/publications/the-world-factbook/geos/ha.html.

6. Skye Justice, "Doing Business in Haiti: Opportunities for U.S. Companies" (lecture, Partners Worldwide conference, Port-au-Prince, Haiti, Jan. 23, 2014).

7. Justice, "Doing Business in Haiti." Used by permission.

8. Laurence Chandy and Geoffrey Gertz, "With Little Notice, Globalization Reduced Poverty," *Yale Global*, July 5, 2011, http://yaleglobal.yale.edu/content/little-notice-globalization-reduced-poverty.

9. "The World's Next Great Leap Forward: Towards the End of Poverty," *The Economist*, June 1, 2013, http://www.economist.com/news/leaders/21578665-nearly-1-billion-people-have-been-taken-out-extreme-poverty-20-years-world-should-aim.

10. Laurence Chandy and Geoffrey Gertz, "Poverty in Numbers: The Changing State of Global Poverty from 2005 to 2015," Policy Brief 2011-01 (Washington, DC: The Brookings Institution, 2011), 4, http://www.brookings.edu/~/media/research/files/papers/2011/1/global%20poverty%20chandy/01_global_poverty_chandy.pdf.

11. Chandy and Gertz, "With Little Notice, Globalization Reduced Poverty."

12. Douglas Wiener (Director, Café Selecto), in discussion with the authors, Dec. 19, 2012.

APPENDIX: NGOs in Haiti and Around the World: An Overview

1. *Has Aid Changed? Channeling Assistance to Haiti before and after the Earthquake* (New York: United Nations Office of the Special Envoy for Haiti, 2011), 4, http://www.lessonsfromhaiti.org/download/Report_Center/has_aid_changed_en.pdf.

2. *Non-Governmental Organizations and Civil Society Engagement in World Bank Supported Projects: Lessons from OED Evaluations*, Lessons and Practices No. 18 (World Bank, Operations Evaluation Department, Aug. 28, 2002), 1, http://ieg.worldbank.org/Data/reports/lp18.pdf.

3. Quoted in Mark Schuller, "Invasion or Infusion? Understanding the Role of NGOs in Contemporary Haiti," *The Journal of Haitian Studies* 13, no. 2 (2007): 97, http://www.hrdf.org/files/schuller-invasion-or-infusion.pdf.

4. Quoted in Schuller, "Invasion or Infusion?," 97.

5. Quoted in Schuller, "Invasion or Infusion?," 98.

6. Schuller, "Invasion or Infusion?," 96, 114.

7. The descriptions in this section rely on the United Nations Environment Programme report: Building Professionalism in *NGOs/NPOs: Key Issues for Capacity Building* (Nairobi: UNEP-IETC, 2003), http://www.unep.or.jp/ietc/kms/data/973.pdf.

8. Oliver P. Richmond; Henry F. Carey, eds. (2005). *Subcontracting Peace - The Challenges of NGO Peacebuilding*. Ashgate. p. 21.

9. Thomas Richard Davies, *The Possibilities of Transnational Activism: The Campaign for Disarmament between the Two World Wars* (Leiden: Martinus Nijhoff, 2007), 87–109.

10. Charter of the United Nations, ch. 10, art. 62, 71, http://www.un.org/en/documents/charter/chapter10.shtml; Grey Frandsen and Lynn Lawry, *Guide to Nongovernmental Organizations for the Military* (Washington, DC: US Department of Defense, 2009), 26, http://www.fas.org/irp/doddir/dod/ngo-guide.pdf; *Working with ECOSOC: An NGOs Guide to Consultative Status* (New York: United Nations, 2011), 1, http://csonet.org/content/documents/BrochureLite.pdf.

11. Frandsen and Lawry, *Guide*, 26.

12. Frandsen and Lawry, *Guide*, 26.

13. Frandsen and Lawry, *Guide*, 30, 31.

14. "Fact Sheet: Non-Governmental Organizations (NGOs) in the United States," US Department of State, Bureau of Democracy, Human Rights and Labor, http://www.humanrights.gov/wp-content/uploads/2012/01/factsheet-ngosintheus.pdf.

15. Alex Rodriguez, "Hobbled NGOs Wary of Medvedev," *Chicago Tribune*, May 7, 2008, http://articles.chicagotribune.com/2008-05-07/news/0805060608_1_civil-society-russian-authorities-russian-president-vladimir-putin.

16. "India: More NGOs, than schools and health centres," OneWorld South Asia, July 7, 2010, http://southasia.oneworld.net/news/india-more-ngos-than-schools-and-health-centres#.VXPhLc-qqko.

17. Schuller, "Invasion or Infusion?," 103.

18. Schuller, "Invasion or Infusion?," 105; Vijaya Ramachandran and Julie Walz, "Haiti: Where Has All the Money Gone?," CGD Policy Paper 004 (Washington, DC: Center for Global Development, 2012), 20–27, http://www.cgdev.org/files/1426185_file_Ramachandran_Walz_haiti_FINAL.pdf.

19. Schuller, "Invasion or Infusion?," 98.

20. Schuller, "Invasion or Infusion?," 99.

21. *Budget of the United States Government, Fiscal Year 2013* (Washington, DC: U.S. Government Printing Office), 152, https://www.whitehouse.gov/sites/default/files/omb/budget/fy2013/assets/budget.pdf.

22. "Non-Governmental Organizations (NGOs)," USAID, http://www.usaid.gov/partnership-opportunities/ngo.

23. "Non-governmental organisations," European Commission, Department of Employment, Social Affairs & Inclusion, http://ec.europa.eu/social/main.jsp?catId=330.

24. *UK Review of Competencies of EU institutions* (London: CAFOD, 2013), 1, https://www.gov.uk/government/uploads/system/uploads/attachment_data/file/212196/CAFOD.pdf.

25. *DAC in Dates: The History of OECD's Development Assistance Committee* (OECD, 2006), 7, http://www.oecd.org/dac/1896808.pdf.

26. *DAC in Dates*, 42–45.

27. "Official development assistance (ODA)," OECD, Glossary of Statistical Terms, http://stats.oecd.org/glossary/detail.asp?ID=6043.

28. "Haiti," Global Humanitarian Assistance, http://www.globalhumanitarianassistance .org/countryprofile/haiti.

29. "Haiti," Global Humanitarian Assistance.

30. "GDP (current US$)," World Bank, http://data.worldbank.org/indicator/NY.GDP .MKTP.CD.

31. Dan Coppard, Mariella Di Ciommo, Daniele Malerba, Kenn Okwaroh, Karen Rono, Tim Strawson, and Robert Tew, *Official Development Assistance (ODA)* (Bristol, UK: Development Initiatives, 2013), 1, http://devinit.org/wp-content/uploads/2013/12/di-data -guides-oda-09-10-12-E.pdf.

32. "Strengthening the Global Partnership for Development in a Time of Crisis: Where Are the Gaps?," UN Department of Public Information, 2009, http://www.un.org/ millenniumgoals/pdf/fact_%20sheet_where_are_the_gaps.pdf.

33. Coppard, et al., *Official Development Assistance*, 32–34; "Strengthening the Global Partnership," UN Department of Public Information, http://www.un.org/millenniumgoals/ pdf/fact_%20sheet_where_are_the_gaps.pdf.

34. Laurence Chandy and Geoffrey Gertz, "With Little Notice, Globalization Reduced Poverty," *Yale Global*, July 5, 2011, http://yaleglobal.yale.edu/content/little -notice-globalization-reduced-poverty.

About the Authors

Daniel Jean-Louis is founder and president of Bridge Capital S.A. international investment firm, and owner of Trinity Lodge in Port-au-Prince, Haiti. He teaches at Université Quisqueya and speaks and trains internationally on entrepreneurship and development. He serves on the board of the 100K Jobs in Haiti initiative. Previously he worked as national manager of Partners Worldwide and has coached and served as a consultant to companies and international nonprofit organizations in Haiti. Born and raised in Gonaives, Haiti, Jean-Louis is a graduate of Liberty University and lives with his wife and two children in Port-au-Prince.

Jacqueline Klamer is regional director of Partners Worldwide for Southeast Asia and speaks internationally on sustainable economic and business development. Previously she worked in global operations management for Partners Worldwide, and prior to that lived and worked in Haiti as a consultant to networks of entrepreneurs in business training and development. Her articles on Haiti and its opportunities for business solutions have appeared in various online and print publications. Klamer is a graduate of Calvin College and lives in Metro Manila, Philippines.